Boundary Songs

Boundary Songs:

Notes from the edge of the Lake District National Park

DAVID BANNING

with drawings by Iain Sharpe

First published in 2020 by Chroma Editions
101 Thornton Road
Morecambe
Lancashire
LA4 5PG
Tel: 07929 930001
www.chromaeditions.com

ISBN 978-1-8380915-0-7 (PRINT)
eISBN 978-1-8380915-1-4 (eBOOK)

For JH, IS and TLS...

Abbreviations used in the text

AOR - Adult Orientated Rock
BNFL - British Nuclear Fuels Limited
CWT - Cumbria Wildlife Trust
FLD - Friends of the Lake District
LDNPA - Lake District National Park Authority
NT - National Trust
OS - Ordnance Survey
SLDC - South Lakeland District Council
SSSI - Sight of Special Scientific Interest
SUV - Sport Utility Vehicle
UNESCO - United Nations Educational Scientific and Cultural Organisation

Carlisle
olway
irth
Caldbeck
Cockermouth
M6
Bassenthwaite
Lake
Penrith
Lake
District
National
Park
Derwent
Water
Crummock
Water
Ullswater
Thirlmere
Whitehaven
Shap
Buttermere
Ennerdale
Water
Haweswater
Grasmere
Wastwater
Seascale
Coniston
Water
Windermere
Kendal
rish Sea
Silecroft
Millom
Arnside
Barrow-in-
Furness
Morecambe
Bay

A lady stands underneath a great picture in a large entrance hall...

Her dark features lit by the red orange glow of an open fire
Crackling and sizzling in the gloom...
Nearby, awaiting inspection, a row of body armour lines up
On the walls and adjacent rooms
Several other portraits of those that followed...
Towards the half-light,
She paces over broad wooden floorboards.
With each step a scent escapes, gently returning souls to life.
A chalice held beside a cluster of unlit candles the size of long metal cylinders...
Fondling the high lace ruff of a dark dress
Decorated with gold jewels...
Putting the goblet down carefully, she lowers herself onto a chair
Adorned with a canopy.

Suddenly the silence is broken...

"The Boundaries call forth to forget our cares...
Beyond the smoke and ashes of earlier ages,
I can see God's moonbeam hanging like a morning mist over Lakes and Dales.
Touching the eyes of places in fashions of old, like a rebirth,
Now a new spell has been cast and I must ignite Westmoreland again.
Honouring the past, seeking those same marks that once bared my initials.
Whereby calling at the former estates and ancient landes of mine inheritance...
Pure in spirit, amongst the darkest of shadows
I have crossed over a great ocean of time,
To offer up prayers to my tenants upon this great perimeter..."

"The original idea of our national parks was fine; it is greed which is wrecking them, whether in the form of tourist developments, business interests or sheer folly."

(Fay Godwin *'Our Forbidden Land'*)

"That haunted figure on the road seemed just right at the time - like a phantom..."

(Francis Bacon in *'Francis Bacon (New aspects of art)'*)

Contents

Timeline 14
Introduction 17
This is Valley End, my only Friend...the End 19
Plumgarths to Gilpin Bridge: *Everything is in front of you* 26
Gilpin Bridge to Lindale: *The true starting point* 46
Lindale to Greenodd: *And the church bells softly chime* 60
Greenodd to Broughton-in-Furness: *I just don't know where it came from, it's never happened to me since* 70
Broughton-in-Furness to Whicham: *In the midst of its own darkness* 82
Whitbeck to Newbiggin: *Sombre winds in a fuzz of doom* 96
Newbiggin to Gosforth: *'Gebdaeth forae' [Pray for...]* 108
Gosforth to Ennerdale Bridge: *The edge of darkness* 120
Ennerdale Bridge to Cockermouth: *The death of hope and despair* 138
Cockermouth to Bassenthwaite: *The past is prologue* 152
Bassenthwaite to Hutton Roof: *In the gentle throes of daybreak* 164
Hutton Roof to Pooley Bridge: *Thou shalt not poop!* 180
Pooley Bridge to Keld: *"There must be some kinda way outta here"* 190
Shap to Plumgarths: *Here's where the story ends* 200
Natural Versus Cultural 210
Acknowledgements 216
Select Bibliography 217

A590, Abbey Flatts, Abbey Park, Abbot Hall, A66, Addison Wood, A591, Allerdale, A595, **an**cient, Appleby, **area**, Armathwaite Hall, Ashstead, Askham, Aspatria, Backstop, Bampton, Barrow, barrier, Bassenthwaite, beacon, Bigland Tarn, Birkbeck Fells, Blakeley Moss, Black Combe, Blindcrake, Bonnie Prince Charlie, border, borderland, borderline, bound, **boundary**: line, bounder, Bootle, Borrowdale Volcanics, Bowscale Tarn, Bowston, Bransdale, Bridge End, Brexit, Brigsteer, Brougham Castle, Broughton-in-Furness, Burneside, Butting, cairn, Caldbeck, Calder, Caldew, Carboniferous, Carrock Fell, Castle Head Hill, cherry pick, Cinderbarrow, circuit, circumference, Cistercian, coast, Coastline, Cockermouth, concave, confine, continue, Cop Stone, county lines, Cow Snout Wood, Crake, cross, Dacre, date line, demarcation, Derwent, district line, **dividing**, division, Duddon Bridge, Dugdale, Dunmallard Hill, Eaglesfield, Eamont Bridge, edge, Ehen, Elba Memorial, Ennerdale, end, escarpment, Eskmeals, EU, exterior, fence line, Felldyke, Fellside, fence line, flanks, fold, Foulshaw, Friends of the Lake District, fringe, front, frontier, Garnett Bridge, Gilpin, Gosforth, granophyre, Great Picture, Greenodd, Greystoke, Gutterby, Helton, heritage, Hesket Newmarket, High Cross, High Murrah, High Street, Hodgson's Green, holiday lets, Hollowgate, Holmrook, horizon, Howe Hill, Hutton Roof, indefinable, inland, inmost, inner, Irish Sea, Irton, Isel Hall, John Peel, jutting, Keld, Kirkland, Knightrider, Kokoarrah, Lady Anne, Lake District National Park Authority, Lamplugh, Lanthwaite Bridge, Leave, Levens, limestone, liminal, **limits**, Limitary, Lindale, **line**, Line of Control, liner, Little Dicks, Longlands, Longsleddale, Lonnings, Lowick Green, Lowther, March, marchland, Mardale, margin, **marks**, marque, Matthew Rudding, Meathop, Mere, Millom, Milnthorpe, Mockerkin, Monbiot, Monks Bridge, Moor Divock, Morecambe Bay, Motherby, Muncaster Castle, Mungrisdale, Murley Moss, national park, Nature Vibe, neighbouring, Newbiggin, No Deal, nuclear, Old Red Sandstone, offset, opposite, Orthwaite, out, out **of** bounds, outer boundary, outline, outlying, outsider, outskirt, Pardshaw, partition, pass, peak, pele towers, Penruddock, Penny Bridge, perambulation, perimeter, peripheral, periphery, phase, Piper's Hill, Plumgarths, Ponsonby, Pooley Bridge, procession, property line, protruding, psychogeography, Radio Cumbria, Redmain, Remain, Risebarrow, River Caldew, River Mint, River Sprint, rock, Roudsea Wood, Rubicon, Scarside, Seascale, second home syndrome, Sellafield, Selside, Shap Fell, shoreline, Silecroft, Skelwith Hill, Slate Hill, Sosgill, Soulby, Sparholme Wood, Spunham, Stagecoach, stake, sticking out, Storm Desmond, Storm Ophelia, Stribers Brow, surface, Swarth Fell, Swinside, Terma, terminal, terminate, terminator, the Fern, **the** place myth, Thornship, threshold, Toadpool, Townson Hill, toxic, transport, trespass, Ullswater Way, Ulpha, Unesco, Valley End, verge, vortex, Waberthwaite, Western Lake District, Westmorland, Wet Sleddale, **Which**am, Whitbeck, Wickers Gill, Windscale, World Heritage…

The Mail
Tuesday
TERROR
ACCUSED'S
"LONELY"
-CHILDHOOD-
- COURT

The Mail
Thursday
FLOOD
CHAOS

The Mail
Monday
TEEN
ATTACK
CALLS FOR
ACTION

The Mail
Monday
SPORTS
CENTRE
PLAN
HOPE

LAKES
HERITAGE
'NOT AT
RISK'
The Mail

The Mail
Saturday
8-HOUR
HOTEL
HOSTAGE
DRAMA

The Mail
Saturday
CLIMBER
DIES
IN 300FT
LAKES FALL

The Mail
Tuesday
PRINCE
CHARLES
PRAISES
LAKES

The Mail
Wednesday
FREE
FLOWERS
WORTH
£12.99
www.nwemail.co.uk

The Mail
Saturday
RAIL BOSSES
'SORRY' FOR
UPGRADE
DELAY
www.nwemail.co.uk

The Mail
Saturday
SEX ATTACKER
CAUGHT BY
HAVE-A-GO
HERO

The Mail
Tuesday
POLICE
PROBE
ATM
THEFTS

Timeline

1820: Wordsworth claims the Lake District as "a sort of national property, in which every man has a right and interest who has an eye to perceive and a heart to enjoy."

1884: James Bryce MP begins campaign for public access to the countryside by introducing the first freedom to roam bill to Parliament.

1894: Thirlmere dammed and flooded submerging the villages of Armboth and Wythburn. Creating a reservoir for the city of Manchester.

1931: Government inquiry recommends the creation of a 'national park authority.'

1936: Forming of a voluntary sector Standing Committee on National Parks (SCNP).

1938: Campaign to Protect Rural England, 'National Parks' Film shown in UK Cinemas.

1945: White Paper on National Parks – part of the Labour Party's planned post-war reconstruction.

1949: National Parks and Access to the Countryside Act - Government passes an Act of Parliament to establish National Parks to preserve and enhance their natural beauty and provide recreational opportunities for the public.

1951: Lake District designated a national park.

1954: Sellafield, close to Seascale on West Cumbria coast (incorporating original nuclear reactor at Windscale), opened by the Ministry of Supply.

1957: Coniston to Foxfield railway line closed to passengers.

1960: First full time Lake District National Park warden position created.

1965: Lake District National Park opposes Manchester Corporation Water Act – for the abstraction of water from Windermere and Ullswater along with the construction of a pipeline down Longsleddale.

1966: First Royal visit from Duke of Edinburgh, 22 July.

1969: Brockhole opened – the first ever national park visitor centre in the UK.

1971: Major upgrades of road network – creation of A66 from Penrith to Keswick and Cockermouth.

1972: Keswick to Penrith railway line closed.

1974: Lake District 'Special' Planning Board created on 1st April after formation of new Cumbria County Council.

1977: The SCNP becomes the Council for National Parks (CNP).

1981: Lake District National Park leases 18th Century Duddon Iron Furnace.

1985: Lake District first bid for World Heritage Site status rejected by United Nations Educational, Scientific and Cultural Organisation (UNESCO)

1995: Environment Act - Gives national park authorities the duty to seek to foster the economic and social well-being of local communities.

1997: Lake District National Park Authority (LDNPA) formed – replacing 'Special' Planning Board. New logo designed based on Britain's favourite view from shores of Wastwater.

2001: Outbreak of Foot and Mouth Disease crisis spreads to Cumbria in March – 98% of national park designated 'infected'. Footpaths, bridleways, access to fells and woodland closed.

2001: 50th Anniversary of Lake District National Park – "Partners in the Park" Mayday celebrations held at Brockhole and on the Glebe, Bowness-on-Windermere.

2002: January, Cumbria declared 'free' of Foot and Mouth Disease

2007: Richard Leafe appointed LDNPA Chief Executive in June.

2008: Cumbria Tourism starts discussions with outdoor industries about the Lake District becoming the 'Adventure Capital of the UK'.

2008: Low Carbon Lake District initiative launched.

2009: Natural England begins consulting on whether to extend the boundaries of the Lake District and Yorkshire Dales National Parks.

2009: November brings record levels of rain causing severe flooding in Cockermouth.

2010: Coalition Government elected, cuts LDNPA's budget by 28.5%

2011: December. NuGen announces plans to build a new nuclear power station at Moorside (to the north and west of the Sellafield complex).

2012: 93% in favour of amendments to the two national park boundaries after third and final consultation.

2014: Culture Minister Ed Vaizey announces third UNESCO bid for World Heritage status.

2015: National Grid unveils plans to erect 'giant' pylons connecting proposed Moorside nuclear power station to the electricity network.

2015: December 5. Storm Desmond causes severe flooding with collapsed bridges, main roads washed away and significant damage to properties.

2016: June 23. EU Referendum, UK votes to Leave by a 51.9% to 48.1% margin.

2016: August 1. Lake District National Park Boundary extensions approved, growing by 3% – an extra 27 square miles.

2017: July 9. Lake District National Park awarded World Heritage status by UNESCO.

2018: November 8. Toshiba scrap plans for a nuclear power station at Moorside and resolve to take steps to wind up NuGen.

2019: June. Friends of the Lake District submit formal request to Natural England to extend the southern boundary between Grange-over-Sands and the Irish Sea Coast at Silecroft.

Introduction

Since 2008, my own timeline has involved toing and froing from south to north, north to south – London to the Lakes, the Lakes to London. Here and there, but always in-between. Always on the verge of leaving. A disconnected rootlessness nourished by an unfixed estrangement. Suspended on a passageway above the void, all eyes all sides. Renting a succession of overpriced rooms either inside or outside the national park. Low wages racking up zombie debt from an assortment of jobs in poorly led arts organisations. Over ten years of relentless displacement. An unsustainable future made more tangible with globalisation, digitisation and isolation, urban and rural transience, hiding away with no control over your life. Existence without essence, the eternal outsider.

In a febrile political climate, I started to develop a fascination with the national park boundary extensions. The lure of towns and villages on the perimeter and where the national park was headed had started to form. A push to the peripheries, escaping a tide of traffic flowing relentlessly in the opposite direction. On trips out to the West Coast or across Shap Fell and beyond to the northern and southern boundary of Cumbria's civilisation. It seemed that the only way to make any real sense of how things had ended up the way they had would be to go out and explore the margins in more detail. Perhaps some of these places could provide answers to my own fog of rootedness at the same time.

Graham K. Dugdale was the Lancaster Guardian's intrepid columnist responsible for the weekly Walk this Way feature. In 1996, he produced The Lake District Boundary Walk, a guidebook split into fifteen individual stages. Printed in black and white with a collection of hand drawn maps, he had devised a long-distance walk that would be virtually devoid of other similar minded individuals. I'd found it buried in the local studies section at Ambleside Library. Almost immediately it became my insurance policy during repeated sorties out to the edges. Although the colour photo on the cover of the track from Longsleddale below Buckbarrow Crag leading to the Gatesgarth Pass seemed a strange choice compared with the actual topography I found on the boundary. As were claims in the introduction about the kind of people enthused by hiking and rambling – from boy scouts to bishops, or toddlers to terminators!

However, like Dugdale, I envisaged a solitary journey, but one inhabiting a rarely spoken of and perhaps even forgotten landscape. Made up of some 160 odd miles where meeting others would prove as rare as catching a fresh water herring. Like a modern day gypsy landslide on the run from all the touristic honey pots of a so called 'vibrant' national park. In search of stories, ghosts and encounters filtering upwards from the boundary well. Dugdale recommended doing it all in one journey, drawing up an itinerary averaging out at ten miles per stage. Due to ongoing work commitments, my own strategy needed to be a lot more flexible. And there wouldn't be any B&Bs or any free handouts of bread and tea either. Instead, I embarked on weekly forays, typically on a Monday or a Tuesday, carrying on from where I left off on the preceding stage. Doing it this way, I envisaged it would take about four or five months through the onset of winter. To get round the logistical headache, I would often drive to the end of each part first, before cycling back to the start, locking the bike up ready to commence walking the whole stage. Returning to pick up the bone-shaker I nicknamed 'Knightrider' on the way back. With an increasingly less frequent service during the day, I only managed to use the Stagecoach bus service a couple of times. On one occasion, I invited a couple of friends along to take a few pictures and film a derelict garage near Silecroft. This episode induced a brush with the local mafia, which also revealed some of the darker un- dertones at play. Most trips began from the few square feet I rented for a hefty monthly packet near Windermere, in the heart of the national park, where letting agents "care about you and your property". A small enclave, made up predominantly of either second homes or holiday lets, most of them predictably empty during the week.

As I started to venture further round the boundary, my written notes became entwined with song lyrics from an assortment of groups, like old memories dancing in circles around me. The whole landscape awash in a musical bric-a-brac swivelling in dark pirouettes. Driving south along the Rayrigg road or north on the A591 towards an assemblage of Blackpoolized tourist traps offering boats and stuffed bunnies, chocolate and fudge, chips, burgers, swans, Gore-Tex, ice creams, kebabs, pizzerias, bars, amusements and pubs. Love the Lakes, turn on, tune in and trip out on the water. Each time as I journeyed further and further away from the main routes, fells would diminish in the rounded out landscape. Often speculating if another, more real form of Lake District lurked behind the up-lifted middle.

Touching the boundaries, a sense of unredressed melancholy bled through echoing silences. During a series of wanderings voices started to emerge from unimaginable depths. Floating over fields, above the roar of rivers, along unkempt hedgerows, filtering through dense woodland, before reassembling into the darkened shadows of modern life…

This is Valley End, my only Friend...the End:

A puddle near Silecroft... "What you doing there?"
"Just a bit of filming" "...in a puddle?"
"Yeah, I like to film them – is there a problem?"

Apparently, some folk don't take too kindly to the filming of puddles. This unexpected revelation came from Richard, when we met up at a layby on the A5093 near Hodgson Green Farm. The altercation had occurred across the road. Near a group of three containers positioned close to a hedge and lone pylon.

"There he is, over there." Richard pointed at a tractor in the field opposite.

"What did he say?" Julian asked.

"He couldn't believe I wanted to film a puddle. I didn't realise you have to ask permission to do that sort of thing now?"

No safety or surprise in our elaborate plans. Desperate after a ninety-minute drive from Windermere, I had wandered off for a secretive call of nature beside some bushes. Completely unaware that I might be creating another pool of discord. Eventually I caught up with Richard and Julian as we began the short walk to our destination, the 'eye sore' of Valley End garage. 'In the out of the way places of a push-button world'. To our left, a blanket of ivy reclaiming the power of an '80s style BT phone kiosk. A little further up the road, the site of a former Austin Rover dealership facing the A595 at a busy junction, under the domed skyline of Black Combe. In the '70s, British Leyland had around ten other franchises dotted around the West Cumbrian coast. Rubbing shoulders with state-sponsored nuclear weapons. Behind the garage, trains shipped flasks containing highly radioactive fuel rods from Sizewell and Dungeness to Sellafield further up the coast. Long hair, sideburns, kipper ties and flared trousers. T-Rex and Led Zep. A country embracing European collaboration. But the song has not remained the same. The national park confirmed Valley End's road to demolition in 2012. The end of everything that stands. Time to make way for ten new dwellings. Supposedly only for locals.

Richard Skelton, musician, artist and keeper of lost words. Hands in pockets, limitless and free. Surveying the pre-demolition sights, sounds and smells within reach. Tall and slender, black jacket, blue jeans, flat cap, camera and tripod. He'd arrived first, despite a two and a half hour drive down from the Borders. Julian Hyde, gatherer of fragments on relentless walks against obliteration. A former colleague in the summer rain, layered up in black and grey waterproofs, eyes everywhere riding the highway west, armed with sandwiches and a golfing umbrella. Valley End on the edge of

Silecroft had been calling us for months. Blood simple, under threatening south western skies. Three men circling each other, there were no clean getaways. We stepped over a trampled down wire fence onto the cracks of the forecourt. A nostalgic purity flowing into our deepest hearts. Derelict, deserted and abandoned, collapsed dreams reflected in tarnished windows – Metro, Maestro or Montego? British cars to beat the world…

"What d'ya think you're doing?"

As if by magic, a voice gnawed at us over the fence. It came from a little old man who reminded me of the mysterious shopkeeper in Mr Benn (minus the moustache and Fez). He appeared dressed in a 1970s smart-casual handcart of dark brown. I'd noticed him ferreting up and down the driveway of a bungalow adjacent to the site.

"Just taking some photos my friend. Is that OK?" Julian replied.

"Have you got permission? You know the chap who owns the land won't be happy about it if you haven't."

"It's all going to be demolished soon though isn't it?" Richard cut in, after setting up to film a doorway and flaking letterbox that looked like the grated surface of a Dubuffet canvas.

"Now look here, he doesn't like anyone crossing over onto the site. He's a queer sort; gets easily offended; owns the building just up the road. There'll be a white Jag parked up outside if he's there."

"Have you got his number?" Richard asked.

"No, he's ex-directory."

"Well, I've come a long way to do some filming here. And we're only taking a few shots. We won't be long."

As the old man shrugged his shoulders at Richard, I noticed a thick plastic bag full of maggots in his right hand. A hush ensued. The silence before the strike. I watched the old man scamper off inside a glass porch behind a polished Rover hatchback.

Cobbles, broken debris and sand, edging out across the reddish-brown soil. The sky began to glow orange and blue illuminating several heaps of slate chippings, rubble and gravel. Now only a few signs remained as evidence of the garage's former life. The deadly deception. A large blue 'diesel' logo clung to its lofty position on one of the pebble-dash walls. Once green, now thought a killer, spewing out black carbon and toxic emissions; dirty, noisy and dangerous. Underneath it, the word 'Sigh' spray-painted with looping extravagance. A burst of traffic roared past on the A595. A convoy of HGVs loaded up with Burlington aggregates from the quarry at Kirkby-in-Furness. All headed up the coast road, running parallel with the national park boundary towards Whitbeck and beyond. I stood leaning on a bathtub turned over on its side. A handful of stones gathered in a slimy pool of water angled at 45 degrees; elsewhere, a string of weeds, tyres, wooden crates and rusted machinery. Dense thickets of wild brambles spreading out in the bulged and buckled mud. By my feet, earthed in the muck, a double plug-point split down the middle.

A skidding sound announced the arrival of a huge 4x4. In a desperate land, executive Sport Utility Vehicles (SUVs) with a commanding view over the rest of the road. Solid and handsome in a Polaris white colour; attracting dirt like a magnet. In control, stitched in leather; the swollen bonnet snorting beside a metal gate.

"Right, c'mon you lot – get out! What is the problem with you people?"

"You come down here and start offending vulnerable old folk..."

Predictable and expected – when the old man had disappeared, we knew he'd be straight on the phone to the landowner. And there he was, staring sourly at us. Scratching his receding hairline with a Jaguar wristband. A stout, rotund exterior clad in Jacamo's finest blue and buff. Any occasion, stay ahead of the game, baggy sweatshirt and loose fitting Union Blues. Memory and desire, a stranger's hand rattling the bones.

"I must get that bloody fence up; I've had quite a few signs nicked off here before."

"Hi there. We're only here to take a few pictures. That's all. Nothing else."

"I don't care what you lot are up to, you'd better get off here now, I own all this you see. It's mine. Only the other week, I caught two buggers trying to make off with the bath over there!"

After a tense few moments, a muted approach seemed to lighten things a little. All the while Richard kept filming. I decided to try holding the landowner's attention by engaging him in more conversation. Julian lingered. Flushed with hyper-awareness, an eerie reflection in a corner of the former showroom windows. Running hands through his hair, hanging around the verge debris recording porno mags, squashed beer cans, cellophane and black bin bags. What's your fetish – Submissives, Knicker Lovers or Lady Boys? A natural selection of George Shaw's rude mechanicals. It's not the boundary's fault...

nothing, like something, happens anywhere.

I hung on, listening to the landowner's self-importance for nearly half an hour. The old man even joined us at one point and mentioned something about the Japanese 'birdwatchers' he'd had to deal with at a 'bang and burn' range just up the coast. Walking amongst Valley End's ghosts; intertwined on rusty railings above the forecourt, the year it opened – 1967. A piece of iron crafted at the house opposite, previously a blacksmith's. Forged in a new world of cash machines, the QE2, and the exciting sound of Radio One. We lent on the metal gate observing Richard quietly assemble more textures and whispers. Touching from a distance on the outside.

Sometimes the toot of a horn provided a welcome distraction from the repeated questions about where I came from and what kind of equipment we used. With the landowner seemingly compelled to acknowledge most of the traffic filing past. Still, persistence paid off, as I learnt the site had been a Shell garage in the 1980s combined with an Austin Rover franchise. Despite all the flag waving and Britain is Best slogans, the cars soon became badge-less, and the dealerships quickly vanished. A MOT/Breakdown Recovery Centre followed, although the shutters came and went abruptly in the early 2000s. This despite talk of more trade amidst rumours of a new bridge over Morecambe Bay, connecting Millom and Barrow. Then a long hiatus when the land was put up for sale before the wait for planning permission. Engagement finished, we said our goodbyes. Fear and mistrust at the base of living rock. Wheels turned away from themselves, rusted with resentment and exhaustion. Left behind in darkness beside the murmur of the road.

Afterwards, a quick debrief down the road at a café in Millom. Post-industrialism on the periphery, spaces where the great popularity of the national park can breed indifference. Whilst we gathered ourselves in the doorway, a chubby guy behind the counter looked us up and down...

"Are you lot bird watchers or a boy band?"

Eyebrows raised, we laughed while contemplating the menu in silence, before ordering tea and coffee. It looked like there weren't many other Kerchings at this time of day. In a corner hidden from view, a set of brown plastic chairs and a Formica table-top provided some respite. High above, Blu-tacked on lined paper, a sign hand-written in black marker pen...

"Do **Not** turn radiator off, if you are too hot move seats..."

We'd landed back in the zone, circa Valley End in the 1980s. With the jukebox playing *Flashdance*, *Simply the Best* and *Footloose*...hit the ceiling, or tear up this town...

"Where d'ya wanna go? Shoe shop an' that?"

A couple of mothers with babies wrapped in fleece blankets promptly got up and left. Not paying attention, I spilt a mouthful of tea from a big white mug onto the wooden flooring. Thoughtful on my left, Julian twizzled a small Saxa salt container. Opposite, Richard tried to locate a socket to recharge his camera. Lose your blues, everybody cut loose. No Love Lost on the Outer Ring. Cumbria Tourism's Adventure Capital reaching out to the Western Lake District. The place myth peering over the boundary rope. Feeling bewildered in a search for the unknown, it felt like our adventures belonged to an area out of step and out of time. Continued exclusion a million miles away from golden daffodils and outstanding universal value. The struggle to find points of reference amongst high chairs, Fizz Wizz and Haribo Starmix. Freshly made toasties (on white or brown Mother's Pride tasting of cotton wool). Sepia photos of knickerbocker glories. Cartoon caricatures, cheese and yucca plants in large blue and green pots. In the window by the door on the way out, a chef figurine issuing a thumbs-up. Yet unlike Valley End's future, this place on the West Coast, home of the 'true Cumbrian people', had survived...

PLUMGARTHS
TO GILPIN BRIDGE

A NATURAL GATEWAY
WHALE'S JAW BONES
A CASCADE OF FAST CARS AND FREEDOM
THE CARBONIFEROUS STRANGLEHOLD
LIVE, WORK, INVEST
HIGH QUALITY 'AFFORDABLE' HOMES
NATURE COLOURED WITH ENAMEL PAINT
MYSTICAL GEOGRAPHIES
A GREAT BUSINESS
THE LONGEST CUL-DE-SAC IN THE WORLD
NOTHING IS ILLUMINATED
THE SOCIAL ORDER IN STONE
PLUMGARTHS TO GILPIN BRIDGE

Everything is in front of you:

A roundabout shaped like a pear…
To the north, a natural gateway signalled the mesmerising power of lakes and mountains. Head west towards the ferry at Bowness and a tub-thumping ride on the undulating Crook road awaited. Turn east to descend back into the auld grey town itself. Or drive south on the Kendal bypass, and the multi-lane M6 offered a swift exit back to the kind of urban decay most people have temporarily escaped from. Plumgarths (also known as 'Toadpool' on modern day OS maps) is one of the most used road junctions in the national park – but is it really a roundabout? You'd be mistaken if approaching from the direction heading south out of Windermere on the A591, through Ings, past Staveley and Burneside – on the slight incline leading onto it there was a lack of roundabout warning signs. No need to stop or give way either. Unless you decide to perform a 360-degree turn in order to reach Kendal. Then, you must halt and give way to the traffic on the A591 moving south at a fair lick from Windermere. Adding to a general sense of confusion, a spate of signs for Kendal North and Kendal South competed with a late flurry for the Town Centre.
What an oddity, how apt…

At the end of August 2017 my journey began there, although it could so easily have started hundreds of times already. Most folk who visit or live in or near the national park boundary follow sections of it unknowingly every day. But from now on I would be acutely aware of its twists and turns, as I sped away from Windermere, ignoring the flirtatious advances of the River Cowan. Up and down, like a crawling king snake. Twisting right then left, past a turn-off for the curiously named hamlet, Heaning Mislet! It's either an expression of annoyance, a Friends meeting place, or both. Standing proud beside a brightly lit garage, St. Anne's chapel at Ings eased into view next to the Watermill Inn. It also highlighted a first encounter with the name Bateman. Every detail matters, even the ones you can't see, or wouldn't normally notice. In 1743, Robert Bateman was an English merchant at Leghorn, in Tuscany, trading in the age of European expansion. Discovery and exploitation in the Atlantic Mediterranean. A world formed in the Middle Ages setting in place the economic foundations of the early modern and modern eras. Buy cheap and sell dear. His generosity led to a substantial rebuilding of the church in its present form. A portrait still hung on the north wall of the nave, whilst his coat of arms was positioned over the door leading into the tower. He is thought to have sent marble, from the famous quarries at Carrara in the Apuan Alps of Tuscany, which graces the chancel and sanctuary floors. Legends soon arose of his murder by a ship's captain on a journey home to his newly built house at Reston, near Staveley. The church even gained the Wordsworth stamp of approval in late 1802, when Dorothy (visiting along with her beloved brother) noted the floor and communion table surrounded by Old Testament imagery. If the doors are open, come and marvel at the marble. A little further on from the church, I got my first true sense of the boundary's vigour at Plantation Bridge. Here, it was fixed and started to gather pace. Before it passed a disregarded folly erected in 1814 on Monument Hill, within spitting distance of Plumgarths.

Boney went to Elba...Away, a-yah! But Boney he came back again...

Intended as a memorial to the exile of Napoléon Bonaparte on the Island of Elba, the lonely obelisk was bankrolled by another Bateman – one James Bateman of nearby Tolson Hall, whose family were thought to have had connections with an old whaling skipper. A trace of these former links still survives on the opposite side of the A591 (near Plumgarths), at the bottom of Gibson's Farm. Here so-called whalebones shaped like a pointed archway adorn a secluded wooden field gate. Although other rumours claim they were the gift of a Norwegian pulp supplier in the early 1900s. During the early years of the national park, they became a well-known landmark for travellers riding on the old Ribble double-decker bus service... next stop, "Whale's Jaw Bones!" Representing a passing from the dirt and noise of factories further south to the open air and freedom of the north, with its abundance of hills and mountains. Once a frontier between different ways of life, nowadays the bones have become almost obsolete. Symbolising the long decay caused by shifts in season and climate. Whether they are the real thing or not is still anyone's guess.

One of Napoléon's many nicknames was 'Caporal la Violette' – the Little Corporal and violets. Amongst the numerous tales that sprang up throughout his colourful life, his own compatriots are believed to have given him this one while he was living in exile on the Mediterranean island of Elba. They envisaged a return in springtime as the violets started to bloom. Displaying them proudly on their lapels in a coded sign of defiance. But the colour also harked back to the Reign of Terror, when sunsets were purple and on fire. And the clouds would surround the fervent colours everywhere. Bateman's own commemoration plans were declared nineteenth century fake news once the 'Day of Violets' arrived on 26 February 1815. With plans for a commemorative plaque hastily kicked into the long wet grass after news leaked out of Napoléon's escape from his island exile. Boney landed a few days later at Golfe-Juan on the French Riviera. Supported by a loyal band of over 600 soldiers, who then marched across the foothills of the Alps on what became known as the Route-Napoléon. Arriving triumphantly in Paris, the so-called Hundred Days that followed counted down to his last hurrah at Waterloo. The history book on the shelf is always repeating itself. After another hundred years, Bateman's forgotten plaque finally emerged when Charles Cropper, of Ellergreen, paid for it to be mounted on the monument...

"In honour of William Pitt,
The Pilot who weathered the storm,
Elba."

At the top of Hollins Lane I sat in my car tucked in next to a wire fence in the lay-by. Heavy splashes of rain knocked out four beats to the bar on the windscreen. In the rear view, a steady stream of trucks headed towards Cropper's paper mill down a route designated for widening. Sobering times and sobering budgets imposed by reduced Government funding and a spiralling pension black hole – choking off the recovery. Not to mention the devastating effects of the 2015 floods. In the late eighteenth century, the growth of traffic from mail coaches and tourism (fed by increasing numbers of newly published travel guide books) required better road maps throughout England. The arrival of the Ordnance Survey (OS) undoubtedly signalled a further move forward from county mapmakers, as a new industrial landscape took shape. Then, in 1770, a few decades before Bateman's embarrassment was built, London cartographer Thomas Jefferys produced a landmark map of Westmorland. Surveyed a couple of years before by John Ainslie (and perhaps another of his colleagues, John Donald), it displayed a level of cartography far superior to anything produced beforehand. On it, Kendal had the beginnings of a street index and five tollgates were shown surrounding the town, including one by Plumgarths to the north (the present A5284 Crook Road / A591 roundabout). This one actually survived for over 200 years after the Plumgarth (via Crook) to Windermere Turnpike Act of 1761. Before it quite literally went pear-shaped, it was demolished. In its heyday everything passed through, from carts and gigs to carriages, phaetons and mail coaches. Until steam trains on the Lancaster Line started to easily outstrip coaches from the mid-to late 1840s onwards.

Back in the 21st century, 'Fern on The Wireless' was asking Cumbria to join in the conversation. On Digital or FM, the things that affect your life. Sandwiched between a healthy slice of mid-morning riff-o-rama from Starship. The so-called 'Killer Clown' craze, where it's not right, and it's not fair. Or the crumbling infrastructure and plutonium stored in degrading plastic bottles at the 'Ugly Duckling'. Don't you remember? Radio Cumbria's pseudo Alan Partridge played the mamba, keep listening to the radio... Through a gap in a windscreen dripping with condensation, I spied shiny and new German hatchbacks and saloons, Land and Range Rovers, Shogun 4x4s, artics and then the 555 whooshing past. Not forgetting the army of Sprinter and Movano vans in close attendance, kicking up mud, engines whinnying like old nags. I decided to leave the warm humidity and shelter of the car to explore the rim of the roundabout. But after turning the corner, I soon discovered there wasn't a pavement, only a sodden grass verge scarred with huge tyre tracks, probably from unruly HGVs. My awkward sliding footsteps were greeted with a few disgruntled looks from the stream of vehicles passing by. Thoughts wandered haphazardly. A place off-limits, nothing for anyone to see here, in amongst the muck and dirt; the lord of the landscape releases only harmful pollutants on this part of the boundary. I ploughed on regardless, pausing beside a large black road sign to stare down the barrel of the dual carriageway. Eyeing up a cascade of fast cars and freedom. From this angle, the bypass looked like a runway. Memories were left at Plumgarths; a natural gateway to the south or the north...

Soaked through, I trudged back on the opposite side to where I'd left my car. After a few yards someone yelled abuse out of a white van. Temporarily losing balance, as it caught me completely unawares. I soon recovered and flicked a belated V-sign in response to both the idiot racing off uphill and the putrid weather. But it didn't end there. Plumgarths now had me in its sights. Back at the car, before pulling away, I counted two ambulances and three police cars speeding towards Windermere. I soon discovered why. At Ings, a roadblock had been installed on the A591. Closing off traffic on both sides, with a solitary policewoman on hand to advise a queue of hacked off motorists. After waiting about ten minutes in line, my turn arrived.

"Hello sir. Local?"

"Yes, no... well sort of."

"Erm, OK – and where are you trying to get to?"

"Well, the other side of Windermere I hope. Is there no way through here at all?"

"Afraid not sir...We're having to send everyone back towards Kendal and the roundabout at the top of the Crook road. Trouble is, a lot of them don't seem to know where or what Plumgarths is! Take it you do sir, yes, no?"

A week later, Plumgarths was quietly lit, with the surrounding hills bathed in gentle apricot sunshine. Raising an eyebrow, I pulled over in the layby at the top of the A5284, and let out a breath I didn't realise I was holding. Cutting the engine, the traffic noised loud, creating a formidable backwall. Crawling out of the car, I stood for a while sniffing the fresh southerly breeze before lacing up my boots. Sizing up the pink boundary outline on a segment of OS Map at the same time. But then, just before setting off, wheels span and smoke rose. The devil was wiser. "It's time to repent," he said. From out of nowhere, a huge gunmetal grey VW almost knocked me into a hedge, attempting an impromptu U-turn. High on diesel and gasoline, the impatient fiend sped off towards the M6. Stunned, I just rolled my eyes and turned to face the soft landscape unfolding to my left instead. In the middle distance, I noticed a train sidewinding in waves of motion underneath Benson Knott's bulging waistline. So, where are you heading? To my right, a gated entrance across the Windermere road led towards High Helsfell farm. Just south of the roundabout, near the limestone ruin of a sixteenth century barn, the former site of a fortified hall or pele tower. On the dual carriageway, people flew by in the traffic's boom, seeking an escape route out of or into the Lakes.

I decided to check my trusty backpack one last time, rummaging through a selection of biscuits, bananas, OS maps and my trusted camera. Until finally setting off, progressing down an uneven grassy bank forming a half-baked pavement. It was littered with empty beer bottles, soft-drink cans, banana skins and sweet wrappers. All presumably tossed out of bags like mine in a mad rush to get somewhere. From here everything in front was a nostalgic dream. Moments were frozen in time on this, the ultimate heritage trail. Elsewhere, nettles, thorns, black and red berries, thistles and dandelions competed for the afternoon's dying light. I passed a 'To Let' sign at the top of Lane Foot Farm, a reminder of civilisation's priorities. It was situated next to a new housing scheme, built on land provided by South Lakeland District Council (SLDC), according to a gleaming new steel plaque. Solar panels adorned a mixture of grey semis, pebble dashed into a post-industrial collage.

Suddenly, I felt a real sense of the boundary's loss. Powerless to its departure, pulled out from underneath. Gone in a flash, avoiding the auld grey town altogether. At Helsfell Hall it split off for good. Continuously zig zagging along the open pasture, melting into dark shadows upon dry stone walls, the arteries and veins feeding the boundary. Shooting up into the seams of Kendal Fell, before resting on a wooden bench atop Kettlewell Crag. Golfers marked their cards, completely oblivious to the close proximity of the line. As police sirens disappeared into Kendal's mirth, in corvid corner a lonely jackdaw eyed up a flagpole. Below, the distant murmur of traffic played on, in heavy stereo. Above, pig-shaped clouds ate up the sky. Ahead through two small areas of woodland a cave held a secret. Some thought it might even have been the 'Last in England'. Inhabiting the woods. Watching in silence, roaming without your knowledge...

How pretty the flowers are about here...how sweetly the little birds sing... never leave the path to run into the wood...

Extraordinary excavations: a skeleton found lying amongst the stones. The time of the Helsfell Wolf dates back to the twelfth century. Cumbria's ecological past, present and future connected not by a huntsman, but by a Victorian archaeologist, John Beecham. Extensively cleaned, rearticulated and preserved, the precious bones form the centrepiece of Kendal Museum's 'Predator' showcase. For now, the UK's largest carnivores can only be viewed as remnants from behind glass display cabinets. Large packs of landowners are thought to be stalling the great rewilding project championed by the likes of George Monbiot. But in places like Yellowstone in America, the wolf is revered as 'a painter of mountains'. During the Civil War in the 1640s, one of Helsfell's most famous inhabitants was dubbed, 'Robin the Devil'. Rising off the lake of fire, from Holme House on Windermere, a taste for revenge led him on horseback into Kendal Church. Once inside, the elusive Parliamentarian Colonel Briggs gave him the slip, before he lost his helmet after striking his head on the west door. Situated high up on the church walls, 'The Rebel's Cap' (an old helmet with accompanying sword) has since marked the sequence of events.

Continuing uphill from Beast Banks, the provincial landscape echoed with more sounds of yesterday. In July 2009, an ancient monument, the Greenside Lime Kiln, was protected, preserved and saved from dereliction. It was dedicated to the memory of Dr. John Satchell (former Chairman of the Kendal Civic Society) whose own fiery passions safeguarded the link between the lime-burning industry and the Kendal to Lancaster canal. Lime – the great fertiliser of the age recovering the acidic soil of Cumbria for agricultural needs. The so-called 'Black & White' waterway derived its name from the transportation of coal from Lancashire, whilst stone and lime went south to various other parts of the country. In earlier times, local limeburners carried out much smaller scale operations, before the area came to be enclosed and administered by the Kendal Fell Trust. Preserve the best of the past; promote the best of the new – snuff, shoes and mint-cake, a town for all seasons. Set back from the pavement, the limekiln was a large structure of dressed limestone, with a wide, shallow round arch and two square draw holes lined with firebricks. The irregularly shaped front arch of the kiln had been caged behind bars, offset at an angle to a row of well-to-do Georgian terraces. Their cool silver-grey colour hewn from the limestone quarries that once peppered the southern tip of Kendal Fell.

John Wesley and the Quaker George Fox are said to have visited in the nineteenth century, whilst another George began his career there a little earlier in the mid 1750s. But Romney, the leading society portraitist, went on to find fame and fortune in a new city risen from the ashes of the Great Fire. Once established, he developed a lifelong obsession with Lady Hamilton, his eventual muse. Genius and talents respected in the shadow of the French Revolution. Classical poses mixed with modern allure on 60 portraits of Lord Horatio's mistress.

I stood a while longer, reading through the various information boards on the site before pausing to take in the view over Kendal and beyond. Below, the town's swirling panorama of ragged ashen-coloured buildings displayed a highly distinguishable persona – rock type. Here, in the ocean basin, layer upon layer, fine-grained and monotonously grey. In 1820, Jonathan Otley, a humble clockmaker from Keswick, described the three great belts underlying the Lake District's central region as: "Clayslates (Keswick), Greenstones (Ambleside) and Greywackes (Kendal)..."
The volcanism of the middle, which formed the rugged Borrowdale volcanic rocks of the central national park, ends here. Out on the fringes, the national park boundary subsides into limestone, muds, silts and sands as the mixture of debris encircles the central core. In rock terms, as in recent British history, the middle has been squeezed.

Only the New Red Sandstones from St Bees to Millom break up this Carboniferous stranglehold. From the Furness Peninsula, the Eden Valley and the Solway Plain, to the major towns of Carlisle and Penrith, the red bed of Permian and Triassic sedimentary rocks buried the mountain core in a reddish brown hue. Today, glowing lowland soils, field walls and major build-ings reflect the former arid desert environment that once deposited them.

Over the auld grey town towards the modern-day business parks on the A6, bright lights glowed eerily radioactive. At street level, the modern rain-soaked pavements were in flux. Once, local craftsmanship extended to wool, paper, gunpowder and marble polishing, along with carpet and brush making. In the early nineteenth century, an industrial quarter sprang up below the former Castle hunting grounds. Soon, the town reverberated with the power of textile mills and a canal ironworks. In the shadows of the industrial North West, needle trades flourished and King Cotton reigned in Lancashire. The arrival of barges changed the layout of the town for good, when it finally spilled over across the River Kent and the small factories and terraced houses that started to appear near Stramongate Bridge were of course built in local stone from the quarries on Kendal Fell.

As the manufacturing of textiles, iron founding and shoemaking declined in the twentieth century, local government administration, tourism and culture stepped in to plug the gaps, but specialised to services and ghosts of industry were left behind. A first taste of globalisation's increasing lust for low prices had left gouges on the landscape. Rubbing bad charms with holy fingers. On this particular afternoon, a dull grey blanket enveloped the buildings below Greenside. Slowly, I moved down the rocky steps edging towards the town. At the corner of High Tenterfell, objects and images began to fade away. I suddenly felt alone in a darkened room with headphones muted and subtitles on. Shrouded in fog, a struggle towards communication. Mediaeval pathways, burgage plots and the ancient village of Kirkland. A stage set for slaughter on the slopes of Beast Banks. The black emptiness echoed where herds used to be the keepers of men.

Taking a detour from the Boundary, I clambered onto my bike and freewheeled into Kendal's grey mist. On the pavements a familiar gang of shufflers were out in force, clogging up the one-way system. A Lowry painting made flesh; ancient paths and Georgian façades competed with a multilevel Wetherspoons. Miles Thompson's honeycomb of stone, once home to council offices, originally Kendal's public washhouse and baths. Inside, get as much cheap, cheerful food and drink as you like. Download, order, enjoy. No need for newspapers, the beermats overflow with slogans about Brexit. On the walls and by the bar another form of self-serve nostalgia is available on tap. Whilst other pubs have closed and people moved away, around ten charity shops have snuck into a small enclave next to the Town Hall with a handful of betting and coffee shops – may the odds be ever in your favour. Welcome to Britain's High Street malaise, the 'clone zone.' Everything in its right place: burgers, baristas, betting slips, bargains and the boarded up. Around the time of the national park's creation, Kendal's rush hour meant hundreds of sheep rattling down the high street. But then cars came along and now, if cattle pass through, they are loaded on trucks. Following a one-way route to the out-of-town supermarkets, where parking is free and unrestricted.

A week later, I headed out in the car towards Scout Scar and the Brigsteer Road. Sitting in traffic that crawled to a whimper on the climb out of Windermere through Ings and Staveley. After a journey seemingly without end, the long line swiftly vanished at the gateway of Plumgarths. Relieved to see an open road, I lent gently into the right-hander, pointing the headlights at the bypass runway. At the top of the bank, a breath of sunshine engulfed the car. I took my foot off the gas slightly, pulling the visor down near the turn-off for the quarry access road, but here the entrance was barred. They'd even installed a human checkpoint with a triple A dangling from his lanyard. The King of Hi-Vis powered by bright waistcoats and bibs on the perimeter. Hard hat, tabard and torch, be anyone you like but charge them for access. Today, Boundary Bank Business Park didn't belong to the town. *Live. Work. Invest.*

The cheesy schmaltz on the Living in South Lakeland website about quality of life, connectivity, transport links and business vibrancy rang a little hollow as I drove on. The Boundary actually underlies the surface of the former quarry area. A site currently trapped in an ongoing hiatus between the Lake District National Park Authority (LDNPA) and the SLDC. Whilst the national park has accepted a future incorporating waste management, the council believe there is more scope for employment development... All the people...So many people...Quietly, in the shadow of hidden depths, the quarry sinks back to nature. Any future proposals are subject to a development management process. Millions of years in the making, squashed, tilted and uplifted. Taste the waste – will it be auld grey, red stone or a metallic high-tech colour? Take a new route straight through the 3 Rs: reduce, reuse and recycle. At the beginning of a sharp incline, leading to a left-hand turn at the bottom end of Bradleyfield Farm, is a site designated by Story Homes for 34 high quality homes. Leafy Brigsteer Road, one of Kendal's most sought after areas. Sustainable and integrated. Delivering a mixture of new terraced, semi-detached and detached dwellings, with twelve of them labelled 'affordable'.

Affordable...

A term the Government define as – 'No more than 80 per cent of the local market rent (including service charges, where applicable).'

But for many languishing on the National Living Wage, this political hot potato isn't actually 'affordable' in any real sense. Still, the vibrant national park understands the acute need of so-called 'affordable' housing, yet they do not build houses. Instead they try to make sure any new-builds or conversions meet the needs of local communities. Hand in hand with quality design and sympathetic materials. The national park's needs comparable to the widening gap between local incomes and house prices. Cumbria's unique 'Fit for Purpose' Housing Strategy. Drafted during the heyday of Cameron and Osborne's age of austerity in 2012, Cumbria Housing Group's Section 106s template was designed to speed up any 'hot potato' agreements. Development Control. Cross-boundary relationships. Traditional settlement patterns. Rural service centres, villages, cluster communities and the open countryside. Evolve and adapt, meeting the needs of key service centres on the edge, just outside the national park's cultural associations and spectacular landscape.

The bend at Bradleyfield eventually opened out to a long straight stretch of road. Nestled between the sprawl of Kendal and the limestone escarpment of the National Trust (NT) managed Scout Scar. Sediments of limestone deposited in warm tropical seas; that drifted northwards to form the fringes with sandstones, gritstones and coal. At the mushroom viewpoint a panorama spreads across the central core of 120 hills and mountains in the Lake District, Yorkshire and Lancashire. On clear days it extends across to the Victorian landmark of Blackpool Tower, or the vast intertidal mudflats of Morecambe Bay. Kiss me quick before the sands of time shift and scour away the shoreline for ever.

The Brigsteer Road marked the spot where Richard Leafe heralded the Boundary extensions approved back in 2015. Now sheltered by the national park's warm embrace, fell runners, cyclists and dog walkers can share paths with the promise of a thriving cross-border community, from Helsington Barrows down to Sizergh and across the Lyth Valley. Whilst the soothing tones of their new chief executive sing out above the noise of the dual carriageway below. I parked up at a layby opposite a new wooden waymarker for Barrowfield and Scout Scar. Lacing up muddied boots, I turned my back to Kendal before setting off on a gentle stroll towards Warriners Wood.

In an idle corner of the new boundary I found the national flower of rubbish. 'Witches' Knickers' suspended in shining barbed wire and tangled around steel gates and wooden posts. Dry stone walls embellished with flattened beer cans. Circles of abandoned black sacks, squashed cans, coffee cups, sweet wrappers and takeaway cartons sprinkled like confetti on the side of the road. Left behind, a dithyrambic row of noise, symbols and song. Right to Roam and rampage where you like. About thirty yards on, a pair of skimpy black knickers adorned with love hearts hung loosely off the branch of a birch tree. Tossed out beside a shrivelled up condom. George Shaw's nymphs scrabbling round the limestone ridges with no clothes on. Touching the wild, porn dogs sniffed the wind for something new. Nature coloured with enamel paint. Don't look back, just try to forget. Walk away, walk on. Better protected. More beautiful. Accessible for all...

Continuing on, I followed the route of communication. Almost every other vehicle that passed was either a 4x4, sport utility vehicle (SUV) or delivery van. A handy cut-through pearled with a sea of manure and the voices of songbirds. Above, telegraph poles kept watch over fields scattered with paving blocks and natural decay. Puddles shimmered, leaves danced, whilst the roots of trees twisted and curved into surrealist shapes. I was reminded of the phrase 'Exultant Strangeness', a description of the Pembrokeshire coast by the landscape artist, Graham Sutherland. Educated at Goldsmiths, the London-born artist became driven by repulsion at the growth of industrialisation. Sutherland defiantly documented the natural world with sketches of rock formations and tree roots on the back of envelopes. In 2013, Kendal's Abbot Hall gallery put on the North West's first exhibition of his work. The paintings burned into my retina a series of brooding landscapes; rocky and fractured. Redesigned by esoteric backdrops and otherworldly images; always provoking and feeding the imagination.

A stray mongrel suddenly flew out of the shrubbery adorning the stone wall on my right. Back into the present the dog's tongue lolled out of the side of its mouth. It stood there panting for a second with a broad smile. And then its small, but powerful hind legs propelled it back into the foliage and out again. Before my eyes popped open it was gone in a blur. Off the rabid beast skittered towards the dirty puddles gathered by a sharp bend in the road. In the field opposite, I started to detect a faint whistling sound. Motioning with my right arm towards the wall, I looked up and called the dog back. Ears pricked, it pivoted sharply and scampered through a wormhole in the stones.

Down through a dip in the road approaching Warriners Wood, a male pheasant ran the gauntlet directly in front of a Land Rover. Flushed out in the headlights. Somehow it escaped to the other side with a manic explosion of feathers. Shaking my head, I wondered why they don't just fly away. Entering the ancient wood on my left, I eased cautiously onto a slick and wet floor. Almost at once, a cycle of seasons hundreds of years in the making began to circle. Mystical geographies evoking a spirit world full of Pagan and cultural concerns. Replacing old ways of life with a new sense of dignity for the downtrodden. Wooded areas covered with green velvet where beasts of the chase were protected. Local myths, legends and folklore. Firing a treble shot broadside that broke the enemy line at Trafalgar. The whole world drifting away through the hearts of oak.

I stood perfectly still for a while, shrouded in strong vapours which crept with a trace of mint. Velvet moss, the green life of change mixed with a mosaic of autumn leaves. Birds performed secret dances and announced my arrival between the silences and shivering breeze enfolding itself around a sea of tree barks. Outside, beyond the stone walls, a mechanised drone of rubber on the western boundary tarmac. Stepping over rocky outcrops of limestone, a rectangular shaped wood sloped gently eastwards. I followed the contours of a permissive path dominated by fallen branches of ash, sycamore and hazel. Natural detritus carpeted on loose slate.

And yet, with each step I felt a lingering sense of being watched. Pausing beside a couple of twigs forming an X shape, I detected movement about thirty yards ahead. It came from the inside of a hollow tree. A few seconds later, something climbed out and issued a final goodbye to the sky, passing birds and clouds. A twirling silhouette slowly formed out of the olive coloured floor. It moved towards me just as the crying wind dropped to a whisper. In the stillness, deer no longer dared to tread. Even the faintest footstep would have echoed in eternity. Enthralled, my eyes fixed on the shadowy figure advancing with the grace of a seventeenth century noble-woman. Full of health and toil, she emerged as a light haze broke through the canopy. Until she stood barely a yard away, hair brown and thick, reaching down to her calves. Black eyes quick and lively, with a round face and dimple on her cheek.

"Walk with me a while?" she asked and held out a hand gloved in lace. Moving closer I stretched out until our fingers almost touched,

"Of course, it will be an honour..."

She led me out through a corner at the right-hand bottom of the wood. Over hills and mountains we floated together on mad, moaning winds. Watching the light of the earth change and unfold in golden shadows. As the wind lashed, her grip tightened above the bridge over the Eamont at Brougham Castle, near Penrith. Loitering, escaping over the lakes and streams at Whinfell Forest. Then she smiled and pointed at something gleaming near a high wall.

"There, I can't believe it's still here...the Hartshorn Tree, from the time of King Baliol."

By now I had fallen slightly behind, but managed to catch her up circling round Caesar's Tower at Appleby. In the darkest dark atop the castle ramparts, contemplating the magical patterns of the constellations. With eyes serene, still and bright. I scratched my head trying to figure out the time. Next to me bathed in angelic light a dream softly creeping, she stared out into the void. As if contemplating an end, eyes fixed on a vision, she began to tell me the story of an Indiana Jones type who became the Queen's Champion...

He was made the Most Noble Order of the Garter, a trusted advisor. But he was a selfish man, who preferred to choose the intrigue and play of the royal court over spending time at home with his family. Over many centuries he had inherited lands through well-judged marriages and sovereigns indebted to him. The largest of these areas covered a swathe of the north-west of England. On her majesty's service he sailed to faraway lands. Swashbuckling, buccaneering and plundering in her name, for some a blessing, for others – a curse. Raids that earned him even more favour and even more treasure for the royal coffers. All throughout, his poor wife, Meg, was treated badly, whilst he remained a virtual stranger to their only surviving child, a daughter. Barely fifteen when he died, she was left only a modest sum, whilst the entire family estates were passed to the man's brother. At a stroke they made him an Earl, who then set about cruelly barring the mother and daughter from entering their rightful inherited lands. In resolute defiance, a 'Great Business' followed covering over three hundred years of family history...

A long pause buzzed like a fridge. Scraping her shoe, she looked down at the fresh scuff marks on the stone floor.

"Is that what happened to you?" I asked.

"I took my leave of him on Greenwich Heath...when a little before his death he had promised to my mother and I that all his lands would come to be mine."

A sudden gust lifted the long, thick hair out of her eyes and I glimpsed a few tears ignited by the pale moonlight.

"But all those moments were lost in time. Burned like a match and disappeared. Now like a rebirth, a new spell has been cast forth. My journey resurrected upon these curled clouds." Suddenly she turned, and reaching out, plucked a pearl of fire from the night sky. Tinged with excitement, I beamed back at her,

"Please tell me the name of such a spiritual creature as you?"

But then smoke ran up my nostrils as the red-orange glow seemed to penetrate and rap my deepest sadness. Sensing the mesmerising effect of the flame, she wagged a finger in front of my stinging eyes.

"Down I have plunged towards earth, answering the calls of my former tenants through the smoke and ashes of ages past. And now together we must ride the boundaries of old Westmorland to the curve of infinity."

Inside a vivid shaft of light we departed once more. Hiding amongst the clouds, the name Isabella floating over and above the formidable barrier at Brough. Along the sky riding the romantic ruins at Pendragon, until the heavens thundered and the earth trembled. Covering her face with a lengthy cloak, she quickly accelerated away and broke through a gap in the enveloping mists. Rushing on, heading down towards Sedbergh, easing right over the sleeping elephants, above another set of castle ruins on top of a drumlin. A little further on a wide river offered views into a mass of grey. Stopping briefly on the mowed lawn of a fine historic house, she motioned me to follow through a set of iron bars and wooden shutters. Slightly nervous, I slipped through easily enough into a box room off the main entrance hall. She closed the door behind me and pulled out a long candle from one of her pockets. Igniting it with the end of a finger, the light seeped into the surrounding area. It covered the whole side of a wall in front of an enormous triptych that stared back, illuminating our souls. I took a step sideways and smiled in awe. There in both flesh and oil. Over eight feet high, with each end panel four feet in length, the monumental 'Great Picture'. Using a combination of portraiture, text and symbolism, the image skilfully depicted Lady Anne at various stages of her life. Whilst presenting the two brothers and parents of her ancient aristocratic family.

Turning to face me, she broke the silence...

"Do you know what the poet Gray said when he visited mine and my mother's tomb?"

Looking upwards with eyes closed, Lady Anne continued…

"She swept, she hiss'd, she ripen'd and grew rough, at Brougham, Pendragon, Appleby and Brough."

As she broke off, a glow returned and caressed the night through the Georgian windows. Moments later, souls of the dead bathed in the light and flew off to scatter embers over the moon. Suddenly the ceaseless swirling faded and I began plummeting down. Falling as far I could until there was nowhere but the Brigsteer road once again. Time passed and I awoke alone beneath a hedge with the autumn wind hollow like a gun. A phrase recurring as in a dream.

Preserve your Loyalties, Defend your Rights…

A week later in the car heading south on the A591, I passed a solitary jogger inching back into Kendal. Head down, phones on, eyes to the floor, block-rocking beats on a long stretch of pavement near a couple of garages, a tile showroom and Travelodge. One last chance to pay the tourist tax before the motorway lottery adds on up to £10 per fill up. Round the next bend a foodie haven out on the edge, Low Sizergh Barn owned by the NT. Its name heralds the arrival of Scandinavian settlements in Cumbria during the ninth or tenth century. Ancient variations of Sizergh include: *Sigarith*– Old Norse for dairy farm, with the second part *erg* – a Norse-Irish term for shieling or hill pasture. These days it marks a modern family-run tenant farm adjusted to the rhythms of diversification, with wooden floorboards and colourful display baskets showcasing local produce and crafts. Mixed leaves and Growing Well. Farming with the future in mind. The key buzz words: sustainability, seasonality, traceability and cutting food miles. Of course, hand-picked means a little more expensive, but a much more whole- some alternative to the one-stop-shop machine age. Once raw milk was taken by cart to Kendal, but now you can watch the changing face of moo cow farm in the milking parlour. There's even a vending machine in the car park where unpasteurized milk flows straight from the teat.

Turn left out of Low Sizergh and you soon encounter fourteen acres oozing with luxury and the wow factor. Once the plaything of Victorian aristocrats and the Sisters of Mercy, now the Villa Levens Hotel is equipped with five-star furnishings. Brettargh Holt, its original name was later transferred to the formidable roundabout near Sedgwick. Here, the A590 forms a large part of the southern boundary as it heads for the Lake District peninsulas on the longest cul-de-sac in the world. At the head of the river, at the source of the sea. Back in 2011, a walk on the dark side from Barrow led to a Bond-style chase in the early hours. A drunken teenager in some kind of domesday machine. Ignoring repeated signals to pull over, a stolen bus ended up wedged in the middle of the roundabout. Turning left onto Nannypie Lane towards the Sizergh underpass through two worlds and the roar of big machines. Stepping stones washed away by the shape of water at the old ford crossing the River Kent. A hamlet acquired by the Wakefield family who established old and new gunpowder works near the riverbanks. Dum-dum bullets and shoot to kill, I hear Empire down. But in the interim years after the Great War, output fell significantly until the New Sedgwick Gunpowder Company Ltd ceased production in 1935. Nowadays the site of the Kendal Caravan Club, it is set in woodland owned by the NT. *Nuts in May* campers enjoying nature to the full in a small slice of heaven.

I carried on, following a serpentine back lane full of large pot holes with skeletal hedgerows sporting new Grade Ones. About twenty yards from the underpass entrance, I parked up opposite a barbed wire fence next to a new NT gate sign. A couple of dog walkers emerged out of the square block of concrete backlit by a screen of white rays. Inside the outdoors, built for adventure. Geared up in complimentary Mountain Warehouse and Karrimor boots, jackets and backpacks. Put off by the presence of a camera hanging round my neck, they looked straight through me. Neither one of us knowing or caring where the other went. Crossing over the road, I noticed a few daubs of graffiti underneath the A591's reverberations.

Lady Killa…
Jamie T = wanker…
Fat Cow & Pot Head…

Not exactly the politically charged statements of Banksy's Existencilism or gang members marking their territory. Instead, I sensed a bunch of bored kids relatively new to the art of swearing. Nothing is illuminated inside these in-between spaces. Yet, the further you go into the darker depths the more seductive they become. Vehicles came and went outlined against the light as they advanced towards the centre of the black hole where I found myself lingering. A dark box brooding away like a giant shipping container underneath the entrance to the national park's beating heart. Here, near one of the three boundary extensions, I'd found a total contrast between the gloom of the old and a portal to a better, brighter world.

At the top of the lane, nostalgia for the light led towards the entrance to Sizergh Castle. Turn right at the T-junction for over seven hundred years of history. Sir Walter Strickland, a new Knight of the Bath, rewarded for his services in Border warfare. Every man dies, not every man truly lives. Westmorland is mine, it owes me a living. The door to the past pulsing with dark Elizabethan oak panelling, wall-to-wall family portraits and a vast array of period furniture and armoury. Always be mindful not to get pounced on by an overzealous room guide trying to jazz up the Strickland backstory. The sort who drove Alan Bennett (another institution) to write the play *People* about the "sense of unease" he felt when visiting similar stately homes owned by the NT. I decided to become a voyeur at a safer distance via several tours of the castle and gardens on YouTube. Sentimental dreams awakened on a four-or-five minute journey through the real Fortress Britain. The social order in stone complete with a Classic FM soundtrack, for all you people out there…the song's over four hundred years long and repeats three words over and over again…

niman bæc wealdan

During the fourteenth century, wealthy landowners started to militarise the Lake District fringes. Pele (or peel) towers arrived with walls up to several feet thick to fortify manor houses as a defence against Scottish border raiders (after Bannockburn). Unique to both sides of the border, these castellated ramparts surrounded the central core and marked out the boundary edges. Casting a stain of red throughout the air, bathing the buildings and surrounding landscape. Their spirits left only death and destruction. Some of the remaining towers, like those at Muncaster, Sizergh Castle and neighbouring Levens Hall, were later incorporated into the stately homes of today.

Returning to the car, I realised the end of the beginning was now in sight, as I pulled out and eased through the underpass. Turning left, where a turnpike linking Kendal with Milnthorpe once led to the Ulverston to Carnforth section. A sharp right just before the Strickland Arms pointed towards Levens, a small township in the Heversham parish that skirts the southern boundary. Its name derived from the Old English words: *Leofa, Leoffwine* or *Ness*, meaning a 'headland'. A place you don't live in, but 'on'.

The narrow road round the back of the Strickland Arms spiralled slowly upwards, flanked by coppiced woodland and an old crumbling wall draped in spongy moss. The cover from the canopy opened up past the Duke Plantation and Heaves Hotel, whilst the road continued to hug the limestone outcrops on Sizergh Fell. At the brow of the hill before Heaves Farm I passed an unsteady cyclist staring ahead in disbelief – a day when giving up is surely easier. I continued my route onto Whitegate Hill past Sizergh Fell Road, until it began to slope gradually downhill towards a rendezvous with my old friend the Brigsteer Road. We met again, serenaded by sites of species-rich grassland and shrub on the edges of non-surveillance. Stirring the calm from out of nowhere, where illicit tales are hidden behind darkened windows. Secret pleasures and passions aroused by the sexual energy of woodlands.

I entered the village from the narrow top of Lowgate on the gentle run to the Village Institute at the junction of Levens Lane. A venue for the whole community, with a gripping monthly agenda comprising WI meetings the Brownies, Appalachian dancers and budding water-colourists. All users must keep off the gravel driveway though. The breaking news on the community website had details of a new village hall. I pulled over to check out the view across the Lyth Valley floor to the brooding limestone headwall of Whitbarrow Scar. Although strangely, I found myself watching a man striding out to the post box merrily whistling as if calling up shades of his youth. It all felt a million miles away from the photos of sunken hedgerows, roads and farms in the wake of the 2015, 2009 and 1967 floods. When the arm of the sea burst onto the valley floor and turned the fields into a nocturne of blue-grey. No one can ever forget that musty, dank smell in the dreaded aftermath. Keep the pumps running when the water comes rushing, who knows when nature will call again.

Turning to a sea of tranquillity on my right, I gazed out on a landscape more reminiscent of a Constable or Peter de Wint. In one of the earliest images of Levens village, (the undated painting *Cottages at Beanthwaite Green*), de Wint used hog brushes loaded with several different colours and swept them across the canvas in thick impasto. He would later go on, though, to be remembered as one of England's chief watercolourists. In the early 1800s he also dropped by Levens Hall to instruct the owner Mary Howard how to paint. Amongst the estate's other artistic connections is a short period from May to November 1971, when the reclusive West Cumbrian artist Percy Kelly was offered a short-term tenancy at Levens Park Cottage. During a period of hardship after his first wife Audrey divorced him, owner Oliver Robin Bagot offered the place at the northern end of the park for a generously low rent. It was here that Kelly wrote the Letters from Levens to Millom poet Norman Nicholson, (published in David Cross's book – *Cumbrian Brothers* in 2007), which included lavishly illustrated paintings and drawings in his own inimitable style. Kelly famously did not paint for monetary gain. To him, a day without drawing or painting would lead to depression. This was outsider art as compulsion, drawing as natural as walking. Before his short stay at Levens, Kelly lived for twelve years at Glen Cottage in the Solway coastal village of Allonby. Similar to many other wealth pots in the glorified theme park, a father and son looking for a good investment later bought the cottage and restored it as a contemporary holiday let.

For many, Levens is first glimpsed from a car windscreen travelling eastwards along the A590. Groups of light-coloured houses blending into a ridge overlooking the Lyth Valley to the west, with the estuary of the River Kent and Morecambe Bay to the south. Situated beside the damson valley where the outside world is kept at a safe distance from the trunk road. The community website reinforces this happy oblivion. An economy previously reliant on agriculture and the dark stuff of peat is now a hotbed: Litter picks, quizzes, wine and nibbles, gentle exercise and apple-pressing, plus B&Bs, pleasant walks, cycleways and fish & chip takeaway vans. Once considered a vital heat and fuel source, now even the soil yawns out here. In a fleeting hinterland on the edge, satellite anthems are full of rural incantations. Sipping tea, twitching curtains and musings on the way to holding a cake knife. Against the distant whir of traffic, seasons roll slowly by and the gates are always open.

GILPIN BRIDGE TO LINDALE

NEITHER LIVING NOR DEAD
A PURPLE COOL BADGE
RICHNESS & DIVERSITY OUT OF TIME
THE AGE OF THE FAKE
RIDING THE BOUNDARIES, 21ST-CENTURY STYLE
ADDING TO ITS OWN CORPSE
MOSS RIGHTS & LOST HISTORIES
GOLDEN STEMS WAVERING GHOSTLIKE
TRANSITORY TRUTHS & UNTRUTHS
STILLNESS & REFUGE
THE PLUNGE TOWARDS THE DEEP
ISOLATION, TREATMENT & CURE
GILPIN BRIDGE TO LINDALE

The true starting point:

Back at Brettargh Holt roundabout about to hit the southern boundary. Junction 36 to the blood and fire of Hell's Kitchen. Barrow – from the Old English beorg, meaning a hill or mound. Yet for some, the hill is a hell. The end of the world trading in the county lines of Victorian tenement blocks. On problem estates gangs of cuckoos peddling drugs to the poor and beaten down. Nuclear sounds silenced by the fallout from years of austerity cuts. A headstone etched with shipbuilding's global decline and the uncertainty surrounding Trident's renewal. Locked out of opportunity, rhythms of panic, craving, nothing, time...

The A590, perilous route of an old nineteenth century turnpike road constructed across the impassable bogland from Levens to Grange-over-Sands. Now it is a slow burn, lined with draining ditches into one of the most deprived areas in England. Back in 2009, after several years in development, Barrow Borough Council announced an eight-point Strategic Community Strategy. Borne out of consultations with local people and various public and private organisations, it set out a long-term approach loaded with acronyms: LAAs (Local Area Agreements), LSP (Local Strategic Partnership), CSP (Cumbria Strategic Partnership), CDRP (Crime and Disorder Reduction Partnership). On the cover of the document's forty pages, a tree formed out of hearts.

Love Barrow. A place that people love...

Multilayers beckoned after the first exit following the old alignment of the A6. Passing a series of heritage and road signs: Sizergh Castle, a Wedding Fayre at Villa Levens and the Lake District peninsulas. Single to dual track, pinch points playing catch-up with a lack of investment and connectivity. "The Home of the Early Riser" marked a first appearance for the champion of all sizzlers. Out in the middle of nowhere, neither living nor dead, Tarantino's *From Dusk 'Til Dawn.* The showdown is on. How far can too far go? Burgers, bacon and beans piled up with streaky onions, chips and spam. The bee's knees under a shower of rain and dodgy gas canisters. White vans and lorry drivers knocking back mugs of tea overlooking the drained mosses. Wheeling behind them other tradesmen's shadows on the go-slow between speed cameras.

Next up, a large boulder signified you were officially inside England's largest national park. But this was an old marker, installed long before Lord Gardiner hammered a brand new logo onto a wooden field gate. Striking nails and palms on the August 2016 boundary extension celebrations at Sizergh Castle. Think deeper. Complex issues communicated through interpretation. Wasdale Head framed in a purple cool badge. A more colourful modern national park emblem.

Discover. Explore. Inspire...

Fresh approaches without a hint of green or russet brown. Drawing nearer to Gilpin Bridge, legends from the reign of King John assembled across the valley floor. Four sharp tusks wallowing in the muck and grassy track northwards along the edge of Helsington Barrows. Deep in the dark a monstrous brute infesting wild thoughts near the hamlets of Cleabarrow and Crook. In nightmare's grip, villagers and pilgrims shuddered with fear en route from the old chapel on St Mary's Holme. Desire and horror damned at the cult of the ruins of the Holy Cross at Plumgarths. Strength, courage and ferocity. In ancient times, Artemis, the goddess of hunting, mountains and forests, sent beasts in fits of chilling vengeance on the ephemeral human race.

On the banks of a stream, the heroic moment arrived. Foam and fresh blood drove the monster to fury, as Richard the rider on horseback attacked with a blazing sword and the sound of a bugle. In a flurry of movement, the final coup de grâce heralding nobility and wealth after the wild boar was finally overcome. Life and death. The epic combat between man and animal. Throbbing within the passions of lavish, expressive hunting scenes painted in luminous colours by the Flemish artist, Peter Paul Rubens. For his brave exploits, Richard De Gylpin bagged a new coat of arms featuring a black furred boar and crescent moon on a gold background. He was also granted most of the land around Kentmere. Now the name Gilpin reverberates as a site of memory throughout the tranquil surroundings of the valley just off the Crook road. Where modern pilgrims pay to explore private woodlands, a golf course and the Wild Boar Inn, said to mark the spot where the spirit of the beast rests.

Indicating right, I turned off the A590 at the junction for the A5074 Lyth Valley road, a route trickling back to the inferno of Bowness. Gilpin Bridge. Last outpost for the Windermere-centric bubble and start of my first proper stage. After skirting Levens, the boundary enters the Lyth Valley via Sunnyside. A narrow road dissected by the long and straight Brigsteer Causeway, banked up over Levens Moss until it terminates near the flood-pumping system at Gilpin Bridge. I parked up on the downslope of the bridge over the River Gilpin. Directly opposite, a group of light grey pebble dash houses sported a thick beard of ivy along one end. A sharp left turn marked the point where the national park trails the current under Sampool Bridge. Flowing out towards the River Kent Estuary where it joins hands with the Winster and Bela onto Milnthorpe Sands. Meeting points. Two young strangers at the garage under suspicion of committing a series of Satanist murders. Brought together after a mishap with a Norton Big Four on the station forecourt. George and Edna. Driving off down the A5074 in Red Robbo's humble Mini. Great cars and a great deal more. Jorge Grau paying homage to Romero's classic zombie horror on the side roads of Levens.

Under big empty skies, remnants of a former seabed reared up into a vast block of hard limestone that dominates the gentle valley. Whitbarrow Scar, a carboniferous escarpment commanding the southern boundary. Rich floras of equatorial swamps and sedimentation forming a horizontal structure on the periphery of the national park. On top of bare pavements, fissured tongues thump and sheen through chills and spills. Hard rock meets soft rock on the margins. Igneous and metamorphic versus sedimentary along a rim of imperfections punctured by the estuaries of Morecambe Bay. Richness and diversity out of time. Everything turning the other way round. Fifteen miles away to the north-west, the lofty King himself, Scafell Pike stares into the flare of England.

The air was hazy and damp as I stood on the corner of the dual carriageway just past the Gilpin Bridge Inn. Close to a spot where an old smithy used to service local farmers, repairing tools, cart wheels, shoeing horses and sharpening shears before it was demolished in 2001. The inn itself has had a somewhat chequered past. Starting off as a 17th century coaching inn, immoral use led to its closure in the early 1900s. Squelching through another layer of history, known colloquially as 'T'peat fella', Charlie Shaw, was a local who used to carry peat to Kendal during his time working the ground at the inn.

In-between the spaces of the traffic's swirling roar, I waited for the right moment to present itself. This was the first time I had brought Dugdale's 'epic adventure' along with me. Taking a keen interest in the first nuggets of advice – visit the Lyth Valley when the damson crop is being harvested and don't get too loaded up on booze before setting off! As I looked up at the aggressive multitude of cars, vans and trucks rumbling by, a Ford hatchback emblazoned with purple go-faster stripes and a national park logo turned off the dual carriageway in front of me. The Fiesta's metallic silver egg shape forming a blur of impressionism towards the direction of the inn and garage. Far from the centre, drifting across dual carriageways, riding the boundaries 21st century style into puddles of oily water.

Skipping over the busy road, it was just after ten o'clock when the stage proper began. All the while keeping a close eye on the time, in order to be in Lindale by 3pm to catch the only 530 bus heading back. I set off in the direction of a sign for the ospreys at Foulshaw Moss, before taking a sudden left at a Cumbria Coastal Way footpath marker. Immediately a dead-end stared back. After hacking my way through a wave of tough knee-high grass, a small hollow hidden behind pockets of silver birch opened up on the left. Roll up, roll up...Welcome to Taylor's Funland on tour, please ask about today's great deals. A Big Top Bonanza beside the A590, full of modern circus vehicles, from smaller vans to heavy road locomotives. Almost every circus act you might need at the crack of a bull-whip. Fun packed days with the Greatest Showmen in Cumbria.

Today any magic tricks or buffoonery were put on hold; with only an eerie silence ringing out across the open dell. Further ahead, on the other side, more trucks were positioned at right angles just off the muddy track. Reared by those that care, supplied to those that know. A stationary butcher's lorry in front, opposite the entrance to a nondescript field. Assembled near the gate in thoughtful repose, a handful of black cows sat chewing the cud surrounded by deep muddy cavities. Plopped down haphazardly, staring at the void between the odd telegraph pole.

"Ye stupid bastard..."

I looked back at the circus vehicles and noticed a mechanic in blue overalls hopping around on one leg, surrounded by a selection of tools on the floor. His eyes were wide and burned through mine locking on with a haunted gaze. From behind the butcher's van a mongrel ran out, ears pinned tight with tail between its legs. Quickening my step past a line of tractors a breeze picked up and carried a nauseous soup of fertilizer. Hovering over my head it grabbed me by the throat and lingered. I dug into the pocket of my puffer jacket and tugged on the zip a little, pulling it over the top of my nose. But the horror and mystery of the land tightened their grip until I looked up at Whitbarrow in despair. Approaching from nowhere in a misty haze, a rouge and cream coloured coach temporarily blocked out the powerful pong. 'Edinburgh Tours' ornamented in gold block lettering running down the sides. Adding another layer of intrigue, the empty coach appeared to be driverless. I shivered as it passed, before continuing on down a long, practically straight metalled right of way, the myth of Rome in stone. Could the smell of isolation and threat be the decimated corpse of the Devil himself? Galloping out to meet the ghostly figures of occultist schlock.

Overhead a series of high-pitched chirrups from a handful of jackdaws competed with the repeated howls of hungry herring gulls. Plunging and circling round something just out of sight in the first of a set of rectangular shaped fields. Lining the route towards Foulshaw Cottages to the left, Gilpin's watery tail curled into a looping G shape. Pouring its heart out into the River Kent, whilst on the opposite flank, wet as the evening rain, Stakes Moss transferred itself into the remnants of another drowned world. Formed during a period of huge climatic change at the end of the last ice age, lowland raised peatbog adding to its own corpse. Moss rights and lost histories.

Peering into the abyss to see what's lurking underneath a Jackstraw of birch trees. Foulshaw Moss. Beyond the horizon lies the secret to a new beginning. Landscape reimagined as a nature reserve, footsteps on wooden boardwalks invoking the past. Ballard's Doctor Kerans gazing down into Ginny Greenteeth's sea of total memory. Descending towards much-sliced earth against the spectacle of cold, damp desolation. Fleeing the world, shielded from the heavy metal thunder of the A590. A process formed over thousands of years, preserved in acidic water. Layers of sphagnum moss up to ten metres high developed into vast peat domes, rising high above the landscape. The destruction of the bog people's dark stuff in favour of an unrenewable energy resource. Turbary rights, hard times and unhappy poverty. Personal use and profit as opposed to the environmental impact. Transforming the nature of the economy. Burning fossil fuels to warm pots and the world.

Deeper, deeper, deeper…

Cutting and selling versus cutting and using. Shaped by the back-breaking work of digging up animal skeletons or mutilated bodies with the soil and rocks. A landscape swallowed by the bog, emptying the past into the heart of darkness.

In 1996, the raised bog at Foulshaw was dually recognised, as a Site of Special Scientific Interest (SSSI) and by the European Union's Habitats Directive as a Special Area of Conservation. Since 1998, the site has been owned and looked after by the Cumbria Wildlife Trust (CWT), and now represents one of the last surviving remnants of a habitat rich in wildlife and history. Spreading out below the bulwark of Whitbarrow just inside the national park boundary, it is the kind of peaceful retreat where you can watch concentric ripples form in the beauty of life, surrounded by the soothing tones of birdsong. In the pinks, reds, oranges and greens where animals and plants flourish, the bog is slowly being reclaimed.

As the removal of conifers planted around the margins entices back sphagnum moss, cotton grass, cranberry and bog rosemary. From the osprey viewing platforms a flat barren landscape is draped in a yellow-brown glimmer from swathes of common reeds. Their golden stems wavering ghostlike, calling across a carpet of sweet-smelling moss. On the other boardwalk a throwback to the New World depicted in the scarred landscapes of Paul Nash. In the stillness, beams of light shine down on mounds of earth and solitary tree trunks form lifeless crucifixions where the music is elsewhere…

On a separate visit to the moss a few months later (on a dull February afternoon), the CWT blackboard had chalked up an impressive list of recent sightings / activities on the site:

- Canada goose
- Fieldfare
- Raven (nest-building)
- Red deer
- Woodcock (near barn)
- Marsh harrier (Female)
- Red kite (2)
- Jack snipe
- Merlin
- Peregrine
- Buzzard
- Lesser black-backed gull (4)
- Pink-footed goose
- Albino red deer
- Little egret
- Kestrel
- Sparrowhawk
- Blue tit
- Great tit
- Cole tit
- Great spotted woodpecker
- Chaffinch
- Robin
- Wren
- Dunnock
- Stonechat
- Crow
- Mute swan
- Teal
- Mallard
- Grey heron
- Snipe
- Redwing

Following Dugdale's route to Foulshaw Cottages, I noticed the buildings were both dated from 1951, the year of the national park's creation. Forming overhead the heavy sub-bass from a biplane pulsed like a memory from the future. On the road to High Foulshaw, wide open grey skies turned darker and grew more overcast with each step. The only hints of colour came from the odd bit of local traffic. A light blue egg delivery and red post office van contrasted with the glistening pearl black of a Nissan SUV. Looking out across the endless flatlands, nothing existed apart from the odd 'members only' camping and caravan site. Cutting in, a sharp westerly breeze propelled a putrid stench from the flood ditches into the enveloping atmosphere.

Drifting in and out of an unwell arena dominated by barbed wire fences and piles of corrugated metal stacked up to plug gaps in the corners of fields. A long straight road. Mud and shit. Old and battered 'Men at Work' road signs. Nothing to be done. Habitat was the great deadener out here. Neither land nor sea, just muddy creeks across four hundred hectares of salt marsh. When I eventually reached High Foulshaw Farm, a substantial milking shed was being consumed in a green miasma. Sheep and dairy cows chased by the Four Horseman of the Apocalypse. Ghastly sacrifices and pictures of death still haunt people from all over the community and beyond. Mention of the dreaded word, 'Confirmed', brings back the year of empty and silent fields under skies of broken hearts.

Shortly after passing the farm, another wooden waymarker for the coastal path heralded a commune with the grass embankment running parallel to the Kent. Built in the traditional way and designed to protect the low-lying community from flooding. My sodden boots sank slowly into a series of oval-shaped puddles next to the gaping wounds imprinted into the muddy soil by huge tractor tyres. Twisting and writhing, I then had to fight my way through clumps of nettles and brambles until a clearing opened up a right-hand swoop of the estuary. Looking at the OS app on my phone I could trace how the Irish Sea pushed north-easterly from Hest Bank towards a narrower point at High Foulshaw and Halforth. Running in-between, Holme Island and Blackstone Point guarded the edge of the boundary entering Milnthorpe Sands in front of the Arnside Viaduct.

Further off, facing Morecambe promenade, the western cliffs are closed in by the imposing limestone promontory, Humphrey Head. A dangerous place at the mouth of a bay filled and emptied with transitory truths and untruths. Effigies cut in stone from fourteenth century folklore resting in a quiet corner of nearby Cartmel Priory, with a wolf carved at their feet. Local whispers still claim it to be 'the Last in England'. Chainmail and metal armour chasing around Cartmel Forest and England's largest lake until the hunt closed in upon the rocks at Humphrey Head. Flung over a gaping chasm, a spear dipped in true love brought a violent end to the ferocious creature. As the shadows started to fall, the fear of who you call fades away...

After making my way up onto the elongated embankment I was greeted by a noisy welcoming committee. First the deep musical tones of the unmistakeable curlew accelerated through the strong breeze. Out of its downcurved bill the song repeated a series of rising '*gui*' notes ending in a trill. Then, hundreds of Swaledales lined up in a single-file procession.

Far, far away...

As if lured with a magic pipe, looking for a portal to open wide. Never ride the lonely road, above all at sundown. Reflection's song searches the sky in bounds of drowned obscurity. Across the sands, dazzling silver met leaden greyness where mudflats thicken the darkest of nights. Idle tides, lying damp and desolate under heavy skies. Stillness and refuge, those rare and deceptive features. A quiet beast of prey lurking in the watery desert. Shrouded in a blanket of mist, Robert Nelson standing upright bathed in the abyss. Like a dream staggering from the Ship Inn at Milnthorpe, clutching a half bottle of whisky. Not found until the next morning by his brother Stephen. Staring out into the Irish Sea in silent expectation, sent to another place by the ebb and flow of changing tides. Awash in morbid death, the pasty hollows in a magical grip, gobbling up any unsuspecting victims. Expunged like wreckage, spitting out bones of the dead. Recognised by her boots alone, Smith the nailer's wife damned to infinity, with half a face and one arm missing. Narrowing shores and funnel effects. New Year's Eve 1787, trading lives in exchange for the ocean's roar. Swilling tides playing the blues of Kings written on marble tablets in the aisles of Beetham Church.

Another lamented youth, Thomas Barker of Cartmel, met his own Waterloo three days after Wellington's famous victory in 1815. Yet still many chose to take their chances on foot, despite a ferryboat service crossing the sands (originally between the Dixie's and latterly the Ship Inn to Foulshaw). Until one dismal night brought about the ferry's demise forever. Sinking into oblivion, two boats with up to sixteen adults and children on board, rowed across the sands by the landlord of the Ship Inn. In the night's fatal rhythm, the pull between land and water, thrown out into the bay and swept upstream. Voices silenced by the plunge towards the deep. In the broken waves, parents, uncles, aunts and their children all lost. Rushed to the black void, bodies remained hidden until the receding tide.

After the Great War during the 1920s and '30s, any heatwaves furnished the sands with a much more upbeat reputation. Large numbers of pleasure seekers flocked to soak up the sun at Westmorland's 'Little Blackpool', until the Art Deco styled pier, pavilions, cinemas, shops and stores of Morecambe flexed their extra pulling power. As I approached Middle Foulshaw Farm, the Sandside limestone quarry dominated the view of Haverbrack Bank across the estuary. Situated next to a dismantled railway junction at Hincaster, I noticed a curiously named feature 'The Dog Hole', a few miles south-west of Milnthorpe. Positioned on the same slopes, lying about two hundred feet up. Originally known as the 'Fairy Hole', it was partially excavated by a Dr Jackson in 1912. Then, in the mid-1950s, members of the First Milnthorpe Scout Group chanced upon it, and discovered a larger cavern below the primary entrance. In the 1980s, Tom Clare (Cumbria's chief archaeologist) closed off the cave with a metal grill to protect the findings.

After a further gap of some twenty years, a team led by Clare from Liverpool's John Moores University conducted more excavations. Found in amongst three designated zones was an assemblage of items, generally Romano-British in origin, including: Bronze bracelets and rings, Iron axe-heads and brooches, glass and jet beads, fragments of pottery and stone plus a few cockle shells. There were also thought to be twenty-three human skulls with a few red deer antlers. A vast accumulation of animal bones comprised numerous dog skulls, along with the remains of sheep, ox, pig, wolf, horse, red deer, fox, badger, cat, rabbit, mouse, roe deer, bat, vole and mole.

Further over to the left of the quarry, on the lower slopes of Beetham

Fell, a former pele tower dates from the fourteenth century. However, Dallam Tower boasts a range of other features – from an eighteenth century deer park and woodland, natural rock and water gardens, to nineteenth and twentieth century ornamental gardens. Continuing on the embankment still trailed by the confused flock, I kept my eyes peeled for a circular bath coated in an 'exotic hue of green slime', as described by Dugdale. To my surprise, I discovered that even after a gap of some twenty-odd years the solid tub had survived, although now its round shape looked more like a cheese vat. Amid concrete and clay, nature still finds a way. A wooden crate and piece of red wire mesh protruded out of the pitch-black sludge gathered in its belly for good measure.

Shortly afterwards, Arnside Knott and the Kent Viaduct came into view. As I veered off to the right, a barrier deep in shadow bulked up with piles of abrasive rock confronted the bay. Approaching the dark rocks, I noticed the distinctive black and white plumage of a couple of oystercatchers at rest on top of the causeway. Their orangey-red bills opened to a V shape, but the wind carried off their song into a misty void. Upright and proud, the artificial barricade, a shield against the constant volley of rubbish and pebbles hurled by the Irish Sea. Sutherland – 'the Cézanne of metamorphoses' - claimed shadows had a presence along with certain rock structures which are embodied with their own kind of personality. Just before he died, Derek Jarman compared shadows to gladiators in his autobiography, *Chroma, A Book of Colour* – June '93...

Everything is but a shadow of a golden past.
The colours will fade in the twilight of history.

Rocks, forever changing over millions of years, are recycled into other rocks. A subconscious embedded with dinosaurs and other ancient life forms which walked, crawled and swam over them. Other objects had been washed up and left temporary calling cards. Forming a colourful dash of plastic bins, bottles and food wrappers, piles of tyres, scrawny bits of wadding and squashed up cans. A loose barbed-wire fence in tandem with pockets of ferns and heather hemmed them all in. The jutting jaw at Birkswood Point marked the spot where I started to leave the fortifications and buried ghosts of the sands behind. Time was now very much against me though, especially if I was to make the 3pm bus at Lindale. Thankfully, the swarming cluster of angry clouds had not yet been given the command to unleash hell. I upped my pace and headed out towards an outcrop cloaked in gorse.

Getting closer to Crag Cottage, a chain of rocky knolls crossed over

100 million years of geological history. Then, out of the prickly bushes on my right, I detected the strange, yet wonderful sight of a movie camera on a tripod spinning round in circles. The jerky movements mirrored those of Vertov's experimental cinematic classic, similarly without any sign of an operator. I stood for a moment, rooted and transfixed. Sadly, the stop motion display only lasted a few more seconds until a man with a long grey beard, decked out in khaki-coloured fishing gear, sprang up. The look of confusion on both of our faces passed off aptly in silence. After not seeing another living soul since overhearing the bad tempered circus mechanic, I surprised a couple negotiating a small footbridge over the Kent Channel in Crag Wood, just after skirting the cottage. This small piece of woodland led out onto the open boglach of Meathop Marsh, following an electric fence – 'sure to put a spark in your step' (Dugdale's words).

My pace naturally increased again after a quick time-check underneath the dark clouds. A series of wooden field gates proudly displayed national park badges on them as I moved forward towards the Meathop Road. On my right, a clump of woodland named *Ulpha* – (Old Norse for wolf) – echoed with gluttonous shadows and silent freedom. I could feel the stench of the bog approaching Meathop Moss, a large expanse of raised mire, and another SSSI owned by the CWT. On the small incline at a cross-roads, I turned right onto cycle path no. 700 towards the quiet retreat of Meathop.

Only a few years before, the same outskirts of the Cartmel peninsula became another temporary hiatus, between the yo-yoing odyssey from south to north and back again. My planned accommodation had fallen through at the eleventh hour, so I began frantically trawling through the Spare Room website. This eventually led me to a charming three-bed-room cottage with a landlady sporting elaborate coloured tresses similar to a Mrs Slocombe creation. Except she had a Border terrier (like Pepper, the one Sir Walter Scott allegedly gave to Wordsworth at Dove Cottage), instead of a much talked about pussy. No doubt sensing the desperation of my plight, she initially wanted to charge £1,200 for just two weeks rent! After nearly falling off the kitchen stool, I did manage to negotiate her down, although she still made a handsome profit out of my misfortune. Day and night, the entire kitchen area used to be awash with blowflies buzzing round saucepans, plates and cutlery; often, to avoid the black haze, I would step outside the back door and stare out across the Moss. Off into the bosom of the national park, where mountain spires peeked through shifting clouds and the periodic troop of traffic droned on the A590's stony shores. Most of the time Mrs Slocombe stayed cocooned with Pepper in her bedroom across the hallway. But on one occasion she caught me on the hop…

"Oh, before you go out, I just wondered whether you fancied accompanying me to a special event at Abbot Hall tonight? It's a walk round their fabulous Canaletto show by the curator from Compton Verney. I've got a spare ticket, one of my friend's has just had to cancel at the last moment."

She thought it would be good if we got to know each other better. But sometimes the torture of a ruined love drops on our eyes like tears. And in this one in-between moment, I sensed both of our souls had dreamed of one thing, but offered another.

At the edge of the village, I paused to look at some posters on the Witherslack, Meathop and Ulpha community noticeboard…

Gentle Exercise Wednesdays at Lindale Village Hall – Keep Fit and Have Fun!
Garden Plants & Party – Grange-over-Sands
Sunday Mass – Milnthorpe and Arnside.

Set within a delightful wood about seven miles from Lake Windermere, the main building on the Meathop Road used to be the Westmorland Consumption Sanatorium. Led by the impulses of a member of the Royal College of Physicians (Dr William Smith Paget-Tomlinson), it opened in March 1900, and proposed to treat the 'consumptive poor' in a businesslike manner: isolation, treatment and cure; fresh air, rest and relaxation. Sickness had become the vacation of the poor. The other white plague on the margins of the Lake District. Here, patients learned about the danger of common flies and the benefits of fresh air and ventilation. However, after the Second World War tuberculosis could be effectively treated with antibiotics. This significant development gave a clear path to the rise of modern day thermal health spas. Many sanatoriums subsequently gained new purposes as: museums, hospitals, holiday homes and housing developments. Typically, a number of holiday cottages, chalets and retirement homes at the Meathop Grange development mark the location of the former sanatorium, officially closed in 1992.

Entering High Wood on the lower slopes of Meathop Fell, a small shaft of bright light pierced through a dense canopy of birches and spruce. Just ahead an elongated cross shape formed in front of me on the narrow track of road. A sharp right turn led down to Low Meathop Farm, where a jumble of stacked-up tyres, rusted machinery, metal poles, animal feeders and twisting plastic pipes jostled for attention with an army of nettles. Like a bookend to the beginning, I hacked my way through a barely discernible path, until I came out next to a newly-built wooden footbridge over the River Winster. As in towns across the country, a car showroom offered the keys to insoluble dreams, with a set of flowing banners and a wave of 4x4s and SUVs arranged in lines. Beside the bus stop, young types in suits pitched new lifestyles to young and old alike. A wealth of experience flying sideways through time. Tearing up the A590 on the mean electric line. As I sat down after boarding the empty 530 bus, the only real interaction on the whole stage came when the driver proffered a begrudging grunt in my direction. Feeling the lag rounding the corner after getting off at Gilpin Bridge, I stopped for a second, mouth open. There, parked directly behind my car, almost nudging bumpers – the silver national park Fiesta...

LINDALE
TO GREENODD

DRIVING ON THE FAST SIDE OF SLOW
SOWING, REAPING & GARNERING
FIRING UP THE BURNING BONES OF THE EARTH
BREAKING THE BOUNDARIES OF GLACIATED
SILENCE
A BITTER NAUSEA FILLED WITH DECAY
SPANGLED WITH MORE EFFICIENT FORMS OF
VIOLENCE
CONSERVING OR REBUILDING
THE DREAMS OF EXILED SOULS
LINDALE TO GREENODD

And the church bells softly chime:

Lindale – carved into the lower slopes of Newton Fell, a jumble of narrow streets with quaint houses bearing names evoking a past filled with Drovers, Peat Cutters and Millers. Driving on the fast side of slow. The Au- togedden of the A6's central spine. A former wasteland for heavy, large and wide loads grinding up the sharp gradient towards Ulverston and Barrow-in-Furness. On a tortuous route mired with unsatisfactory alignment. Steep hills meant more gas until modern industrial needs called for a high-speed bypass. Then, in the mid-70s, a series of improvements and realignments allowed Lindale to sink back into quiet obscurity. The arrival of a new economic lifeline for the Furness region eventually linked up with the A591 and M6. Before the internal combustion engine, extra horse power was often needed to pull stage coaches up Lindale hill. Riding on anything, a vital connection made in the village. With the summit reached, a rest and some feed in the Hay Loft at the Royal Oak Inn or 'The Top House' until the next duty arrived.

Blue-chip motor retailing appeared in the early seventies to coincide with the A590's expansion. Quality and integrity feeding social image and persona. The power and control to take you where you want to go in life. Opposite the village's modern temple of dreams, a tall black obelisk marked the grave of John 'Iron Mad' Wilkinson. The push and pull between the present and the past. A 'father of iron', whose birth in a cart on the way to Clifton market gave rise to a local prophesy, 'Som tyme bee a girt man.' In 1741, at twelve years of age, he moved to Backbarrow, where he went on to establish a forge and furnace at Wilson House, close to the River Winster. In the 17th century, the area surrounding the Furness fells became recognised as a centre for iron-making, burning charcoal produced within the woodlands at Low Wood, Cunsey, Ulpha, Colwith and Coniston. But the hammers of the Bloomforge were eventually silenced in favour of another fuel. Coal – cheap and plentiful, especially after conversion into coke, when a greater weight of iron ore meant more could be smelted in the blast furnace.

Marked by fate, a spectacular wooded gorge foretold the birthplace of the Industrial Revolution. Wilkinson's single-arch design heralding the world's first iron bridge erected over the River Severn at Coalbrookdale in 1779. Rising high; tall chimneys and interminable serpents of smoke to change the world. Sowing, reaping and garnering. A legacy commemorated by an eerie absence sealed inside twenty tons of cast iron. The representation of post-industrial decline embedded with the hopes and fears of Coketown. Dickens' Hard Times, belching out capitalism's more grotesque inequalities.

Summoned by an ancient bell from Cartmel Priory, Irish labourers built Wilkinson's Georgian mansion – Castle Head, half a mile south of Lindale. After changing hands a couple of times, it was turned into a residential Catholic Boys school in the early 1900s, before the house found a new purpose as a Field Centre. This ultimately merged in 1997 with the Field Studies Council charitable organisation.

In 1847, Elizabeth Gaskell wrote a short story, *The Sexton's Hero*, published in *Howitt's Journal.* Images of death, isolation, endurance and non-violence were central to a tale draped in Gothic imagery and the symbolism of fighting the forces of nature. Lindale itself, St Peter's Church at Heysham and the desert sands of Morecambe Bay provided the setting...

"You can see Lindal, sir, at evenings and mornings across the bay; a little to the right of Grange; at least, I used to see it, many a time and oft, afore my sight grew so dark: and I have spent many a quarter of an hour a-gazing at it far away, and thinking of the days I lived there, till the tears came so thick to my eyes, I could gaze no longer. I shall never look upon it again, either far-off or near..." (E. Gaskell, *The Sexton's Hero*, p102)

After riding the A590 westbound to the Meathop roundabout, I turned off onto the B5277, crossing over the River Winster towards Lindale. It was early September when I pulled up at the small village (population around 550) opposite a waterfall known as The Weir, about halfway up the gill. A man-made obstruction dammed the beck which used to feed a mill pond now long gone. I watched the water's milky flow and listened to a gentle murmur beside a set of temporary traffic lights. Long echoes rebounded against one another, redundant in the afternoon's lonely dreaming. Moving further down the road between the dark shadows on the pavement I came to the village store/post office. Hogging the front window, a square-shaped noticeboard displayed a miscellany of services pinned randomly along the edges. Business cards, creased up flyers and laminated posters. Local, affordable and reliable: gardeners, handymen, electricians, personal trainers, dog groomers, equine and canine physiotherapists, balance and wellbeing treatments, stonemasons, dry-stone wallers and mechanics.

But the four C's (Come on in for Coffee and Cake and Chat – and tea and hot chocolate and sandwiches!) Blu-tacked to the door were off the menu until the following morning. The time had just crept past one o'clock, when the store closed for the afternoon.

I had a few more options to play with on the X6 bus timetable for the return from Greenodd, the end point of the stage. Heading out of the village, a wooden lectern overflowing with colourful graphics framed the entrance to Lime Kiln Wood. According to the blurb, the small piece of privately owned ancient semi-natural woodland housed over 80 species of trees and other plants. A trust (formed by local residents) still harboured ambitions to renovate their dilapidated kiln. A future buried in the past, firing up the burning bones of the earth. Newer evidence of regeneration was already evident in hazel coppicing that had produced stumps barely a couple of inches off the floor.

Turning right at the board, I entered the leafy expanse of White Acre Wood instead. Here, occasional bursts of early afternoon sunlight flickered through the blooms and branches like illusory images of William Morris wallpaper patterns swarming through the woods. Spilling out in elegant designs sunk into the softest cushions of the national park boundary. Stirring up a storm of leaves, I tramped uphill accompanied by the soft falling melancholy of a willow warbler's song. Hidden from illumination, the muddy path was dissected by stone walls encrusted with the darkest of green moss. At the top of the path, a mild breeze lifted the shade and filled the (B5177) Windermere Road for a brief second or two. Another set of tem- porary lights shone their emptiness into Lindale's soft embrace.

Through a gate-squeezer stile, ascending the slopes of Hampsfield Meadow, a new vantage point opened up over the estuary and southern Lake District. Regional dips, fault lines, dissected plateaus, limestone escarpments, domed skylines and craggy outlines created a complex geological map. A multitude of shapes, appearances, fascinations, colours, textures and structures up to 500 million years after the main event. Rock piles of lavas, pyroclastics and volcaniclastic rocks ejected and blasted, breaking the boundaries of glaciated silence. Halfway up the field, next to an old feed shed, a small group of Holstein dairy cows looked primed and ready to charge. Out over the estuary another dark horizon gathered, adding to the blare of menace. Turning sharply on my heels, I caught the silhouette of a shadowy figure marching speedily down the left-hand side of the field. Deep into the fissures of buried memory with soulless eyes and a polythene bag. Staying close to the field fence and escaping a world of undying dreams. In pools of brown mud, I descended a grassy hollow with boots getting heavier drop by drop. It came out onto a small track surrounded by soft undulating fields separated by clipped hedgerows and metal gates.

Further ahead, farm houses built in local grey stone merged with new forms of angular architecture. Building on the past, the old meets the new. Spatial sequences for glossy magazine features. With views of the bay behind I passed Home Farm, before a sharp left fork gave way to High Hampsfield Farm. Elsewhere on the horizon, a Union Jack fluttered in the breeze. Conflict always perishes in the brotherhood of flags, but in the unfolding fabric I sensed only a bitter nausea filled with decay. Sheer driving pleasure raised the standard on the driveways though, with Bavarian-owned BMW superminis and a couple of Honda 4x4s. Sunk to the depths of its soul, the former power of British carmakers' overheated in all those unreliable engines. Before the burning ashes of a venture capitalist Chinese takeaway condemned a sorry tale to the breaker's yard. Now a new form of nostalgic departure is adding further ballast to an already struggling ship. Headless and all alone, bring on the dancing horses...

On the descent into the Cartmel Valley, a surprise view opened up after a pinch in a pretty buttercup meadow beside Great Wood. Ash and hazel dominated within the thickening woodland; although I spied some juniper, the abortive mother's ruin, survivor of the last ice age and one of three native evergreen species. There on the outside looking in at the Furness Fells glazed over with an iron-oxide wash. Off into the far distance, a huge, dark concave saucer shrouded the central massif. It reminded me of the tense moment when the Mothership hovers menacingly over the White House during the film *Independence Day*...

On the squelchy slopes of Hampsfell, rounding the north-west edge of Great Wood, a flat patchwork of fields interwoven with hedgerows was punctuated by pylons stretching out beyond the horizon. In the middle distance, soft chimes caressed languid skies from the little white conical spire of St Peter's church at Field Broughton. Passing Heaning Wood on the left, a weightless blur fell in front of my eyes. Led by instinct and senses working overtime, velvety black wings, red bands and white spots hypnotise and enrapture. The striking wings and undersides of the red admiral butterfly in distinguished, playful rhythm. Out into a world of sweeping motions continuing northward through the migrating breezes of North Africa and continental Europe. Turning remorselessly upside down, nature's enchanted heart so fragile, and yet so misunderstood.

Near the road junction at Four Lane Ends, I came across a Grade II listed Georgian mansion, Broughton Lodge, set in three acres of self-contained parkland and woodland. After its conversion into apartments during the 1980s, high flyers tempted by a life of stately style were invited to come and play at being the country squire. Grandeur and space, tucked safely just inside the national park boundary.

Yet barely a mile down the road, a story eight hundred years in the making has been curiously overlooked. Despite a call to prayer echoing from mediaeval times, Cartmel Priory's rich culture and history stands alone. The story began at the end of the seventh century, when St. Cuthbert and all the deserted Britons were exiled to the fringes by Northumbrian King Ecgfrith. It's easy to miss the peaceful village, even if the ancient village streets are perfumed with sweeter, natural ingredients. The Old Post Office serving up sticky puddings made from: toffee, ginger, banana, chocolate and toffee apple. Yet a day at the races offers an alternative flavouring on spring or May Bank Holidays. Here they come, clearing hurdles with aplomb, galloping straight past the shop...

At a blind corner of Green Lane ahead of the entrance to Broughton Lodge, a cyclist appeared out of nowhere, catching me unawares. Unfortunately, I'd accidently wandered into the middle of the road just as he was zooming past.

"Watch it you idiot!" he shouted, riding off shaking his head tapping on the pedals even faster. His considerable bulk decked out in full Team Sky jersey, shorts, gloves, cap, socks, matching shoes and helmet.

"You're not on the Tour..." I yelled after him. As I watched his thin wheels finger the ground past Longlands Farm, days filled with whooping crowds of commuters on the smoking roads of London span round in my mind. Every morning or evening, a vast immensity of riders on their own grand tours running red lights and steaming through pedestrian rights of way. Scoffing at any country bumpkins or confused tourists who dared to stop.

Stepping over a stile into a large open expanse of grassland, the presence of a pot-bellied robin drew my attention back to more pleasant things. It looked at me inquisitively, like a Royal inspecting their land. With each glance and twitch of the tail, it edged a little closer than before. Except, suddenly our little moment of intimacy was over...after I'd stopped to see if I could tempt my new friend with a piece of sandwich. Overhead a harsh, raucous call of craa! craaaaaw! sent the robin scurrying off. Carrion crows – one of the eight species of corvids breeding in the UK. Occasionally migratory or nomadic, mostly a squabbling mass of monochrome raw energy and intelligence.

My favourites are the jackdaws (*corvus monedula*), always flapping excitedly, noising loud and cheerful, fashioning chuckles from dawn to dusk. I once had the pleasure of watching one trying to devour a bag of Cool American flavour Doritos thrown away beside a park bench. At first it kept looking at me, as if to say, "Naff off mate, they're mine." Then a dance broke out with the crumpled bag of crisps before it got stuck between the support struts and the bench itself. Next a strong gust of wind blew a page of tabloid newspaper over the poor jackdaw's head. How I laughed when the front sheet of *The Daily Star* bobbed up and down every time it attempted to waddle off...In the fable, 'The Jackdaw and the Pigeons', a jackdaw paints himself white from head to foot to disguise himself as a farmyard pigeon. That way, he can get to eat the same large amounts of food as they do.

At first his cunning plan works, then one day he forgets himself and starts to chatter uncontrollably, immediately alerting the pigeons to his deceit. They gang up and start pecking him so unmercifully that he has to escape back to his own flock. With all the injuries and white paint still showing though, they don't recognise him, so they drive him away and he is left alone to become a wandering outcast for his troubles...

Approaching the tiny hamlet of Green Bank just below Field Broughton, the boundary announced its presence on a narrow road waving a complementary mix from the verge. The yellow and purple of lesser celandine and mellow thistle blended seamlessly with the neutral whites of meadowsweet. *Giu-giu-giu-giu*...pierced from above, sending tremors congealed with blood through the fields and hedgerows. Out of sight amongst lofty perches, the agile *accipiter nisus* tinged with a brown or blue grey glaze patrolled the landscape in-between the bushes and trees. The highly controversial but painfully shy sparrowhawk lavished with a history mired by game-rearing interests, persecutions and pesticides. A smaller version of the goshawk, it has been nearly lost from our skies on a number of occasions.

However, with the loss of many gamekeepers in the two world wars, numbers recovered, before the introduction of various harmful chemicals into their food chain almost wiped them out. Now protected, they are to be found in woodland habitats across a vast range of countries from tropical Morocco to the arctic forests of Norway, and east to Japan. From this moment on, whenever I heard those familiar *giu-giu* cries, a compulsive excitement arose, watching the sublime elements of power and terror. Bird of prey; take me on your flight. Perhaps it had something to do with my own fascination for human catastrophe, which although frequently anomalous, often reveals moments of lucidity afterwards. Right on cue, a much deeper sounding menace temporarily restored man's control. The voices in the sky were silenced by a low flying Tornado spangled with more efficient forms of violence. Slicing a route through the ice-scraped valleys off into a world all gone to war...

Continuing on, a Union Jack-shaped tree with a Conservatives logo clung to a stable door at a farm on the road to Barnsley Bottom. Amongst the repetitive strains of electioneering, enclosure rubbed shoulders with allotments thickened by silence. In the fading light of mid-afternoon, the great allotment unfolding on my left looked more like a great wound. Exposing the sort of desolate imagery typically found in a Sutherland painting than one set aside for growing. Deep into the cracked earth touching shadows of beauty and ugliness, delight or horror. This was an eerie primordial atmosphere of fallen trees, serpent-like roots, severed branches and twigs. Sustainability piled up in a blighted landscape linking economic, environmental and social values. Cutting and burning, preventing woods from regenerating and destroying the places where animals and plants might live. Absent administrators making a new world in Monbiot's No Man's Land, tucked safely out of harm's way on the margins. Conserving or rebuilding. Public funds shelling out for ecological destruction, whilst other budgets (including national park ones) are slashed. An ever evolving masterpiece...

Feathery ferns, shoulder-high nettles, pylons, telegraph poles, barbed wire and drooping cables offered an embrace of dereliction along the route to Outley Mosses and Grassgarth. From here, I waved a temporary goodbye to the boundary and joined up with the Cumbria Coastal Way again. This led me through the dark and dank smelling High Stribers Wood, a shimmering mass of ash and oak. Under the grey canopy a silence rustled through the limestone woodland, following the transition of time, like ghosts writhing in a tomb.

Curving left, the boundary gnawed the dreams of exiled souls, dissecting Roudsea Wood and Mosses National Nature Reserve before spilling out onto Greenodd Sands, our next rendezvous point.

GREENODD
TO BROUGHTON-IN-FURNESS

SUMMONING ANGELS WITH DIRTY FACES
SOULS CALLING TO THE DEEP
THE MUFFLED DRUM OF THE GREAT UNKNOWN
POOLS OF DEPARTURE ALONG THE BOUNDARY'S EDGE
THUNDERING LIKE A CORRUPTED MONSTER
A SPY, COUNTER-SPY
INTO THE SPREADING BLACKNESS
SCRAWLED WITH ROCK AND GRAFITTI
STRIPPED NAKED BY A FESTIVAL OF EMPTY GESTURES
GREENODD TO BROUGHTON-IN-FURNESS

"I just don't know where it came from, it's never happened to me since..."

Within half an hour the music had been channelled onto a baby grand piano through a long and sleepless night. A universal prayer played over and over until daybreak. Summoning angels with dirty faces. The gift of music fired up after half a bottle of champers and a couple of toots of coke. Loaded revelations declared on Desert Island Discs from Fleetwood Mac's singer songwriter, Christine McVie. A journey of gold dust launched from the old market village of Bouth, just up the road from Greenodd – a name of Scandinavian origin, with the '*odd*' meaning *ness* (a headland), translating to 'The Green promontory.'

In waking light, I met the morning at the end of a no-through road. Against the growling purr of the early commute, songbirds sang in bright sunshine like never before. Opening the car boot, I picked up Knightrider's heavy frame and set it down on the pavement ready for its inaugural outing. Immediately a strong sense of doubt rose within my mind. Could I really drag this hunk of junk over stiles and farmland and then cycle it back on the lumpy route from Broughton-in-Furness? With no bus service to fall back on, there was only one way to find out...After dipping its toes in the channel of the River Leven, the boundary avoids Greenodd altogether by entering the River Crake, before pulling out at the A5092 near the small hamlet of Little Dicks. From there it keeps to the road. So, if all else failed, I could keep cycling on the main highway until more favourable terrain presented itself.

As I gathered up my things and prepared to set off, shafts of sunlight shone onto rooftops and sniffled into dusty corners. In the salty air, a brief moment of hush walled everything in on the narrow road and felt as blue and lonesome as the skies above. Roughcast and limewashed on the slow drift amongst small terraces and cottages, where tinted windows hid souls calling to the deep waters of the sands. From the quayside, Ships Cabin, High Tide and Sea View kept afloat memories of an illustrious past dried in muddy channels or perilous depths. In the eighteenth and nineteenth centuries, copper ore from Coniston, quarried limestone and gunpowder from Backbarrow all passed through the old port. However, darkened by a much more sombre triangular trade wind – Africa, Caribbean, Cumbria – slaves, sugar, cotton and coal were sent, collected, delivered and received. Opposite the Ship Inn on Main Street, hints of more modern developments, twisted in a looping right turn into a small row of social housing on Sheriff Well Close. Changing negative perceptions, house to home. Within four walls, the promised dawn for bidders to get on the property ladder.

Greenodd's more recent social and economic history shares one major thing in common with Lindale – both have been bypassed. Now, in quiet backstreets, a landscape of loss lingers and bows with a melancholy head. The good, the bad and the indifferent started when the old railway station felt the sharpening of Dr Beeching's axe, officially closing the branch of the Furness line in 1965. Back then, a former viaduct used to carry the track over the River Leven to Haverthwaite, where it terminated. You can still pick up traces of this route if you cross over the footbridge beside the present day A590. Until the 1980s, high volumes of traffic frequently clogged up the overcrowded high street. There were even two petrol stations that used to provide temporary relief from the gridlock and fumes. Only the bravest of souls attempted to reach the end of the world at Ulverston or Barrow. The building of a new bridge across the River Crake eliminated the congestion and condemned Greenodd to the muffled drum of the great unknown.

Half way up Main Street, stone walling creeping with ivy and thorny brambles protected remnants of a broad-stone chamber preserving a hearth at its base. Built into a bank of rising ground (for ease of filling), the former flare kiln is now overlooked by a set of austere grey flats. In the dense darkness, fiery torches sparked associations with castles, churches, corn ovens, villages, dovecotes, manor houses, moats, palaces, quarries, roads, religious houses, towns, town walls and track ways. The ancient fires cooled in the grandeur of the void, and now it is dormant, burnt out, next to a couple of commercial waste bins.

The big splash on the village hall noticeboard offered a unique form of mash-up. Dance or jive to 'Swede Dreamz' (an Abba tribute act) or sample 120 varieties of seed spuds on 'Potato Day'. The hall also featured the sales bumf of estate agents, who invite buyers to seize the day, selling Greenodd as the ever popular village. With a bakery and café, post office, primary school, pub and even a bus stop. For a select few, the 'special stuff ' at the family butchers is half a locally produced lamb or pig – cut and bagged to your own requirements for the freezer. Opposite the hall, next to the chippy, the Crakeside Business Park backs on to the sands and offers much needed employment to locals, selling beer wine and spirits, satellite televisions, agricultural supplies, telecom or garage services and furniture for the home or office.

Back on Main Street, free-range eggs flecked with dirt test people's honesty in a cute wooden box. According to the 'I Live Here' website, Greenodd has an older demographic than the rest of Cumbria, with the majority of residents over retirement age. In recent times, the Crake Valley population has tipped just over the 1,500 mark and is almost exclusively made up of people born in the UK, with hardly any immigrants. Greenodd's post-code actually lies within the Furness Peninsula ward/electoral division, in the constituency of Barrow and Furness, which voted almost 60/40 in favour of leaving the European Union.

"Hi. Just those please."
"Ta luv, that's er, four fifty then."
"Lovely morning. I've just been reading about a dog on your website, guess it's not with you today then?"
"Aye, it's a beauty isn't it… you must mean Millie, she's out chasing rabbits…again."

Just before departing the post office and village store, nostalgia besieged my heart as I picked up a postcard of the tapered view down Main Street. The cover image featured the snapshot of a cosy, not-too-distant past immersed in clear blue skies. It could have been taken decades ago or that same morning. Looking at the blank space on the reverse, I thought about the primitive age before smartphones and the omnipotent selfie. Those same old themes that used to be scribbled down hastily to catch the last post…

Greetings from the Boundary!…Weather – good so far.
Bike – iffy…Not looking forward to the ride back!
Just stocked up on water and flapjacks.
Having a great time, see you soon…

Still a little disappointed to have missed the golden retriever in the village store, I headed off behind the Ship Inn, pushing the bike up the sharp incline of Mount Pleasant Road. About halfway up, noisy kids hugged the edges of a small playground swarming with arms and legs during primary school playtime. Turning right onto Bankside, I stopped at 'The Britannia Inn', a small country pub set back from the main road. Here the advertised bar meals didn't seem to be in full alignment with the new Brexit Britain. The '*Have cake and eat it*': God's Allotment pizza (everything with a bit of goo on it) contrasted perfectly with the 'Backstop': Brit Burger – a more dependable less gooey alternative. I pedalled on…

Up until the 1750s, few people would have attempted to visit the Furness area lying between the Duddon and Leven estuaries. Those foolish enough to give it a go would have found it hard to get anything wider than a horse beyond Kendal. Forming a natural barrier against the Irish Sea, the territory is relatively cut off by rivers and mountains to the north, and by lakes, sea and sands to the south. However, its coastal position played a crucial role in building a prosperous economy, significantly aided by labour and capital from outside the area. Primarily, the charcoal/iron industry blazed a trail throughout the peninsula, from Greenodd, Spark/Penny Bridge to Backbarrow, Low Wood, Nibthwaite, Coniston Forge and Cunsey. But the ironmasters' hand gripped tightly and kept wages low. With furnaces shielded behind trees like modern-day pylons and coppiced areas providing open green spaces, the area was peacefully backward.

On an eighteenth century geo-economic map the land is split into two distinctive parts:

High Furness (1,000–2,600 feet) east, west and north of Coniston Water – Largely desolate common pastures and waste, mainly for sheep farming.
Plain Furness (300–700 feet) South of Coniston Water – fertile for growing crops – malt, wheat and barley, dairy cattle, iron production, wool (Broughton), Greenodd (ship-building, coastal shipping trade with Lancaster, Liverpool, Scotland and the West Country).

Copper ore used to be the main product transported down the length of Coniston Water, where it was loaded onto pack horses or carts bound for Greenodd. The journey involved going over the River Crake at Spark Bridge or Penny Bridge, two of the main sites of interest on the outskirts of the village. The name crake is believed to be derived from the old Celtic (Cumbric) language, where it translates as rocky stream. Yet crake also descends from the Old Norse (*kraka*), where it means crow or raven. Originally known as Crake Bridge, Penny Bridge takes its name from the aristocrat, Richard Penny of Crake Side, whose family were benefactors of the church and the poor, settling where the bounds of the land began at the great ford of the Crake, called Tunwath in the late sixteenth century.

The Duke of Buccleugh was the main landowner, inheriting the lordship and liberty of Furness from the Montagu family, property included the manorial lands of: Egton with Newland, Blawith, Ulverston, Plain Furness, Dalton and Hawkshead. With numerous grand estates elsewhere, the duke preferred to rule from a distance.

In the great age of economic development during Victorian times, the mass movement of slate from the Tilberthwaite and Coniston fells was made possible by the arrival of the Coniston branch of the Furness railway. Slate from the Troutbeck Park quarries also made its way along Windermere to Waterfoot, crossing overland to Haverthwaite for waiting ships at Greenodd or Ulverston. From there it was shipped with other products to Glasgow or Liverpool. Thousands of homes covered every year by sound roofs and solid walls made from Furness industries. Clean lines and beautiful markings communicating a handmade or natural artistry, shaping the Lakeland landscape and towns from locally quarried slate. Now the old connections form shards of memory sleeping in pools of departure along the boundary's edge...

Somehow, whilst soaking up the last strains of mid-September's warmth, I lost concentration and balance. It happened as I was preparing to hoik the bike over a dog-eared wooden stile. Readjusting my feet caused my right hand to brush against stinging nettles. The venom released a familiar cocktail of chemicals. First the tingling pain, then the blisters.

"Shit! Bugger..." the world isn't all unicorns and sparkles...

Clearly bringing the bike had been a huge mistake. Still, it was too late now. I'd come a long way and had no alternative but to keep going and finish the stage. I plodded on under cloudless skies, climbing the uphill track from the A5092 onto sylvan pastures rolling like a healing balm. Staring back at the haze of gleaming sands, a voice whispered and I fell into a dream...

Marked by erosion, the smooth lower slopes stroked my face like a warm flannel until an avalanche of volcanic stone released a weighty storm. A huge pair of talons made out of the upper crags and buttresses of the Furness fells sent the sons of farmers reeling towards the valley floors. Shutting my eyes, I tumbled into an encircling void hugging the walls of a dark chasm with a searing heat rising from underneath. A spark flew out onto glowing pastures speckled with cottages populated by weavers, tanners and blacksmiths. On pathways made out of slate arranged haphazardly, a display of swill baskets, pieces of carpentry and piles of rubble and stone for wall-making. At dawn in the misty hop, groups of children slouched with heads bent near the gates of cotton mills at Backbarrow and Penny Bridge. Thundering like a corrupted monster, the noise of the Leven and Crake twisted round the cheap and manageable dead from the workhouse. In honour of them, I placed a small piece of rock on the summit cairn of Whitbarrow, high above the marshes and meadows of the centre. As the journey continued over hills rolled out like centuries, I grabbed the sizzling wires from a pylon, plugging in to new desires. All along the flood lines wheels were turning round. Holding a lifeline, I swung across a cast-iron structure onto the prominent edge of limestone at Hutton Roof. Poking through the south-east corner, anything seemed possible in those shadowy imaginings...

'Kukuk kukuk kukuk' followed by a clattering whirring of wings. Built for eating, a nervous male pheasant scurried off and hid in a ditch below a line of hedgerow. Turning left amongst dark silhouettes congregated at the bottom of a field, I dragged Knightrider's bulky frame uphill again. Moving slowly between the lines of freshly cut grass strips, cemented shoes waiting to be baled for silage. Crossing over at the top, I entered a beautiful wild flower meadow surprising a lone roe deer who darted off into a small piece of woodland. Amongst the last throes a swathe of marsh marigold, yellow rattle, great burnet, poppies, buttercups and ox-eye daisies – despite the faded scent and diminished glow of autumn's last parade their grace and harmony sung back at me.

After negotiating another awkward stile in the corner of a field, I took brief refuge in a shady lane beside Addison Wood. In the muddy centre of the road a redder shade of leaf on a darker shade of pale. Standing in the middle of Sutherland's *Entrance to a Lane* a visual primer, painted just prior to the outbreak of the Second World War, in 1939. Swirling abstract forms rendered to express the 'intellectual and emotional' essence of a place. The actual lane that inspired the painting can be found on the west bank of Sandy Haven, off the Milford Haven estuary in south-west Wales. Darkness and light. Decay and life. Stripping out the extraneous details and honing in with striking, mystical results. Enclosed in a green lane buried in trees and shrubs, I had once again stumbled upon 'the exultant strangeness' of a particular location.

The painting had also featured in the second room 'Accidental Encounters 39–45', during the Sutherland retrospective at Abbot Hall. Seeing as St Michael's Day was still a week or so off, I picked a few pieces of Devil's fruit from the bramble bushes, ahead of the ancient curse said to make them unpalatable. Between mouthfuls, taking a deep breath to fully absorb the earthy smell of fallen leaves mixed in with the fresh, cooling scent of a nearby stream. Just as a foetus responds to voice and sounds, or in the reactions to light and dark shadows moving from place to place, Sutherland referred to such spots as 'womb-like enclosures' akin to being inside 'a jewel'.

Freewheeling downhill, I picked up the A5092 again and turned left through the tiny hamlets of Crakeside and Thurstonville. In several tight stretches a glut of traffic hissed at my back wheel. Delivery drivers straining to meet guaranteed time slots, large trucks overloaded with agricultural machinery, even a council gritter loaded up with pinky-brown rock salt nipped in dangerously before a narrow bend. This speedy cut-through towards Broughton, Coniston and the old county boundary at Duddon Bridge was evidently no place for the likes of Knightrider.

After passing through Lowick Green, Esps Farm offered a timely opportunity to join a bridleway and escape the rasping engines for a while. Dismounting, I walked down a dipped driveway that curved round to the right. This led to a small compound surrounded by an assortment of buildings set at various angles to each another. A couple of them, shaped like elongated silver jets out of an old Bond movie, turned out to be feed silos for a seething mass of chickens hoarded behind a wire fence. There's nothing more determined than poultry with a plan. Leaning the bike up against the piece of 007 rocket memorabilia, I delved into my backpack for the camera. The couple of shots I managed to take didn't really convey the dancing swarm of prowling roosters and chickens.

"Going somewhere?"

Turning round sharply, I looked up and down the muddy track but couldn't see anyone.

"You'll have a helluva time getting that bike through the gate down there. Been tied up for months."

Looking back again at the main farmhouse I noticed a thin, grey figure hovering next to a tractor. I could only make out his head and shoulders, since a robust stone wall obscured the rest of his body. I always thought farmers were more bothered about shutting gates than opening them.

"You might be right. It's been difficult dragging it this far. I'm just trying to get off the road for a bit. Thought I'd head out on the bridleway for the community hall and the church."

He shook his head slowly…

"Good luck with that! So what's the big deal with my chickens? You're not from the local paper, are you?"

"No, no, nothing like that…I'm doing a personal project in stages, whenever I get time on my days off. Just taking the odd photo here and there for a reminder. Hope you don't mind?"

In the silence that settled, I lost sight of him again.

"Anyway, sorry to have disturbed you. I'll take my chances now and make for the hall. Cheers then…"

There was no reply…

The path leading out of the farm soon deteriorated into a boggy track rutted with deep tyre marks chiselled in the muck. Undeterred, I stopped at a metal gate bound tightly to a large stone post with flayed strands of wire. Sensing the burn from unseen eyes, I simply hurled the bike over in a show of defiance and stupidity. Trying to show no reaction, I watched in silent horror as the wheels and pedals sunk into a deep pool of sludge on the other side.

On a sizeable wooden bench outside the hall, a glimmer of sunshine lit up a tiny square on the closely cut grass. Flicking lumps of mud off my boots, I wolfed down a chicken tikka sandwich, before plotting my next move. After studying the OS map I noticed how the A5092 split Lowick in two, with one half in and the other half out of the national park. 'In, out, in, out, shake it all about', joining hands in the air, 'you do the hokey cokey and you turn around…' With knees bent and arms stretched, a creeping atmospheric mist leaves no distinctive mark except the strange phenomena of myth and mystery. Hung up on the side of a gable entrance containing a stable door, a noticeboard displayed a number of ads trying to inject some life into a fly-blown lung...

Feelgood Singalongs, Daytime Singing Group (popular classics open to all abilities), Li Style Tai Chi, Yoga, Friends of the X12 Bus Service, Hardy Soft Play Hire – Bouncy Castles, Disco Domes, Glitter Tattoos, Mascots, Candy Cards, Sweet Cones and the Lowick Parish Plan (including details on the new 40 mph speed limit!).

Reaching for the handlebars, I grimaced at the pedals and gear derailleur encrusted with clumps of shit. No more marshy fields, from now on I would stick to minor roads instead. Against a backdrop of birdsong rising and falling on a swirling wind, the rattle and hum from a chainsaw took care of business. Hanging out by the boundary line, a killing machine without a face, or a name. Pushing off, I pulled over almost immediately to absorb the opulent backdrop from behind the iron gates of St Luke's Church. Dugdale admired the same picture of undulating landscape on the Furness fringes...
'where Silurian slates contrast markedly with the rugged grandeur characterising the central mountain core...'

The church was a model of elegance, thought to have been rebuilt in the nineteenth century. Constructed out of slate rubble and finely dressed sandstone, it featured angled buttresses, gable porches and stained-glass windows.

Shortly afterwards, a more imposing pair of gates adorned with acorns marked the entrance to Lowick Hall. After the titanic bloodfest at Hastings, extensive chunks of Cumberland and Westmorland were handed out like Kinder Surprise to the first Norman Lords of Cumbria. The small manor house at Lowick represented an estate incorporating a thousand years of feudalism, blood ties, owed allegiances and the rage of northern foes. At the height of the 'Border Reivers' in the mediaeval period, two pele towers were thought to have guarded the site. During the sixteenth or seventeenth century, the old wing of the house formed an extension onto one of the towers, whilst the rest of the building dates from the mid-eighteenth century.

Left in emotional peace, the ties of blood and marriage were finally severed in 1948. Put up for sale on the open market, a celebrated children's author with a walrus moustache and Trotsky's former secretary stumped up the cash and acquired the estate. Arthur Ransome and Evgenia Petrovna Shelepina had first met when he reported on the Bolshevik Revolution in Russia for the *Manchester Guardian*. Apparently, Ransome visited Trotsky regularly, played chess against Lenin and drank tea with their other Bolshevik comrades. *Bratstvo, svoboda, ravenstvo* – fraternity, liberty, equality – professional revolutionaries pursuing totalitarian social domination. They had a cause and causes cause problems. Amongst military personnel and ordinary working people, Ransome found himself in the right place at the right time throughout the cataclysmic events of 1917.

Despite voicing opinions that were 'not red, but at least a reasonable pink', M16 instigated a murky double life by recruiting his services in 1918. A spy counterspy disavowing any knowledge of action. The cinematic reboot of his best-known book, *Swallows and Amazons* in 2016 alluded to these shady adventures. With the Blackett's Uncle Jim Turner (aka Stevenson's 'Captain Flint') pursued by Russian agents with guns, trilbies and trench coats.

Ransome's connections with Lowick began early, during childhood holidays from 1884–97 at Swainson's Farm, Nibthwaite, situated at the southern end of Coniston Water. At Lowick Bridge, his father would often scrutinise the River Crake for places to fish, while his mother painted watercolours. This left the young Arthur free to exercise his imagination running over the surrounding hills and rocks which later populated his famous series of books.

When Ransome settled into his new role as Lord of the Manor in the post-war nuclear age, he moved into a ramshackle, dilapidated house without electricity, water or a phone, but there was a fine view of 'Coniston Old Man', a summit he had once been carried to as a six-week-old baby. After initiating an extensive programme to upgrade the house's facilities (adding two new bathrooms), he and Evgenia Petrovna Shelepina moved out less than two years after the purchase. His only written output during this time was an unfinished manuscript for a thirteenth *Swallows and Amazons* story. Remarkably, Hugh Brogan uncovered it in Ransome's desk at Abbot Hall whilst working on the biography, *The Life of Arthur Ransome*. Brogan also came up with the title, *Coots in the North and other stories*. In the main story, three young Coots – Joe, Bill and Pete stowaway from Norfolk to the Lakes for a lively encounter with the fearless tomboy, Nancy Blackett, acting captain of the *Amazon* dinghy.

Subberthwaite Common is on the Lakes and Dales Loop, a 196 mile circular cycle route that takes in the Lake District, Yorkshire Dales, Eden Valley, Morecambe Bay and West Cumbria. After pushing open the last of a number of metal gates, I gently manoeuvred my own huge grubby tank onto the common and set off into the spreading blackness. Part of the Woodland Valley, the tarmacked road weaves a snakelike pattern through rough undulations richly veiled with bracken and heather, fragmented with rock and speckled by small tarns. Mouldering in its belly were funerary monuments, clearance cairns and medieval settlements with interlinked enclosures. Time stagnated and rubbed over the wings of pheasants pressed low to the ground, running scared in the bracken. By a bend in the road a Bronze Age barrow known as the Giant's Grave kept watch. A large headstone surrounded by a radial wall scrawled with rock art and graffiti dating back to the early 1700s.

*Ho ho ho...*it's still anyone's guess which Titan or hulking troll might be buried there. At a little over 800 feet, Blawith Knott scrapes the clouds and sends shadows along the shore to Black Combe, the Howgills and over the boundary to other peaks in the Yorkshire Dales. With no time to de-tour up to the summit, I picked up some real momentum on the descent to-wards Spunham Wood instead. The plantation on the crest of a hill looked in a sorry state, half of it barren and treeless after a huge bite had been taken out of it. A storm of ignorance stripped naked by a festival of empty gestures.

At Low Rosthwaite Farm more evidence of unique visions was sitting pretty on the driveway. Porsches and Superminis stretching boundaries with intelligent performance, greater power and efficiency, with every mile, form follows function on roads terraced in dreams. Overhead something circled feeling no pity, no pain, and no fear. Pulling over, I experienced the hypnotic movement of two sparrowhawks skilfully using thermals in a lazy, graceful, dashing and extraordinary display. Scanning up and down the hedgerows, the pair of terminators darkened the skies with a sense of im-pending fate. Joining up with the boundary on the final stretch into Broughton, a special magic of ghostly light ignited the A595. Before melting into a lustrous void, cerulean skies eclipsed the Duddon Estuary on the climb over Windmill Hill, shaping a slow rhythm into the autumnal after-noon like never before...

Announcing my arrival, long shadows scattered sorrows onto the fish slabs of the vacant market square. Pausing in the silent bloom by the stone obelisk, I took a much-needed drink and a rest. Contemplating the ride back to Greenodd, where the songbirds sang at the end of the line. Fear-ing the epic struggle as it pulsed like a wave on the lonely road to the lofty heights of Kirkby Moor quarry. From the petrol station a bright yellow house at the end of a lane tinted the forefront of my vision. Buckhorn brought Van Gogh's retreat in Arles to mind, before I settled into a sedate tempo climbing Grizebeck Brow in a state of anguished apocalypse.

Gripped by themes of existence, cherishing each and every vague breath of my burnt-out condition. Dragging Knightrider out of the deep abyss into higher hells, survival became immersed in truth. Beyond the surface the strongest personification of the boundary connected to the spectacle of nature's salvation...

SAY
No Pylons
No Pylons

BROUGHTON-IN-FURNESS TO WHICHAM

A BLACK MIRROR OF ABANDONED FRAGMENTS
LIVING INSIDE A HERITAGE TOYTOWN FILM SET
FIVE GO MAD IN BROUGHTON
RURAL SERVICES IN AN AGE OF EXTINCTION
DULL THE PAIN AND KILL THE JOY
SEDUCED BY THE ROAD IN SLEEPLESS SOLITUDES
BLOOD-BLACK NOTHINGNESS BEGAN TO SPIN
THE SONOROUS ATMOSPHERE OF A FRIEDRICH PAINTING
DREAMY SOULS WHISPER THEIR GOODBYES
SWEPT ALONG IN STRANGE SYMPHONIES
BROUGHTON-IN-FURNESS TO WHICHAM

In the midst of its own darkness:

A black screen…
Nothing…
Just a deep void stared back, mocking my sense of disbelief. The entire voice note had somehow been erased. The power of touch kicked thoughts and observations down into a measureless chasm. Crouched beside Buckman Brow, head in hands, contemplating nearly an hour's worth of lost data. With ceaseless turmoil traffic roared past forming a black mirror of abandoned fragments. Through woods and dales the shadows of voices rebounded against the black tyres on the A595 absorbing light and eroding landscapes. Absences, black holes and the colour of resurrection, what does your soul look like?

In playground speak, I went back to square one. After dropping off Knightrider's creaking frame at Whicham Church car park, I'd arrived under the showy horse chestnut tree in the middle of the 'historic market town square'. Negotiating a winding and undulating mediaeval Furness coastal road as the rural countryside pushed right up to the urban centre. Eyes glimmered on the nature of daylight, with secret rays for livestock market day in Broughton. A living working town in the early October sunshine, an Indian summer bound by a straight line, by the order to prepare for what lies ahead. Positioned above the line, non-linear time viewed the past, present and future simultaneously; life and death could be the same. In the empty square the first cries of twilight drifted towards me as I prepared to begin another amble across the perimeter.

Touted as a mini-London, the model village was decorated with a cobbled square, Georgian facades and yet another obelisk (erected in 1810) to commemorate George III's Golden Jubilee. And Kingdoms rise and Kingdoms fall. A member of the Hanoverian dynasty, the King of a new all-powerful and all-knowing nation, but he wasn't quite all there. Living inside the bubble of a heritage toytown film set, a community of yesteryear rooted in familiar affection but tinted by fear, boredom and loneliness. Some locals apparently still like to maintain the town is as Lancastrian as tripe and onions. With winter approaching in fast thick pants, the square's tableau filtered sleep as though a tomb.

The town's distinctive eighteenth-century character was now protected under the Broughton in Furness Conservation Area – designated by the LDNPA in 1982 'an area of special architectural or historic interest the character or appearance of which it is desirable to preserve or enhance'. On the edge of the south-west corner of the national park, it is also a place of meeting points. The A595 shoots up from Dalton and Barrow, crossing from south-east to north-west through the centre before heading over High Cross to descend into the Duddon Valley, from there it crosses the River Lickle and Duddon Bridge before snaking south to Millom. Ascending the valleys at each side of the steep ridge, the A593 is a spur leading southwards by Torver to Coniston, or the more northerly strand to Broughton Mills and the hills of Dunnerdale and Seathwaite.

In mediaeval times, the relatively unspoilt landscape was populated by the Cistercian monks of Furness Abbey, who worked the iron-ore fields of the peninsula in the early 13th century. Over time, the area became awash with open-cast workings, small bloomeries and forge sites, but now the nature reserves dotted around the Duddon estuary are a growing testimony to how the land is being repossessed. Public footpaths link Broughton to the rolling surrounding countryside, while the town sits on the Cumbria-Coastal Way, a long-distance footpath from the Cumbrian-Lancashire boundary to the Scottish border.

Heading over on the sloping roads I'd been listening to Fern on the wireless putting a damp spoon back in the bowl. Cumbrian back stories, some funny, some tragic. Fern's continuous misbehaviour playing non-stop AOR marked him out as a sure-fire contender for the Grade II listed village stocks. Lining up next to the wooden throwbacks, a row of ancient fish slabs once used for selling the most prized catches from the River Duddon. Opposite, a market hall with lock-up shops dating from 1766 was turned into the old Town Hall, which now houses a community Tourist Information Centre. Originally built in the best of Georgian good taste, it still represents a curious combination of restraint and elegance. Stepping inside, I found no one else around except for a woman dressed in black behind the front desk. She was absorbed in a daydream holding a 'Back in 5 minutes' sign. The look of vacant isolation, staring out beyond all the herdy mugs, maps, prints, cards and local books, reminded me of the despondent couple 'smothering a parrot' in the Degas painting, *L'Absinthe* – minus a glass of the greenish coloured liquid of course. The 1876 work originally shook the London art world with its perfection of ugliness. Disenchanted, cut off from the human family, where brooding emptiness was being reflected back in the mirror on the wall.

Sensing the blank mood out of the corner of my eye, I too felt neither festive nor enchanted. I breezed through racks and hurried off through the out door. Another bit of imagineering for folk passing through can be found on the corner of Princes Street. Tyson's the high-class butchers, grocer and off-licence, imbued with charm and nostalgia distilled into bottles and sold over a rustic looking counter – reality and fantasy – fusing the real with a dream life under a red and white canopy. Knights of the cleaver with knives keen enough to sever the hamstring of an old black bull.

A Holbein-esque portrait of Henry VIII hung on the outside of the Old Kings Head pub opposite. Dating back almost four hundred years, it used to be the favoured haunt of cattle farmers who stopped by to whet their whistle. Sheep farmers on the other hand flocked to the village café and bakery for a cup of tea and a pie. First opened on auction market day in 1928 by a Mr and Mrs Shaw, it has since passed through the hands of several Broughtonians. Entering an unassuming entrance through a set of beaded curtains, it might not have looked much from the outside, but inside bread and pastry discovered an invincible truth. Recent online reviews even managed to avoid the usual pantheon of pettiness and hysteria supposedly celebrating consumer power, but said: "Eat everything! Wonderful find, fabulous, top bakery!"

Taking a seat on the pine furniture, I ordered a three rasher bacon roll on white with black coffee. Looking round all the other empty tables, bold numbers were displayed in the bottom left hand corners. On mine, in heavy neo-grotesque helvetica, a big black five laminated on white paper had been stuck down without any logo or brand awareness. Five Go Mad in Broughton. Next to my corner spot, a shabby looking sofa, couple of armchairs and wood burner offered a cosy and quaint escape to any out of town hipsters craving French vanilla cappuccinos. Above, clinging to the beige and violet coloured walls, a handful of odd sized canvas works gouged in oil gazed back like expectant foundation students before a critique. Thick layers of impasto formed out of the emptiness, conjuring up Frank Auerbach's endless search for new notions of possibility.

Downstairs, sandwiched between mouthfuls of agricultural language and Radio One's Live Lounge, a heated debate between the pot wash and a baker took on colourful shapes. The social media addiction. Sharing and distributing.

"No!! I'm telling you Snapchat is shite. It's just silly crap for kids. Besides, you never keep any photos. At least you get to see a bit of what's happening on Facebook."

Ephemeral constraints versus a juggernaut of detritus in a battle of what it means to exist. People's hopes and fears played out in a fantasy land on a screen somewhere. Thankfully, the bacon roll arrived in no time. Arranged on a placemat fashioned from a chunk of blue/grey slate with a couple of brown-sauce sachets positioned on the edge. Refreshed and full, I stepped outside into the hazy mid-morning directly opposite the unoccupied wooden benches of the Black Cock Inn.

BBC One's series *The A-Word*, a family drama about difference that featured a boy with autism at its heart set amidst fleeting glimpses of the model town. A bus shelter especially built for the square during filming of the drama eventually found its way into the beer garden of the Old Kings Head. Now converted into a quirky wee sun house and smoking shelter, putting two fingers up to the ban on lighting up in public places at the same time. The Manor Arms, another pub close by, featured on screen in the bleak animated film, *The Plague Dogs*, adapted from a Richard Adams novel. Escaping to a different world, it was turned into The Manor Hotel, before freedom beckoned towards an island far out to sea.

Broughton's ancient origins started with mentions of 'Borch', part of the manor of Millom in the Domesday Book. It was later recorded as 'Brocton' in 1196, a name believed to be Old English and meaning 'settlement by the brook'. Intruders and occupiers. Building up layers of history like the band of Coniston limestone composed of sedimentary rocks laid down in the Silurian Period approximately 400 million years ago (known as the Windermere Group).

With Norman foundations, early settlements limited to the valley bottoms eventually opened out to the coastal plain. Similar to the trade centre established at Greenodd in the eighteenth century, ships sailed up the estuary collecting coppice wood from the iron furnace at Duddon Bridge. At one time Broughton was the centre of the wool trade, until the late nineteenth century ushered in the manufacture of oak hoops and baskets (swills), brush handles and wooden shafts for farm tools. From the 1860s onwards, a familiar tale left its heart pierced and burning with the advent of new Victorian boom towns at Millom and Barrow. Dugdale claimed Broughton jogged along in languid fashion with a unique atmosphere few other Lakeland towns could hope to match. Today, like many towns de populated after the decline of rural industry, its main areas of employment are either in tourism or the buying and selling of livestock.

Walking slowly downhill past a succession of attractive holiday cottages, a sleek black Mercedes and an Audi A5 Sportback followed their own rules parked up on the street outside. The ultimate driving machine for those brief encounters before bed and breakfast on a getaway weekend. A little further on, I paused briefly to take a few snaps of shop fronts proudly displaying 'Power without Pylons' posters in their windows. "It's loud and it's strong, they don't want no giant pylons..." So goes the protest song I unearthed later on YouTube by Kirkby ukulele whizz John Woodward. Just one of around 8,000 voices adding support to the campaign against the construction of national infrastructure scale pylons in the Lake District including the Whicham Valley and Duddon Estuary.

Plans to connect the ill-fated Moorside Nuclear Power Station to the UK electricity grid have been rumbling on since 2011. The National Grid's idea to construct a giant steel fence along the western edge of the national park boundary ignited high feelings amongst the local communities affected. Offshore subsea route versus onshore – with the Morecambe Bay Tunnel route. Engagement not endorsement, undergrounding and additional lines. During the 2017 General Election, candidates from all political colours cited landscape disfiguration and the detrimental effect of 50-metre high pylons on areas just outside the national park boundary around the Millom and Furness peninsulas. Yet with this campaign, there was still a lingering sense that, similar to the inevitable fallout from Brexit, the prospect of what is left behind for the next generation could only be one giant leap into the unknown.

On the corner of Station Road, a wall-basket planter stuffed with lamb's wool signalled the entrance to the hard-edged, no-nonsense Broughton-in-Furness Mart. On Mondays and Tuesdays, Carlisle based farmstock auctioneers Harrsion & Hetherington put sheep, cattle and the odd bull through the sales ring. The tracks of time gathered together – a showcase for rural services in an age of extinction. Conserving, preserving and perpetuating one of the last of the old traditions of the British Isles. Dull the pain and kill the joy. Come on; come together for the traditions of our ancestors. Unknowingly, I had stumbled upon the real beating heart of the town. Yan, taen, tedderer…sing a simple melody. Here, inside a private world with a different language, where young and old farmers rubbed shoulders in the hustle and bustle next to a smoking burger stand. Having just filled up in the café though, the perfect storm of fried onions and street burgers brought on nothing but a wave of nausea. Moving swiftly away, I watched sheep marked with magenta-coloured fluid being filtered through a maze of metal gates. Their heads pressed up against the bars after a burst of movement, while a team of auction helpers in hoodies followed attentively, cajoling and whistling instructions.

Heading out of town past the Old Kings Head on Station Road, I stopped momentarily outside the Victory Hall. Built in the last throes of the Art Deco period with a gable-roofed ice blue and white façade, it was designated a National Flagship Hall (one of only ten in the whole of England) by the National Lottery Millennium Commission under its 21st Century Halls for England Scheme. It looked like it could have been plucked straight out of one of Edward Hopper's paintings of New England colonial architecture. Adjusting the contents of my heavy backpack took a while, (sandwiches, banana and bottle of water, chocolate flavour Frijj, camera, Dugdale, waterproof mac, bike pump, wallet, phone, notebook and pens), whilst the steep slope up to the bend at High Cross beckoned.

At High Cross I planned to rejoin the boundary above the estuary, as it followed the A595 over the Duddon Bridge, skirting Furnace and Mount Wood, ascending High Boghouse and another sharp ramp up to Hazel Mount. From lofty heights where thoughts soared and hours passed, daring to think of hollowed destiny; Silecroft and the Irish Sea. In the scattered sun standing on freedom's shore, seduced by the road in sleepless solitudes. Ringed by the surrounding Coniston Fells, Greenodd through Lowick Bridge on to Broughton; a musical poem without meaning. Dying a hundred times, edging back to black, ruling our primitive souls without colour. Blood-black nothingness began to spin...and dreadfully distinct against the dark, a tall white waterfall whispered softly between farms, estates, mansions, quarries, gorges and defensive towers; the futility of words dropping furtive tears into the eyes of streams. All the while, the lone sentinel had been outflanking me. Invincible, almost mythical and shrouded in shade and light, while the sea brought forth an eternity of air as clear as time, unseen but still felt in the mountain's shade.

The High Cross café, terrace, bar and boutique B&B was another bolt hole for business and pleasure. On the crest of a ten per cent gradient overlooking Cumbria's West Coast, real food for real folk feeling frisky wearing low-cut T-shirts. Rocking up to drink chilled fizz with a twinkle in their eye. Opposite, on High Brow's pavement beside a large brown road sign announcing the Western Lake District, I had to make a quick decision – roadside or public footpath. With odds of fifty-fifty, I chose poorly! The path proved a big mistake, as my feet plunged into the unforgiving fringes of the Duddon Marshes. The trusted old pair of trainer boots had finally given up the ghost, captured by the same malignant hand of Conan Doyle's obscene depths. Suddenly thoughts of abandonment were stirred by the thought of another seven miles with ever-widening cracks in my boots and saturated socks.

Desperately looking round, I searched in vain for any crumbs of comfort, eventually turning to Dugdale, my one and only trusted companion...

"Deep gullies hide the incoming tides and the unwary traveller only becomes aware of his rapidly deteriorating position when the creeping fingers of sea water lap about his ankles."

Since the creeping fingers had already infiltrated my own dubious defences, it was time to just shrug the shoulders and get on with it. From the mouth of the estuary at the great divide of Duddon Bridge, a reverse L-shape led out from a periphery into the shining mirror of the Irish Sea. High above on Kirkby Moor, a renewable energy source waved back like an industrialised host of golden daffodils. The swishing of aerodynamic rotating blades from the noisy neighbours may already be doomed. Blown out by members of the SLDC planning committee who rejected another ten years' worth of energy generated from the wind farm. Out here as the echoes dissolved, renewable contemplated an end.

Unexpectedly, the changing seascape inhabited by the iron men of Gormley's *Another Place* sprang to mind; weathered figures being tested against planetary time under the prevalence of a naked sky. All along the drowned shoreline, the estuary flushed out the picturesque. Taking a detour from the boundary, a significant change since Dugdale's day arrived when I came to the sealed-off ruins of the Duddon Iron Furnace – a site surrounded by warning notices (stonework dangerous and liable to falls). From a safe distance, visitors must now stare at the ruins covered with lichen and ferns from behind a wire fence. Bought by the LDNPA in 1981, ten years of restoration works helped save the original buildings, but at present the interpretation boards looked rather dog-eared and uncared for. Built in 1736, the site is the oldest surviving charcoal fired iron furnace of its kind in northern England. It was hidden away down a track which serves the Dower House, a late Victorian country house built on the site of a mediaeval packhorse inn. The former ironworks featured prominently on a national park leaflet, 'Working the Landscape', which included an artist's impression of the huge wheel, turned by water from the river, driving the bellows that pumped air into the blast furnace. Concealment masked the general theme of decay passing through the site.

Eventually a wooden path riven with dark shadows led to a throng of rhododendron bushes. Suddenly, a riot of autumnal colour burst forth from thickets of fragrant sponge-shaped flowers tinged with pink, some blotched yellow and others turning purple and red. The familiar clattering noise of a couple of nervous wood pigeons escaping over the top of the tree cover revealed an azure sky as clear as deepest summer. Stretching out between gaps in the branches, a curling pattern of contrail clouds looked almost as if a vintage guitar lead had been plugged into the sky. In growing silence, edging further under the canopy of Furnace Wood, a dampening mix of conifers with pockets of native broadleaves provided some refuge. Moving further away from the road, warbling birds greeted my slow trudge uphill with a riot of sound as they queued up to sing their day songs at me. My thoughts were now fixed on finding a route through the blackened mossy stone as the path grew more and more indistinct towards the shifting heights.

After closely monitoring the OS app for guidance, I managed to locate a corner stile buried in a stone wall exposing the open fell before Boadhole farm. A great silence descended while passing through its deserted courtyard. Black, damp and shivering, a white eyed collie loosely tied to a metal chain eyed my every footstep. I took some photos of what looked like *Hypholoma fasciculare* (sulphur tuft) mushrooms erupting from a few old stumps, after looking them up online later. Richard Fortey, a natural historian with a lifetime's experience of seeing into the life of things, described October as the mushroom fancier's 'polychromatic pageant'. Just the right amount of rain combined with a perfect dose of sunshine encouraging huge amounts of growth.

After carefully exiting through a wooden field gate, a rough track widened out, opening up an area of pastureland extending out to Silecroft, and far away into ethereal realms. With haunting beauty, the Barrow offshore wind farm emerged with a rhythmic pulse in the sonorous atmosphere of a Friedrich painting – the mystic with a brush. A painter of serenity, whose dreams disappeared after dawn in the low places for his masterpiece, '*The Grosse Gehege near Dresden*' (The Great Enclosure). An image brimming with secret yearning and melancholy, as it sings to the thirsting cries from the past and the future.

Next up, stories in stone entered my soul like a needle disturbed with a wandering hand. Beneath a mighty form, traditions, mystery and a thousand years of struggles bound up with a megalithic ring in the centre of the world. My eyelids were stirred to shut out the dark on a narrow gravel track leading uphill for a couple of miles. Underneath Knott Moor's smooth slopes, the cries of a sparrowhawk plunged the bitter depths as it searched for something's flesh. Beside the path, a weightless skylark hovered briefly above patches of boggy ground sprinkled with long networks of reeds and *cirsium horridulum michaux* – purple thistle.

At Crag Hall, the mystic round of Druid fame announced itself – Swinside Stone Circle, the purpose of a small detour from Dugdale's route. No voice or sound broke on entering the inner group of stones, save for a few bite-sized bleats from the ever-present sheep, answering the odd high-pitched rasp from the crows. Walking slowly between the 55 stones gathered from the surrounding fells, I finally paused beside one of the large portal openings. In patient earth, prehistoric Britons were thought to have constructed the unroofed, wide ring in the late Neolithic age. Other tales spoke of a sleepwalker entering the human world at night. Foul deeds arose when the stones of a new church under construction during the daytime were pulled down. Sunkenkirk, a place where footprints dressed in red carried out rituals or ceremonials inside the remote amphitheatre. Drifting through the south-west corner of the boundary, a breeze swept up the broken pieces of yesterday's life, as dreamy souls came to whisper their goodbyes.

Reclaimed by nature – don't it always seem to go. On the approach to

Graystone House a couple of abandoned cars were parked up waiting for paradise. All the windows smashed in and, on the driver's side, a wiring loom spewed out of the dash like a wagging tongue, an unopened can of Red Bull on the mouldy passenger seat.

Run with me...

Heading downhill on the path towards Hazel Mount and the A595, a plain looking figure loitered by the bushes poking about with big black boots as if trying to bury something.

Run with me...

Getting closer, I realised I had mistaken the woman for a boy as she scratched the curled mess of dark brown hair, in clothes the same colour as a wild wood. A few yards behind, an empty black estate car's engine smelt like it ran on glue and tar.

Run with me...

She immediately scurried back to it after hearing the rustling of my footsteps. Head down beneath the visor, her pale visage quickly disappeared behind the dark shield. Moving with the shadows of the trees, a lingering heat caressed the back of my neck as I passed.

Then the black screen. Nothing...

Let's run...

Under the slopes of White Combe, the devil had gathered the black hour. Yet the first step of pure creation stared back like the face of new art. In my hand, holding darkness still, repudiating nature in the void of life. For a moment, my phone had been transformed into Kubrick's monolith. Fear and curiosity in a cosmic fusion of Arthur C. Clarke's short story The Sentinel and Wordsworth's unobstructed prospect of a lifetime. Feeling reborn, at High Mount, I greeted the boundary again with no recollection of how I'd got there. Crossing over the A595, I leant on a metal gate tied with a flayed piece of string near the farm buildings at Gornal Ground. Surveying the humped white paradox sitting on an ebony throne as it silenced all of history with its bulk. Like a god of the underworld, the whaleback outline of Black Combe gazed into the abyss. Across the misty gloom the ground soon levelled out beyond the gentle slopes enveloping Fox's Wood. As the coastal breeze swirled round a series of hawthorn bushes, birds filled the hush with babbled tunes. On the right-hand side coming into view, a left fork in the road headed down to Millom on the A5093. Breaking off, the boundary kicked on towards the very edge of the kingdom at Silecroft.

Under the watchful eye of White Combe, foot to the floor on a winding rat run, boy racers, red-faced delivery drivers, SUVs and lorries loaded up with aggregates. All seemingly oblivious to the surrounding artist's palette of purple lake, rose doré, raw umber and hooker's green. Walking parallel to the A595, I thought about driving out to Millom after the stage, but quickly decided to put it off for another day. October had already begun to strip the woodland, while the afternoon's long shadows and low sunshine collided to leave new forms of isolation – a blindness that touched perfection. The further away from Duddon Bridge and the closer to the post-industrial West Coast, the more it grew...

At the small village of Hallthwaites, I crossed over an old packhorse bridge, leaving Heron's Pool and Riverside pure at heart beside Black Beck's final resting place. On a tarmacked back lane, everything was suddenly connected and bathed in bright sunshine, save for Black Combe holding hands with its sibling White Combe, brooding away under a blanket of cloud. By The Green houses sporting rhododendrons, freshly cut grass and manicured borders rubbed up against a bare cul-de-sac, which had been tarred with the grey, austere brush of social housing. Crossing over another old bridge by the village hall, I could find no trace of a store mentioned by Dugdale. The main ads on the noticeboard highlighted a variety of upcoming treats and wants instead: indoor bowling, bonfire party, volunteers needed for Age UK, music events, table tennis and a car boot sale. Opposite the hall where the old post office used to be, the 18th century Punchbowl Inn had the monopoly on food and drink with its partner organisation, the Beckstones Brewery. Despite the lack of competition, a quick delve into the non-stop bluster of TripAdvisor revealed nothing but praise. Particularly, the 'great gammon', 'lovely halloumi' and a nice surprise to find a vegan option in West Cumbria.

Following a sign for Lady Hall, I crossed the A5093 and headed over rolling fields looking for a series of indistinct field boundaries. On lines of landscape dissected by telegraph poles, a murder of crows sang blackened cries like fools in love. Up above, the unsettling presence of Black Combe hummed and vibrated with a deathless beat. One of those mountains that chose to show a different face every day of the year. Over a stile onto the grubby track heading for Mire House Farm, a herd of attentive black and white Holstein Friesian cows appeared on the brow of a hill. They'd already taken a keen interest in my backpack and sodden footsteps. Instinctively, I started to moo at them, like in 'Mr Brown can moo, can you?'

A sudden acceleration caught me by surprise until they all filtered out in a long single file. Eyes on the floor, with tails wagging they proceeded to mooch slowly downhill on a muddy channel by a small brook. By now I was sinking up to my ankles again, only this time in a biting mix of grime and muck. The farmer watched it all unfold from the other side of a long gate leading into the heart of the farm. He stood motionless, lapping it up, smirking, with long white hair, tweed jacket and, crucially – a pair of wellies. Next to him, kicking a ball repeatedly at the milking shed, his teenage son wore a faded yellow Brazil top and blue knee-length jeans without once looking up.

"Taken a wrong turn eh?" the farmer said, opening the gate to let the cows through first.

"Looks like it, this map's over twenty years old!" Another few precious moments passed waiting on the other side, as I sank further and further into the mire at Mire House.

"Where you trying to get to then?" he said finally letting me through.

"Whicham Church via…Po House I think it's called. I've been really struggling to pick up any paths round here though. They all seem to be completely overgrown or not there even…"

"Whicham Church you say? Well that's easy enough…just follow the beck down the valley to Bankside. You'll have to go through the Wet Moss first mind."

"Great, these boots have already had it…"

"Aye, the Wet Moss – aptly named, but you'll not find it on any map. It's the in-between place where the lake would have been."

"Anyway, head for Spunham. You'll need to pass through it first to pick up the road. If you can find that you'll be at the church in no time."

Then he looked down at my broken boots and smiled again.

The Wet Moss turned out to be another predictable foray into mushy sludge covered in brambles, thorns and bushes. Most of the paths here on the periphery had been reclaimed. Morale at this point had sunk like my boots to an all-time low, not helped by the dearth of any sugary comforts in my backpack. As my mind similarly wandered into a quagmire of despair, thoughts of the cycle back to Broughton just about kept flagging spirits alive. The national park sold the western Lake District as a land of contrasts, with four distinctive valleys rich in character, scenic beauty and full of hidden gems. The sheer distance between towns coupled with the close proximity of the boundary seemed to have marginalised these out-of-the-way places into shoes of wood.

With my energy fading faster than the light, I wandered by mistake into the driveway of Spunham Farm, sending a pair of caged Jack Russells mad with rage. Their aggression born out of anxiety and fear set off a chain reaction that flushed out a couple of male pheasants, sent a black mob of crows soaring into panic and even turned the heads of a few sheep between mouthfuls of feed. At the brow of a hill, before Wood Farm, the clip-clop of someone approaching on horseback seemed to quieten things down again. My eyes glazed over at the wondrous sight of the female rider's graceful charm leading the black horse on into a sleepy haze. Over on the other side of the Whicham Valley, flecks of disorderly gulls harried the silhouettes of crows as they circled each other riding high on the current. In these dark imaginings the summit cairn of Black Combe poked its nose through a set of clouds, moving like a river flows into the ocean.

Nearing the end on a dry open road scaling the heights to Bankside, everything closed in around a small stretch of woodland, until the slopes of Dog Crag sent shadows falling towards Po House. Built in the Georgian period, the cottage (now a holiday let) basked in the world heritage status of Wordsworth's cultural landscape to help boost bookings. It was once owned by John Myers, a cousin of the poet, who spent some time there according to another of his devoted sister's diaries. On the final stretch to the church, the buzz of a cyclist freewheeling surfaced out of the gloom; a wicker chair was strapped very carefully to the back of her bike. Her Hair a nest of tight blonde curls, and with a large yellow coat flapping in the wind, I thought of the scatty chalet maid Peggy, played by Sue Pollard, in the TV series *Hi-de-Hi*. On my left in the fields leading to Baldmire Wood, a scarecrow dressed in bright, baggy clothes circa Madchester 1990 observed us.

The West is the best...

The West is the best...

Further on beyond the church, opposite the junction where A5093 and A595 met, an abandoned garage near the sands at Silecroft rolled out lost memories in a wilderness of pain.

Unsurprisingly, progress proved slow on the long lumpy cycle back to Broughton. While images from the day flashed through my mind, the last vestiges of energy melted onto the steep slope at High Cross. Consoled by the other side of night, I rode back into lost fragments, spreading infernal and divine into the empty market square. Since leaving the illusory decorated shed of Broughton, strange symphonies swept along by ghosts of the daylight cobbles had been dancing in flames. Far away in this small corner of the world, search light souls sang like the autumn stars...

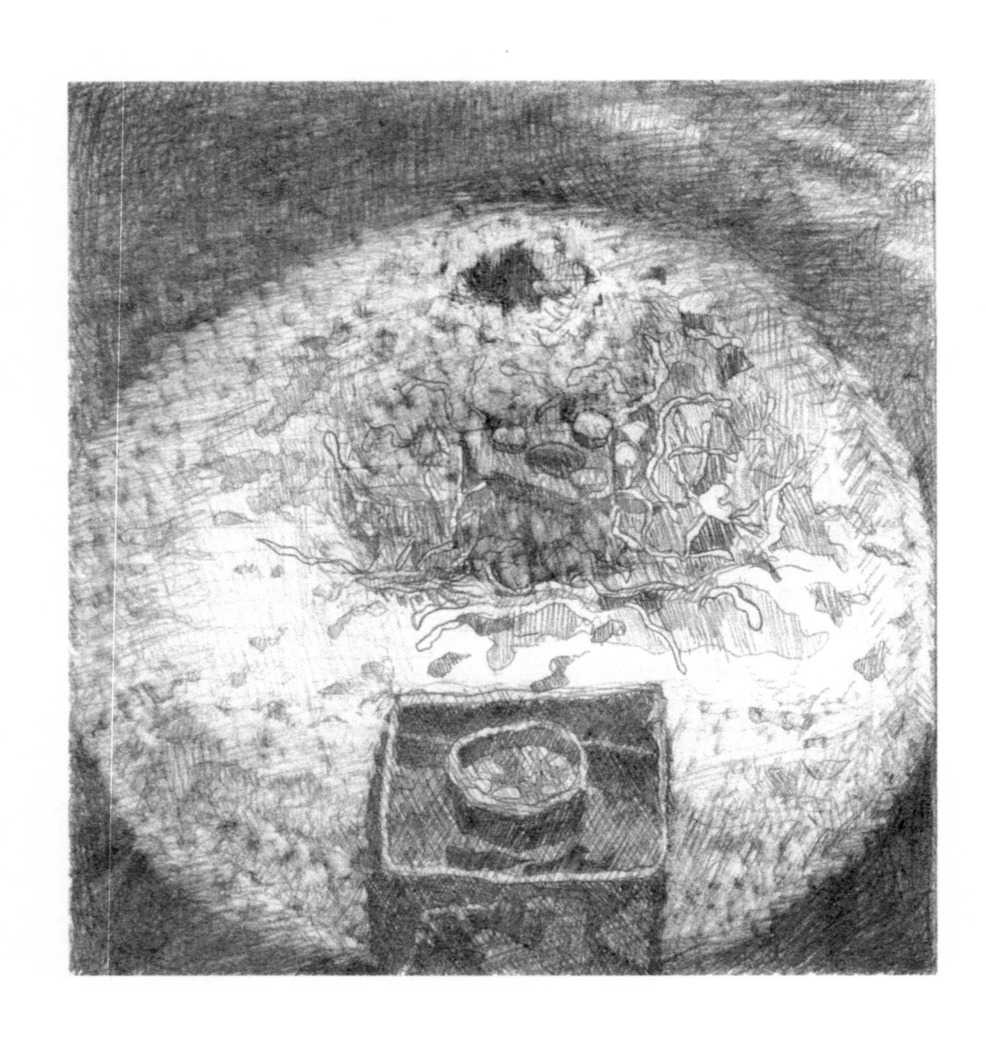

WHITBECK TO NEWBIGGIN

RUBBING SHOULDERS WITH STATE-SPONSORED NUCLEAR WEAPONS
THE SWOLLEN BONNET SNORTING BESIDE A METAL GATE
RUNNING DOWN A DREAM OF SUMMER SUICIDES
DESMOND'S BROWNISH FLAME SWEPT ACROSS THE ROOM
CLONED ARMIES OF BUZZING PYLONS
WRAPPED IN A PILL OF TOXIC WASTE
RED CURLS SWARMING THE SKIES IN FLOODS OF TEARS
WHITBECK TO NEWBIGGIN

Sombre winds in a fuzz of doom...

After the dark undertones during our brush with the Silecroft mafia, storm Ophelia's arrival a few weeks later presented an entirely different challenge...

Hurricane Ophelia: 'Do NOT travel' unprecedented warning issued - KILLER STORM heads towards UK

BRITONS urged to stay at home and NOT TRAVEL as 100mph Hurricane Ophelia prepares to strike the UK.

The day I'd pencilled in for my next boundary stage proper was the one straight after the ex-hurricane raged through Cumbria. For once, a weather headline in the Daily Express abandoned what Monbiot called their 'usual bollocks with bells on' statement and was proved right, after gusts of almost 100mph were reported in some parts of the UK. In Cumbria, this led to multiple road closures, major disruption to public transport and more than a thousand homes left without power. Despite a long list of damage, including fallen trees, roof slates and debris on the roads and overhead cables pulled down, I decided to head out and see how far I could get towards the West Coast.

Initially, strong gusts blew my car from side to side on the open stretches of the A590, but keeping the speed down, I managed to skirt round debris left lying on the road. Eventually, I reached the end of the stage and locked the bike to an iron fence at the C of E Primary school car park in Waberthwaite. Driving back to the foot of Black Combe, I pulled into a layby off the A595, up the road from Whitbeck Church, and sat in silence praying for the dregs of Ophelia to blow over. Pressing the buttons to open all the windows, the invincible form of mountain stood like a rock of jet against the reddish sky. Drowning in its dark, Ophelia's death notes dragged in the last remnants of tropical air and dust from the Sahara. The last time I'd been seduced by a storm of such brutal force had happened almost two years before, when Desmond left a series of calling cards that broke the national park in two...

Then, despite nearly a week of unrelenting heavy rain, McSwailes and I had ventured out, grabbing a quick breather below Alcock Tarn as the wind came up. He'd arrived earlier on a Virgin Pendolino from Glasgow for a boozy weekend break. It was late on a Friday afternoon during a brief dry interlude over Grasmere. We'd met many years before in London, after I'd managed to blag some work experience in the music business. Uncle Rupert's spaced-out plaything, situated just off Fulham Broadway. It was here that we fetched and loaded umpteen boxes of promo vinyl and CDs to a record company stockroom marinated in fungus above a fried chicken take-away. He was a painter doing occasional jobs for cash following the completion of a master's at the Slade. While his best mate, another Scot from Aberdeen, had landed the art director's gig at the main label. For a moment our wings rose and spread in the city streets. All around us everything glistened as the electricity accelerated and we danced fervently into the abyss. Hopes and fears versus expectations. Solo and group exhibitions; movers and shakers; after-show parties; television and award shows; Christmas do's on private islands.

Where to choose...McSwailes moved to Highbury. Whenever sales dried up he exchanged paintings for Ikea furniture and was eventually rewarded with a scholarship to Iceland. Somewhere in the deserts of black sand, nature in its rawest form blew sombre winds in a fuzz of doom. It's easy when you know the rules. It's a free world. Play the game – yeah... But that then, that wasn't McSwailes anymore. Version 2.0 scribbled poems on walls, drew pointillist temple drawings and gathered up studio materials. A short dabble into Walthamstow's grubby labyrinth blew out the last embers of burning ambition. It wasn't happening. The speakers were blown and the hurricane was forming. McSwailes returned north of the border and almost disappeared completely...

Similarly, I'd been running down a dream of summer suicides after escaping from the cruel and shallow money trench. A fair bit of messing around had followed another more painful separation that drained the colour from my eyes. Every now and again, with an awful thirst, I'd bump into McSwailes after moving south of the river to live in Deptford to study for an Art History degree at Goldsmiths. Various jobs selling memberships in the cash for culture world of corporate art followed. Eventually a temporary hiatus at the Wordsworth Trust poured wine across a lake of sorrows. I ran the London Marathon, enrolled on a Lake District Landscape course led by Gandalf at Lancaster University, and began the in-between cycle from the Lakes to London and back again. High and low in a long distance relationship up to Leeds every other weekend burnt down love's machine. Initially, I kept it close and Yorkshire wanted me. In the end, the relentless miserable National Express journeys, coupled with the battle against cancelled trains amid hasty hellos and weepy goodbyes took their toll. Like McSwailes, I retreated...

As the dreamy shadows passed under thunder clouds black as pitch, something dreadful was about to blaze in from the east high above Helm Crag. Like nothing I'd ever seen before, a thick gluey mass hovered over Grasmere, while the sky above burned like fire. Falling, falling...I emerged into a large open field that was already so saturated it had become transparent like glass. As thunder rolled and spread fear into the valley below, I saw something afloat in the rising water. A remarkable image advanced as the form grew and knocked me to the ground in shock. It was a newborn child treading water inside a gleaming bubble...

"Ah sod this. Let's get a beer!" McSwailes straightened himself up and put an end to my daydream, marching away from the rocks by the tarn on a winding path towards civilisation. A modern-day rebel without a cause, dressed in casual outerwear, rocking a half unzipped black Harrington with red and green tartan lining, blue Wranglers and North Face trainer boots. Like Houellebecq, a caricature wannabe Nostradamus and one of his favourite authors, McSwailes had always been hard to place.
Life it seemed, made all three of us blue.

The rain, the rain, the rain now...non-stop it came down in steroids as my dad would have said. Retreating to a couple of locally sourced overpriced hotel bars, we drank away our gloom on hard wooden benches. Two pints for ten notes, cheers! Then a quick dash in monsoon-like conditions brought us back to the cave. A dark, chilly cottage (and former stables) nestled away at the top end of Grasmere, opposite White Bridge Forge with the River Rothay meandering close by. I'd been looking after it for a couple of friends who were away on a six-month travelling scholarship to China.

Turned out the place was as quirky as the landlord, a chemist who stocked up for the winter by running the local am-dram society, drove a bright blue Austin Seven and lived just up the road in a mansion opposite a four-star hotel. Mr Pharmacist, I insist...Within the open mouth of the lounge area, exposed timber beams regularly sprung leaks, while the TV signal was so bad you were lucky if you got as far as the autotune. Often, in the early hours, a succession of soft squeaks from either mice or bats kept me awake, until I could sense the concentric ripples of the afterlife. At least an old piano (perfect for a pissed-up jamming session) took pride of place by the sofa. As soon as we got back, McSwailes threw off his soaked Harrington and started playing rinky-dink melodies from a careworn collection of old folk and pop songbooks. After towelling myself down, I grabbed my guitar and joined in the impromptu knees-up. Thankfully, our drunken boogy-woogy drowned out the waves of chilling rain.

The next morning three knocks on the front door hammered into my weary head. Turning over with my head in turmoil, whomever it was came back almost immediately. Not a peep sounded from the spare room, where McSwailes had crashed after rocking the main stage into the dawn. Opening the top half of the stable entrance slowly, the old chap from next door shook a lake of water off the hood of his jacket.

"Now then...I've been trying to get you all morning! You'd better come and move your car quick, it's about to float off..."

Storm Desmond had duly arrived...After sorting out the car I tried to rouse McSwailes...

"Oi, fella... fella...get up quick! I'm serious; they're bailing out next door! I'm not kidding... you should see the state of it outside!"

"Ugh... what, bollocks, wait...they can't be!"

"They are, I just got drowned trying to move the car off the drive. The water's coming up so high it could be in through the front door any minute..."

"Jesus fucking Christ! What is this sick place?"

What followed turned out to be one of the quickest hangover cures yet, when more than one month's prolonged and intense rain fell between the Friday and Saturday nights. It made our paltry attempts to bail out the gathering flood at the front door using only a wok and rusted spade seem almost as bizarre as the extreme weather. After nearly three hours fighting to stem the tide and with hunger kicking in, I'd popped a couple of mince pies in the oven. But at what must have been around the same time, two channelised landslides below Stone Arthur started to pour a significant amount of debris into Greenhead Gill. The tumbling gravel and larger bed material were then transported down into the River Rothay and deposited along the river corridors, reducing the flow capability of the channels.

With no formal flood defences in place, the Rothay burst its banks. It flooded directly outside the cave, with tides of water spewing out towards Broadgate and the centre of the village. Unbeknown to us, a whirlpool of tears had formed outside our very own sinking ship, now cast adrift from the other properties in White Bridge. My head started to throb once again, and then with pitying fear the ghostly moment arrived when the brown coloured sludge started pouring in through the front door. Startled, McSwailes said nothing on the wooden staircase after a lengthy visit to the upstairs bathroom. Instead, we both watched in awe as Desmond's brownish flame swept across the room and started to bleed under our feet. Defenceless, the power of water spun everything upside down as the intruder turned us into refugees.

For the next couple of hours I was waist deep in muck, ferrying possessions to McSwailes on the stairs. After turning off the electricity, candlelight threw long shadows onto the black theatrical screen of emptied lounge floor and kitchen. Into the night our senses heightened in a psychedelic dream world upstairs. We attempted to block out the surrounding apocalypse by watching Clint Eastwood's *American Sniper* on the laptop in between checking out Beach House's new album. All the while

Desmond blew his last set of cancerous kisses like de Quincey's trembling crocodile. Occasionally we heard the odd swishing noise of a car parting the standing wave of flood water before the small bridge over the Rothay. Their headlight beams formed explosions in the sky that threatened to ignite the dark.

The next morning I woke early to a stomach-churning stench of dank and musty rotten eggs curled into the air with a sweet undertone of smoke. It was a smell that would stick around for a couple of months, like a stop in time. After throwing on dry clothes I raced downstairs, wrapping my nose in the hood of a hoodie.

"Christ! It's all gone!" I shouted up at McSwailes.

Puzzled by the lack of water, the sight of a pair of collared doves perched on the bush opposite the stable door provided a strange distraction. Opening the top part, unrolling like a muddied carpet ceaselessly swirling, I saw the floodwater resting almost halfway up. It was as if the past and future had met to form a new ocean. It didn't take long before I realised the only way to escape the drowned cave would be to climb out of the top half. Positioning a chair to stand on, we legged it over the bottom door and carefully waded out knee-high through the slush. On the driveway the maelstrom had attracted a crowd, some of whom stood around pointing and taking snaps on their phones.

"Screw this, let's get out of here." I turned to McSwailes who'd been eyeing the mob with growing disgust. "People with no hearts make bad enemies."

"Yeah, this lot are seriously taking the piss. Besides, I could really do with eating something."

The drive to Ambleside resembled Jim's walk through a deserted London in *28 Days Later.* Similar to Boyle's post-apocalyptic Britain, the storm's grizzly aftermath had left behind a trail of destruction on the A591, which was strewn with abandoned cars, uprooted trees, broken signs and piles of rubble. Ombrophobia...during the local hysteria in the months afterwards, I developed an intense fear of rain. (Not exactly an ideal condition in the Lake District!) Before the storm came, any amount of droplets used to sing ambient melodies of sweet serenity. After Desmond's destruction, they brought the impinging chaos of discord. Often, to relieve a sense of feeling trapped, I would simply lie down or sit on the floor with doors and windows wide open until the downpour ceased...

Long is the way in and hard on the A595 that out of here leads back to the light...Whitbeck, or 'white stream' was a tiny village made up of a handful of farms scattered around the focal point of St Mary's Church. The simple grade two listed building featured an attractive red sandstone front. Its origins were thought to be from the twelfth century, although it was altered in the nineteenth century. A local legend claimed neither fish nor ducks lived in the white stream, even though cattle supposedly drank in it without care. In the aftermath of a wild night that had seen the heads of traffic lights ripped off, the stream was now being swept along at a frightening pace.

Ever since I'd departed the Georgian façades at Broughton, the coast I'd encountered up to this point felt totally at odds with the national park's so-called distinctive area. Out here the main distinctive features appeared to be cloned armies of buzzing pylons and wind farms. Quarries, dismantled railways, churches and abandoned farms had sucked the land dry, with the odd Neolithic burial site a reminder of the shift from managed hunting to pastoral farming. In reality, the former historic county of Cumberland was now a coastal strip expunged into the Irish Sea, wrapped in a pill of toxic waste. Above the waterline, a narrow piece of low-lying land incorporated the industrial belt to the north; in the middle the haunting loneliness of Sellafield held back the colour of Millom's patterned scum in the rear. The national park boundary formed a great divide created in the mind.

The coastline had in effect been cordoned off from a World Heritage back-cloth of self-contained mountains animated by outstanding universal value. Yet amongst empty roads, isolated houses, bare fells and austere buildings fashioned out of the imposing red sandstone bedrock, a couple of artists emerged from the post-war nuclear haze. One was a lonely Lakelander, the other a beautiful gypsy-like woman with dark green eyes. Both of them painted their native West Cumbria as a dark and moody place. The kind of spot where nostalgic day dreams stirred up thick layers of oil and heavy sombre outlines formed intricate patterns onto gouache, watercolour or charcoal. Percy Kelly and Sheila Fell...a cross-dressing postman awkward to deal with and a miner's daughter loved by all.

"Cumberland is not like the rest of England...It is like no other place," Sheila Fell once wrote cryptically.

From the bizarre and livid sky in the depths of Black Combe, a long stretch of the A595 ploughed a lone furrow through the heart of Whitbeck and beyond. Standing in the middle of the road, I saw a barren landscape that reminded me of the melancholy mirror depicted in Percy Kelly's bold chiaroscuro 'Into the Valley'. Turning to face the changeable backdrop on my left hand side, I thought of driving into the ocean, busy, busy, busy, and laughing in the face of death.

At the Whitbeck noticeboard:
Black Combe Holiday Cottages, Holiday cottage cleaning and laundry service. Urgently needed - Volunteers to help with speech after strokes (in the Millom area), an advert for the Millom Squadron Air Cadets, and a notice for the vacant Assistant Priest position in the Black Combe Benefice...

Setting off in the direction of the coast, with my hood up, a metalled road headed just off the A595 towards Gutterby Farm. Then almost immediately, a short train carrying a series of large grey cabins on top of long flat-bed waggons checked my stride at a level crossing. It was nothing, probably just another load of nuclear waste passing by in the less visible rural wastelands. Edgy and dull, a six-inch valley ran over towards Bootle, where a crowd of black and white cows gathered under a blood red sky.

Even on normal days I imagined not much happened round here. I strode on beside a succession of humming pylons and suspected the wild surf must have brought a special and golden gift for the offshore wind farm! All wet! Shakedown! While dreams walked in the first shadows of winter, ripples in puddles wavered with a sense of renewal. In the tail end of a world on fire, I soon discovered my own limited attempts to record voice notes were nigh on impossible. Ophelia's deafening fury had blown almost everything out.

Down a churned-up path, a wooden gate preceded the sand dunes circled by the salty air. It whipped across a beach littered with boulders on the coastal cliff edge above, patches of yellow gorse tangled with strands of barbed wire swinging freely in the air, as if an invisible hand uplifted it all. Aqua sea foam shame choked on the ashes of the weeping roar. Ophelia was a vampire, sent to drain. Like an exile, I walked in solitude upon Annaside Banks beside the rumbling ocean. Behind me the western flanks of Black Combe slowly disappeared as the cries of gulls floated past a buckled copse of willow, sycamore, hawthorn and blackthorn. In the cold afternoon, I skirted round the Bog Hole, a dark and wondrous basin-shaped depression.

The Cumbria Coastal Way running cold and driven apart by erosion, as the crimson tones started to drain from the skies. Soaring overhead like clouds of fire, skylarks brought back the soundtrack of a childhood filled with walks in sunnier climes on the South Downs. At least the buildings of Annaside farm provided a welcome respite from the freezing bursts of wind. Missing out Bootle, I decided to ignore Dugdale's little detour and took the most direct route on a narrow winding track hemmed in by gorse and brambles covered in red berries. The going proved heavy, passing from farm to farm on sopping wet ground approaching the railway line at Syke Beck. On from there, almost all the other farmhouses I passed through were either deserted or fallen into ruin, adding to an overall sense of seclusion. Lashed by the merciless wind, weary field hands drifted away like a cloud.

Easily the most evocative in the pastoral graveyard was Inmans Farm, highlighted by Dugdale on one of his hand-drawn maps. Lying on the northerly route to the small settlement at Hycemoor, its dark empty shell could only be reached by wading through a ditch of brown sludge enclosed by clumps of piercing thorns, pricking, pinching and tugging at my coat. The remains reminded me of Tate Britain's 'Ruin Lust' show, 'a time machine that released the mind to wander in nooks and crannies of lost ages – and ages to come.' The exhibition featured sketches of decayed castles and forsaken abbeys alongside bombed-out wreckage by stalwarts such as Turner, Constable, Nash, Sutherland and Piper. They were included in the same conversation as contemporary artists like Laura Grace Ford's Brutalist estates, tagged in the same way a dog marks its territory, or Jane and Louise Wilson's large-scale black and white photograph of a derelict Second World War bunker on the Normandy coastline of northern France. Gazing at the exposed frames bulging with branches and weeds, I wondered what had gone so wrong at Inmans to tear the people away. If the leaky skeletons of such places reveal the passage of our lingering past, could they also be a reminder that even though dreams might have vanished, death is not the end...

From the ghostly depths of Inmans' sweet sorrow to the asphalt streets of Hycemoor felt like stepping back into some form of civilisation. Now I was surrounded by rows of bungalows, cars on driveways, wooden sheds, trampolines, garden tools, road bikes, football nets, a defibrillator and then a person! The first I'd seen in nearly three hours crossed the street ahead of me with a Border collie pulling vigorously on a leash. All these things into position, all these things...

Suddenly modern life sped past in a blur when a Ricky's Travel bus tailgated a Tesco delivery van in the heat of the afternoon school run. Escaping the wheels of communication, I turned right onto one of the muddiest paths in the world. It was on the approach to the farm buildings at the Nook. The noise of my splattered boots plodding along surprised a friendly basset hound waddling around outside the gate. The dog then greeted me by throwing its long ears back and letting out a deep bark. The lady owner dressed immaculately in yellow wellingtons and blue dungarees stood about ten yards away staring at a red tractor opposite the pair of us. Beneath brambles, blackthorn hedges and fields of endless bog, Williamson's Moss ran parallel with the old railway path.

This led to the next port of call, the 'bang and burn' of the MoD establishment at Eskmeals firing range. Continuing over a level crossing, I was thankful to reach a good stretch of solid ground servicing the weapons camp. Immediately, a profusion of red warning signs announced the danger of live ammo. As I entered a new zone of surveillance cameras, barriers and flags, the main buildings looked like a glass, concrete and steel Brutalist icon. Rigid lines and cold steel frames added to the austere veneer staring back like a machine gun. Round targets in the darkening countryside, revvin' up engines in the twilight until the red line overload of the danger area. Out along the edges a special form of technology, full of violence and destruction.

Then I remembered the old man from Valley End reminiscing about targeting the Isle of Man as shooting practice when stationed there with his tank crew. He'd also told me about his collection of photos that showed Japanese dignitaries removing magnets from the soles of their boots. Nullifying the cunning attempts to collect scraps off any fired artillery shells. Firing out to sea on the very edge of the boundary, a stage that started with the screams of red curls swarming the skies in floods of tears had a final threat up its sleeve. The rat-a-tat-tat of gunfire!

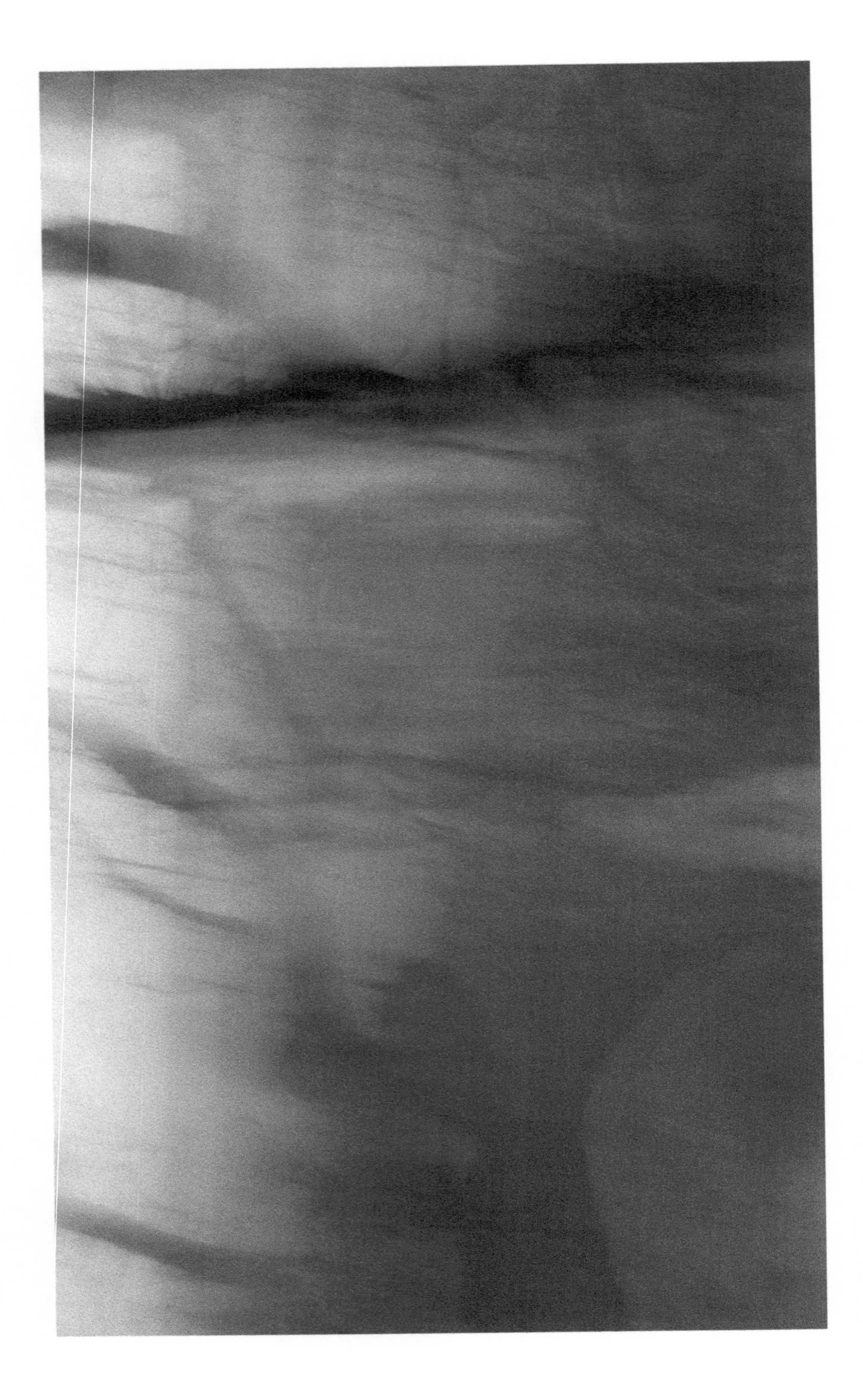

Whenever, whatever

w
an
Buried
afcend
Whole
Lord
theFath
thePr
knowle
rection

us u
hero
n Glor
ave no
oprocee
gether is
elieve o
for the
the Life

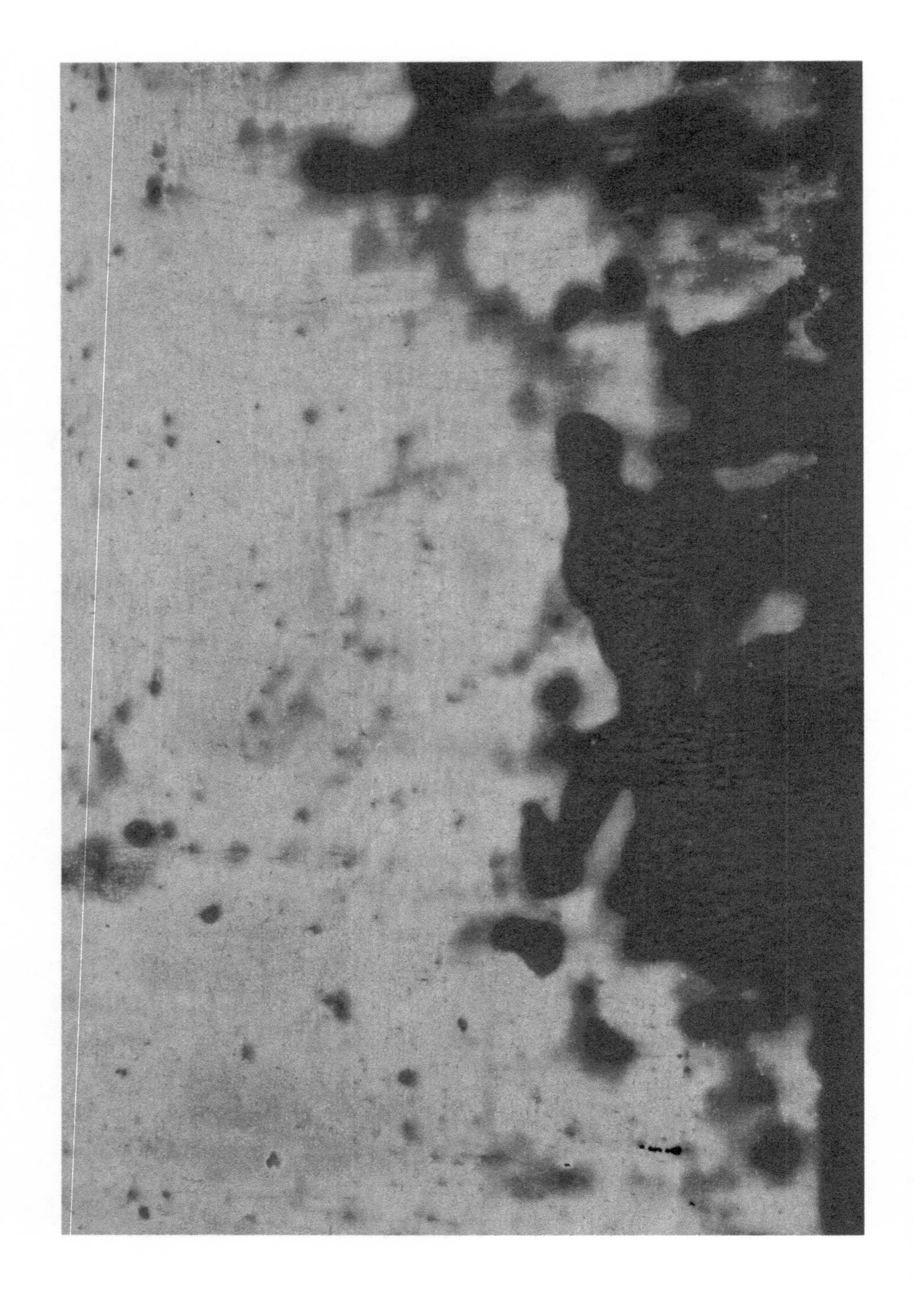

CAUTION
VANDAL
PROOF
PAINT

NO
HEAVY
VEHICLES

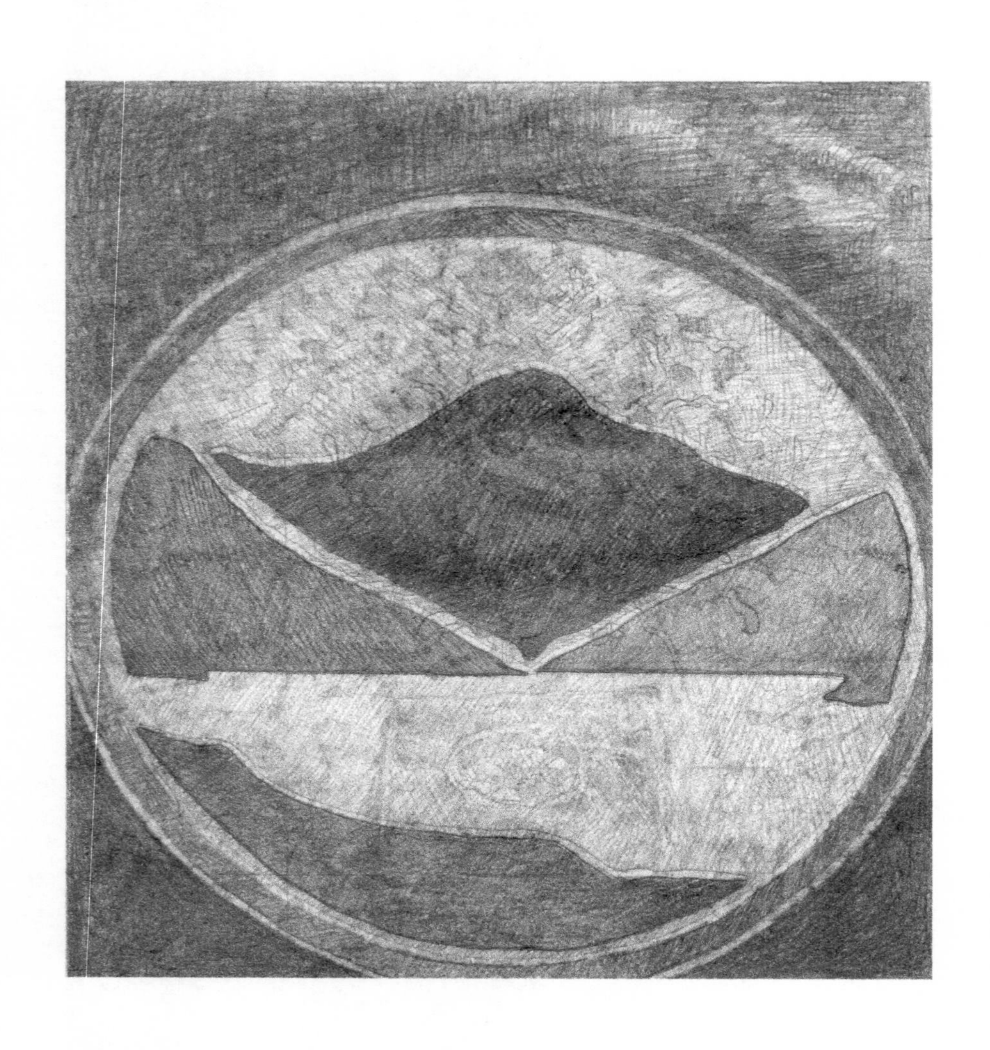

NEWBIGGIN TO GOSFORTH

THE MORNING BREXIT BRAINWASH
UNDER THE CONSTANT THREAT OF TIDAL FLOODS
OLD RED SANDSTONE
STACKED WITH A SAWTOOTH-LIKE FORM
FAULTLINES, FLOODLINES AND FORMER LAKES
THE HUSH OF DANGEROUS CARGO
RESTLESS SPIRITS TRAPPED IN LIMBO
A SLICE OF ENGLISH QUAINT
THE NIGHT RODE IN FORCE
A BLACK FLAG SMILING TO THE NIGHT
NEWBIGGIN TO GOSFORTH

'GEBDAETH FORAE' [Pray for...]

24 October 2017. Half term week with the morning Brexit brainwash in full swing on Breakfast TV.

"Can I have a pint of milk and three packets of Brexit?"

"Clothes, suitcase, now...did I pack the Brexit?"

Brexit...not just politics, it's everyday life – so goes the BBC advert...

Hard-headed and unresponsive, the same images and sounds reflected in the enemy's eyes and ears. But now for the very first time someone had dared to speak out about victory and defeat. Winners and losers. The negotiations were said to be centred on three separate issues, with the border in Northern Ireland the main problem. Political boundaries at the edge of nations where borders are often go unchallenged, accepted and preserved almost as a matter of course. I was relieved to get away from the continual bickering, even though it was a wet drizzly morning. 'Boundary weather' – like the news, everything was cloaked in a thick layer of dark grey cloud.

First of all, the long drive out to Gosforth meant navigating a way through the heaving bottleneck of Bowness. By mid-morning the queue to meet Peter Rabbit and friends had already backed up behind a lorry blocking half of the road whilst a team of two unloaded beer barrels at the pace of Mahler's 5th. After a twenty-minute crawl through the inferno, the A590 moved at a much brisker tempo before I reached the pull up to Cawpthwaite, where a labouring Shell lorry spewed out diesel fumes and slowed the line of traffic almost to a halt. The signal for the radio started playing up until the autotune located Radio Cumbria again, with Fern blasting out Toto's *Rosanna*. Switching it off, for some reason I found myself humming the 'Rah Rah' bit of Gaga's *Bad Romance* all the way into Gosforth instead.

Newbiggin to Gosforth – a nine-mile stage 'chewing on a mud pie' according to Dugdale. The journey really started with a wet cycle from the village car park in Gosforth through a ribbon of grey cloud along the busy A595. Trying to avoid the rotating spray kicked up by an endless stream of vans and lorries through Holmrook, Muncaster and Broad Oak, before the steady gradient at Prospect Hill into Waberthwaite. Exit lines, bones and silence. Arriving soaked through, I had to lock Knightrider on a wooden fence opposite a bus shelter by Newbiggin Primary School again. Evidently, Newbiggin was no cycling Mecca.

Waberthwaite might be tiny and easy to miss when skirting round the West Coast, but its agricultural past boasts a royal nod of approval. Since 1990, the post office and grocers of Richard Woodall has been 'By Appointment to HM Queen Elizabeth II Suppliers of Traditional Cumberland

Sausage'. It started way back in 1828, when a living room converted into a shop began curing and selling hams and bacon. They bred prize-winning pigs with bellies the size of hot-air balloons and exhibited them at the Royal Agricultural Society's International Show in London. Some of their wares were even present at a few key moments in history, going down with the Titanic or pulled up Everest by the Cumbrian based mountaineer Sir Chris Bonington. Time may still be of little consequence in the sleepy sandstone backwater, but folk still come from far and wide to sample bangers made from old recipes and 95% meat.

Padlocking up the bike, the shop, which doubled as the village post office had something of Sid's Café from Last of the Summer Wine about it. Getting closer to the bright red door, I peered in at a queue of customers. Here was a modern-day example of Kendal's Museum of Lakeland Life with actual people replacing a street-scene soundtrack. Real deals, fresh meat, general groceries and other delicatessen items – staged authenticity in the bygone age of retailing. In the pull and charm of such lonely places, small villages are often thought to be a chance to rediscover bits of ourselves.

The name Waberthwaite in Old Norse means 'Wyburgh's clearing'. It's surrounded by the River Esk, which begins a circuitous journey from the Scottish Borders and ends up winding its way around the foothills of Muncaster Castle, where a 250 feet high beacon tower projects a haunting enchantment from the unconscious. The old days are dead and gone days. A couple who I thought must be Japanese tourists emerged from the shop, looking slightly bemused and carrying freshly packed bags. Well into middle age, the man and woman seemed completely out of place, dressed elegantly in a dark suit and a floral dress. The man walked slightly in front holding a camera strung round his neck, while the woman studied the road with a troubled eye. In the silent soft breaths of late morning I watched them pass in front of me and disappear along Stockbridge as if never really there. Like a false awakening for the grey flat-lands populated by buildings hewn out of Eskdale granite. Among the farmhouses, a coastal village lives under the constant threat of tidal floods; the dream is all too real...

The Eskdale Intrusion is the largest exposure of the granitic batholith underlying the national park. Over tens of millions of years, collisions and mountain-building periods meant the upper surfaces outcropped, and the heat that was generated metamorphosed the rocks it intruded. Plutonic rocks within the Borrowdale Volcanics were mixed in with the older Skiddaw Group in a period often referred to as Old Red Sandstone. The main forms can be found at Shap, Skiddaw and Eskdale, the granophyre of Ennerdale, microgranite of Threlkeld and hotchpotch of rocks on Carrock

Fell. Poorly exposed outcrops of granodiorite – consisting of pale-coloured and course grained igneous rock containing quartz – are located in the southern area north of Bootle and Newbiggin. Parallel to the Lake District boundary fault on the western margin, tabular granite sheets were stacked with a saw-tooth like form. Despite intense alteration, much of the course-grained and pale pink textures formed by the intergrowth of sodium and potassium orthoclase were left behind. Until just after the Second World War, many villagers residing in Waberthwaite and its environs relied on the quarrying of granite sets at Broad Oak to eke out a living. But despite the post-war economic boom, the rock of ages sent to equip countless nearby Lancashire towns was closed down for good.

The stage promised to be another trip across fault lines, flood lines and former lakes. From a twelfth century church towards one of the country's most haunted castles. Then a glimpse into the national park's favourite view beside an Anglo-Saxon ninth century cross erected to mark the junction of four ancient trackways. Since leaving Woodall's shop the chill in the air along the solitary path tugged on my coat sleeves. But this was not the only happening in the misty gloom. Birdsong; lyrical, melodic and intimate… my constant companion floating like free-form jazz out of the hedgerows. Through a closely interwoven set of branches providing safe nesting, roosting places, berries and other fruit for fieldfares, redwings, song thrushes, blue tits, finches, robins, hedge sparrows and wrens. The more open hedges attracted the larger and noisier jackdaws, magpies, crows and pigeons.

In Dugdale's time, a survey of landscape boundaries found many hedges near Bootle and Waberthwaite to be degenerate due to a lack of applied maintenance. But these objections have obviously been corrected over time, given the robust appearance of the sculptural forms rising high and wide along the village lanes. At the Grade II listed Newbiggin House Farm, dated 1768 on a heart-shaped panel over the door, the flat ground of the alluvial deposits of the River Esk and its tributary Whitrow Beck, ran past the front of the farm to the north. It was easy to see how high tides might cause flooding if the water built up in the run-off from the fields behind the property. The name Newbiggin or New Town is a familiar place name in the Eden and western districts of Cumbria, with several others sprinkled around Penrith and Kirkby Stephen.

After carefully tackling a metal gate surrounded by deep cavities of mud opposite the farm, I made my way, gingerly at first, on the sloshy Cumbria Coastal Way to Hall Waberthwaite. In puddles marbled with sepia tones the path cut through marshes made up of a series of muddy creeks serviced by the rise and fall of the estuary's tides. Lost in a dream underneath a telegraph pole, I stared out across the marshland into the steel body of the late nineteenth century Eskmeals Viaduct. Drawn to the hush of dangerous cargo covered in metal and cooled by water along the vast structure on a section of the Cumbrian Coastal Line. Just a short walk takes you out onto the mud and sand of the Drigg Dunes where the Esk, Irt and Mite meet. Built on a danger area near the mouth of three rivers, a weekly shuttle service operates between Sellafield and Heysham. It's a lovely day; bring a nuclear flask...

The boundary dips briefly into the Irish Sea from the edge of the coastal sands to circle Kokoarrah. A curious name for a patch of rocky ground formed of glacial deposit extending below the low tide mark. Koko could be an acronym - Keep on Keeping on...according to the Chambers Dictionary;Arrah is an Anglo-Irish expletive of emotion or wonder. The rocks are now included within the Cumbria Coast Marine Conservation Zone. A stretch of approximately 27km that extends just south of Whitehaven, around the Old Red Sandstone cliffs at St Bees Head, to the outlet of the Ravenglass Estuary above the viaduct. Its aim is to protect and support a rich community of marine wildlife including sponges, sea squirts, barnacles, tubeworms, crabs and lobsters nestled within kelp forest and turfs of algae. But you'll need a boat to pay a visit.

By a bend in the Esk, another silence greeted me upon entering the dusky light of St John's Church. Podgy and rectangular, it was a humble building bound up with centuries of devotion. Built in mediaeval times, perhaps replacing an earlier church, it had an ancient cross-shaft in the churchyard, similar to the Irton Cross that would sing a different prayer near the end of the stage. For 800 years, long echoes have filtered out from the base of a solid block of sandstone, once thought to have been a Roman pillar.

Fed by the Esk, Broadoak Beck dissected the saturated ground to Rougholme Farm, which brought the A595 within earshot again. In the wet conditions, wooden stiles and duct boards coated with green slime traversed the blackness under a scrap of dark woodland. Opening out on the other side, chords of thick mist and cloud shrouded the marshy interior of the valley floor below Muncaster Castle. Clumps of grass mixed with thick belts of mud made the going heavy again, as the path almost evaporated in the green wetlands. But with Muncaster Bridge in my sights, I decided to take the most direct route, come what may. Hood up, head down, keep moving. The sound of bells floated out from the castle, peering through an atmospheric mist almost too perfect for Halloween week. By now my frothing boots had developed an unhealthy squelch on every step, then a sudden onset of sharp pain like a hammer blow in my right ankle left me rooted to the spot. After a few moments the discomfort subsided and I was able to continue again. The remnants of an old football injury had come back to haunt me like some of the former inhabitants of the castle.

Reaching the bridge (erected as late as 1828) brought a slow trudge uphill. My pace dropped to a shuffle beside a long line of grumbling half-term traffic on the A595 now with no real pavement. Stuffed underneath bushes and hedgerows I discovered a familiar mosaic of plastic bottles, sweet wrappers, crisp packets, coffee cups, beer and coke cans. All of it thrown out of car windows by scuffers too busy and important to use a bin. At last a wide piece of pavement began just past the North and West Lodges belonging to the estate. Around the same time, a high-pitched fizzing noise pierced the air, from an articulated lorry spinning its wheels trying to gain traction on the sharpest incline.

Muncaster Castle 'midway on the waves' impressively positioned on a spur above the Esk estuary. A mediaeval relic and pele tower that was later reconstructed out of red granite and sandstone to be absorbed into a Victorian mansion. Since 1208, the remote but rugged and romantic castle has been owned by the Pennington family. Anthony Salvin remodelled it in 1862 using red granite and sandstone, adding towers and a roof to the courtyard to create the drawing room. Inside there's an Elizabethan four-poster in the king's room, a vast array of Charles II walnut chairs, Gainsborough's copy of Titiain's *The Vendramin Family,* various family portraits and *A Study of a Boy with Falcon* once attributed to Velásquez. Outside the view from the Georgian terrace has become known as Ruskin's 'Gateway to Paradise'. A phrase attributed to the polymath after he witnessed the whites, purples and blood-red rhododendrons in full bloom amongst the 31 hectares of mature woodland. The rest of the beautifully kept gardens offer a small tincture of the Himalayas, with camellias, magnolias, hydrangeas and maples flourishing thanks to the Victorian plant-hunters; George Forrest and Frank Kingdon-Ward.

But perhaps the castle is best known for all the strange happenings and paranormal goings-on. Restless spirits trapped in limbo, eerie spectres and disturbing manifestations are said to be a palpable presence at nightfall. Sightings of greyed-out ladies, footsteps on stone floors, thumping on stairs, muttered conversations and children crying in the tapestry room; it all sounded like a Stephen King novel made flesh.

The court jester of all the supernatural happenings in the West Coast Overlook was a malevolent sixteenth century character known as Thomas Skelton or Tom Fool. He was the last fool to the Penningtons and a steward of the estate. It was also believed that he knew Shakespeare, who even used him as a model for *King Lear's* fool. But nobody ever heard him, or the sound he appeared to make busting someone's brains out. He kept it all out of sight. Handy with a mallet and broad chisel, he did his master's dirty work under the cover of darkness. But the Esk eventually claimed him along with the brutally murdered Mary Bragg. She soon became another infamous ghostly presence often seen in a long white dress; it was thought the tree under which she died oozed with blood.

More recently, thanks to a third millennium funding project raising £5.5 million, the castle and hotel has reinvented itself as a modern-day magnet for families and tourists. With its out of the way location, it's a long way to go. The tourism economy of the UK's built heritage market, often monopolised by the NT's drive for membership, is an ongoing turf war.

With foolish grins, the annual tomfoolery traditionally kicks off on April Fools' Day with the Festival of Fools, followed by the Feast of Flowers in May. October is, of course, all about the Halloween ghost tours, but in the dark nights of winter, mystical son-et-lumière shows are the main attraction alongside a Victorian themed Christmas market. Nowadays, Tom Fool is also employed to do audio tours, full of family anecdotes and juicy tales. The rest of the extensive 'what's on' includes exhibitions, Himalayan gardens, winding woodlands, enchanted trails, a kids' play area and even a world of owls. Everything to keep the 'are we there yet?' generation occupied. Exits through gift shops come with tacked-on cafés, while weddings, corporate events and celebrations contribute to the products and experiences on offer.

Passing by the far-reaching castle grounds surrounded by woodland at the top of Muncaster Hill, a small track on the right-hand side led to the Branken Wall conifer plantation. Even though the heavy rain had turned to drizzle, I was still grateful for the cover afforded by taking the spongy path. The floor was littered with severed logs, while moss and lichen adorned strips of bark with creeping poetry. Pine needles and the cones of conifers carried a fresh, sharp fragrance, while the notes of midnight souls remained lost in the darkest corners. All throughout the drumming sounds of pheasant wings combined with a familiar thick-voiced and harsh crowing sound. The track led downhill through another plantation and then skirted round the former Muncaster Mill, now a private house.

A sharp left fork out of the woods landed me in a lost world of steam. An evocative rhythm of clickety-clack, clickety-clack rebounded off the tree-wall with the odd woo-hoo whistle thrown in. Here was a nostalgic throwback to the heyday of the industrial revolution that transformed the sonic landscape. Beside a narrow piece of track, I was face to face with none other than the puffing sound of an engine on the La'al Ratty (Little Railway). Running on a three-foot gauge, 'Ratty' has been serving the lower part of Eskdale since 1875, when it transported ore from the iron mines at Boot.

Built predominantly for mineral trains it also carried passengers until April 1913 when it was closed after the iron mines were abandoned just before the outbreak of the First World War.

In 1915, Narrow Gauge Railways Limited acquired the line and re-laid the track with a fifteen-inch gauge from Boot in Eskdale to the coastal port of Ravenglass, an old naval base for the Romans. Since then it has carried granite from neighbouring quarries along with locals and tourists riding on covered or open-topped carriages through seven miles of spectacular scenery to the foot of England's highest mountains. Fast-paced in the age of steam, it's an incredible and unique survival story given almost all the other original mainlines in or around the national park have been closed: Workington to Penrith, Foxfield to Coniston, Ulverston to Lake Side, only Kendal to Windermere has survived. The world's just a train ride.

A firm favourite for families with kids, the Ravenglass and Eskdale Steam Railway has five different coloured trains which resemble another British railway icon, *Thomas the Tank Engine and Friends*. Except Ratty's engines have not been relaunched as gender-balanced and multicultural. Pete Waterman, a self-proclaimed trainspotter and pop's Frankenstein figure (whose creations include both Kylie and Simon Cowell), was invited to officially open a new station and visitor centre at the Dalegarth terminus back in April 2007. At Miteside Halt, I stood for a while at the small request stop, watching the clattering wheels and hissing steam disappear towards the base of Muncaster Fell. Unusually, by the side of the line, there was an upturned boat, which Dugdale had referred to as a clinker-built fishing smack. Now the old wooden dinghy harboured only echoes of its time used as a shelter during the railway's initial years as a passenger line.

After edging round the boggy fields at Miteside and Gasketh farms. I looked back at a smoking backdrop circled with creamy cigarette smoke. A long straight road below the fells indicated the way to St Paul's Church. By now I knew the prospect of meeting any other pilgrims walking the same path would be unlikely. With the onset of evening the light had started to fade sharply. Out of the bleeding field corners, ghosts whispered back and forth across the muddy fissures and walked alone in dark moves of love. Embracing the gloom, the night rode in force while the good and bad sang to the valley below.

As the silence settled once more, I skimmed the horizon under a greying rose-tinted sky, while straight ahead in the distance a small white light flickered like the evening star. It started to grow, holding me in its magical spell for a brief moment. Feeling the weight of my rucksack, I paused again to relieve the throbbing in my ankle. Until, with a final flourish, the car headlights pierced the darkness in brilliant flashes and temporarily blocked my sight on passing. On the approach to the church another car appeared from nowhere and skidded into the driveway of the Old Vicarage B&B. The security light exposed the mist creeping round the building. After the slamming of doors I heard the faint sound of muted voices before the quiet returned.

Digging around in the rucksack I fished out my camera and front bike light to aid my way into the churchyard. Silhouetted against a Persian blue sky, the ancient Celtic Irton Cross stood like a black flag smiling to the night. At ten feet tall it was erected in the ninth century before the Scandinavian settlers started to colonise Cumberland. On a walking tour in 1802, Wordsworth's great friend Coleridge referred to the shrine made out of Old Red as a 'curious fretted pillar'. Without any human or animal figures, it contains the decorations of vine scrolls and step-and-fret patterning, minute interweaving and rosettes. No longer visible due to weathering, two panels of Celtic interlace separated by a narrow panel once held runic inscriptions. In 1863, a mould of the lettering interpreted it as simply, 'GEBDAETH FORAE – Pray for…'

Snapping away in the isolated grave-yard, the netherworld danced across the uneven scattering of headstones and memorials. Exiting the churchyard, I was immediately drawn towards a field gate in the corner. Looking out over Haggs Wood, the pillow-like hills and honeyed grass of the national park's cool badge reflected back. At the end of a rough track, the elevated site of the thirteenth century St Paul pointed like an arrow to the sky. The church was rebuilt in 1857 to replace a former mediaeval building and this was made possible after a lavish donation from Lord Muncaster of the nearby castle. The Victorian construction was designed by Kendal architect Miles Thompson, and features stunning stained glass designed by Pre-Raphaelite artist Edward Burne-Jones, which was manufactured by William Morris.

Brand new second hand. Samuel Irton of nearby Irton Hall laid the foundation stone of the new church in 1856 with a mallet made from a timber in the old church. Nestled between hills and sea, the church also offered a spectacular view into the heart of the Wasdale Valley. Peering in at the drama and beauty of a world heritage UNESCO view. With night almost fallen, I turned away to head off in the direction of Stock Bridge when a small hatchback pulled up and parked directly outside the tower archway.

A plainly dressed middle-aged woman got out and stood holding a candle burning little by little in a glass tube. After hesitating for a moment, I headed to the car. On the way over, a small cloud of steam blew out of her wet hair whilst a flicker lit up eyes circled in hothouse red. Lines of sweat trickling down her forehead made me shiver as we passed each other without a word or acknowledgement. Glancing back over my shoulder, I watched her disappear through a pair of wrought iron gates and into the church. Led by the radiant glow from my bike light on a rough track sloping gently downwards, something in the atmosphere made everything seem exaggerated.

Suddenly a church bell hollowed out the sky, whilst its solitary song sent echoes through the earth. Arousing ghosts of bygone days, the sound complemented the mountains enveloped with white grey puffs of mist. The further I moved away from the church, the more powerful the sound reverberated within the landscape. As a breeze touched my face I saw water coloured gold running from a mountain top. Hiding behind a cresting of rocks, a pair of burning hands dragged a storm cloud over the top of my head. Filling my nostrils, the air was cold and damp, while the ceaseless tide formed a protective blanket in the dark…

GOSFORTH TO ENNERDALE BRIDGE

ONE MAN WITH A CAMERA VERSUS
A STATE WITH NUCLEAR WEAPONS
PUSHED OUT TO THE EDGES OF
EVERYDAY EXISTENCE
LIVING IN THE RUIN OF THE OLD-WORLD
VOICED GEOLOGY IN A PALL OF ENCLOSED
DARKNESS AND ANXIETY
BATHING ITS CLAWS IN ATOMIC DUST
CURLED UP IN AN ATTRACTIVE BUNDLE
OF WORLD HERITAGE
MUSIC CALLED FROM SOULS OF THE DEEP
SUNKEN FIELDS WITH DEATHLESS CHIMES
GOSFORTH TO ENNERDALE BRIDGE

"The Edge of Darkness..."

Calder Gate 8pm...

An intolerable risk. Pushing at the real perimeter. On a clear and serene evening another long drive all the way out to the best of the West. An hour and a half racing against the dying of the light into the dark core of the danger area.

Chernobyl, Harrisburgh, Hiroshima... Sellafield

Chain reaction and mutation, contaminated population. Turning off the A595 at the Westlakes Hotel, I pulled up at an electronic sign, 'Access Road Open', on the edge of Seascale, the nearest town on the doorstep. Swimming in someone else's pool, I accepted the signal and turned right onto a long straight unnamed road. The closer towards Dante's inferno, the more intricate the sonically muted maze of steel fences became. At times it felt like I could have easily been skirting the perimeter zones of Gatwick or Heathrow. Without fully intending to reach it, the dead end of the main gate reared up more quickly than expected.

Uninvited and faced with a simmering brute, the short-stay car park offered a temporary lodge. From there I grabbed the camera, took a deep breath and got out of the car to snap some quick shots. Immediately, I could sense CCTV and hi-vis lurking behind rings of barbed razor wire shielded by boom barriers lit up with glowing red eyes. One man with a camera versus a state with nuclear weapons. Sure enough, about a minute or so later a dream lottery carrying radios wearing reflective waistcoats emerged from the dark horizon.

"Excuse me, yeah, you over there...you can't take pictures you know."

Behind the trio was a small box-shaped white Portakabin protected by another set of barriers off to the right-hand side. A line from the *Darkest Hour* suddenly came to mind (the one about trying to reason with a tiger when your head is in its mouth); fearing the worst, I tried deploying the same level of candour used at Valley End.

"Sorry about that...I'm actually just after a couple of background shots for a university project. I've been taking some photos down the road in Gosforth...guess it was one of those impulsive things to come here too..." I looked down at the camera and bit my bottom lip.

"University? Right, well...I'm afraid you'll have to wait here now. I've just radioed the security team. They'll be on their way up any minute and they'll want a word. Just to make sure everything's in order and take a look at your photos. Shouldn't be too long...couple of minutes maybe. Stay here while I see where they are and don't move till I get back, ok?"

"Of course, no problem..." I shrugged and fastened my eyes on the flashing lights going on and off at the barrier. Then the tallest of the trio disappeared into the heart of the belching leviathan, leaving me suspended at a rather flimsy looking plastic red-and-white barrier. With camera held aloft in my right hand, the other partners in hi-vis curled their upper lips in my direction. They kept me waiting for another five minutes, or possibly more, but I didn't care. Absorbing the fall- out with eyes closed I felt totally intoxicated, like the no tomorrow of pure cocaine. I knew this was a unique opportunity to be face to face with the old monster before global warming, GM crops and fracking moved the protestors on. Into the unblemished night sky, plumes of smoke were being expunged like a Lynchian stage set. The thunderous industrial world pushed out to the edges of everyday existence.

Peering in at a modern dark furnace full of smokestack industry, it was as if I'd been transported back to the Victorian London of John Merrick and Mr Treves. Here in front of my eyes mankind's revenge reared up in relation to the vast sublime images of John Martin's *The Great Day of his Wrath*. Wicked minds, racism, fear and disinformation have cooked up a cocktail of mass destruction. Summoning up apocalyptic forces, splitting the atom with flashes lighting up like a Christmas tree. Radioactivity...it's in the air for you and me, disturbing the silence as the cancer grows.

From the unbroken concrete and steel landscape of Project Servator, two Judge Dredd types in black jumpsuits, bulletproof vests, belts with pouches and elbow pads sporting H&K rifles approached with the tall hi-vis following like a lap dog. Started by the City of London Police, the CNC nuclear factory has been deterring any hostile threats and reporting suspicious behaviour since 2016. Things that make you go hmm...Living in the ruin of the old world. At Mega City One on the West Coast, I sensed a judgement was coming.

"You do know this is a nuclear licensed site and not open to the public?"

"Yes," I nodded firmly.

With a neck like a mastiff, Horatius, Captain of the Gate bent down and positioned his rifle to one side, before nonchalantly reaching into his top pocket for a small pen and notepad which he flipped open at some previous bits of scribbling. After a pause that sailed around the world, the interrogation began.

"OK, why exactly are you here taking photos?"

Looking him straight in the eye, I replied slowly, picking at the edge of the camera strap as I spoke...

"It's for coursework...I do Lake District Landscape Studies. I wanted to take some background pictures for a project about the national park boundary."

He put the pen to his lips and looked back at me for an unnerving twenty seconds without blinking.

"Right, so you're a university student then?" he finally asked.

"Yes."

"And where do you study?"

"University of Cumbria," I tried to smile but only ended up grimacing.

"Which campus?" he asked, scribbling again on the side of his pad.

"Oh, I guess it's mainly the Lancaster campus whenever we have to go in...which isn't that often..."

He didn't move. But continued to stare down at the pad, offering nothing, before eventually looking up and closing it at the same time replying in a slow burr, "I see...well, before we go any further, let's take a look at your photos..."

Tuning into a melody of warning signs, secrecy and guns, picking at the nuclear scab barely a mile or two outside the boundary. The works of the sprawling Sellafield site separated from Britain's favourite view by a narrow strip of the A595. With the national park's vibrant communities only a minute away, wrapped in a comfortably numb bubble of world heritage, where the future of the environment is thought to be in safe hands. Thankfully, the address details on my driver's licence checked out. Seeing that I presented no threat at all, the security sent me away with a stern, but reasonable enough warning. Incredibly though, they let me keep the handful of photos I'd managed to take as well! Thinking they looked way too dark to be of any real use. But then, just as I was about to clear out after scampering back to the car, an older, more portly bald man dressed in a long white coat marched out of the door to a control room door beside the perimeter fence. Tapping on the driver's side window, the glare from the lights of the main gate framed an oval-shaped face with a weary toothless grin.

"You do know you're parked in the wrong place! I was just coming over to warn you about that, but they got to you at the barrier first."

"Yeah I know...oh well...no worries; I've just spoken to them there anyway. It's sorted now, thanks, it was all just a little misunderstanding on my part."

"Yes, yes I can see that...Take it they made you delete all your photos then?"

"Oh don't worry; as I said, it's all been sorted thanks...Anyway, best be off, bye for now..."

I pressed hard on the button for the window to close, revved up the engine, spun the car round and turned back down the straight road towards the thundering growl at Seascale. In the rear view a police car followed about twenty yards behind...

Gosforth above Seascale, heading north, with the promise of yet more boggy fields, more mud, more shit and more of a mess than ever before. The slave to an army of damp and grey puddles marching ahead in the gloomy drudge. The Bay to the Borders. Fern talking 'the A Word' on Radio Cumbria, blasting out Tina Turner's, *We Don't Need Another Hero.* Living under the fear, till nothing else remains. This time I avoided the Lake cruises at the promenade of the main inferno and drove through the engine room of the prosperous, world-class visitor experiences and vibrant communities.

On through the central hub of Ambleside, where dreams can come true, but they're often a bit rubbish. Zipping past the very place where the threat of sound violence was silenced by the small-C conservatives at the Thirlmere Reservoir, before skirting the adventure capital at base camp, Keswick. From there the A66 begins the northern empire and fleets of Eddie Stobart trucks operate with cult status and eye-catching livery throughout the rest of the UK.

Gosforth to Ennerdale promised a Viking cross, the most hazardous facility (in terms of risk) for the public in the UK, the ruins of Calder Abbey and the wettest valley in the Lake District. Looking at the medley of landscape surrounding the village on Google maps, I was reminded of Sutherland's *The Setting Sun.* Landscape tilted vertical, painted from high above, yet also from deep within. Voiced geology in a pall of enclosed darkness and anxiety. Fields of virulent greens, florid mauves and washed-out beige stacked together like slices of bread. Above black crablike claws, the sun leers threateningly over the crest of a hill. Its rays are sharply pointed and green, like corroded switchblades. The image burns through my mind, again and again...I first saw the painting one very cold winter's day at the exhibition, 'Graham Sutherland: An Unfinished World' at Modern Art Oxford. George Shaw curated the show just after he'd been nominated for the Turner Prize, the annual freak show once the favourite punch ball of the gutter-press darlings, now just an institutionalised juggernaut of boredom.

After circling round the village a couple of times, I locked Knightrider to a rusted handrail at the village hall. Inside the main convenience store a dubious vending machine charged naive idiots over two quid for a unique cup of Bisto-flavoured coffee. After one tentative sip I instantly regretted the decision to avoid the lengthy queue of mainly tradesmen at the bakery. Feeling more than slightly miffed, I immediately went back in and bought a Frijj Irish Coffee Flavour Milkshake instead. Up the road at a crossroads, a handful of inns offered a glimpse into a new Brexit utopia, with flags of St

George forming a red and white guard of honour. Even the grub chalked up on the A-boards matched the John Bull-ised theme... 'Freshly Battered Fish and Chips','Cock & Bull Steaks' and a dish somewhat brazenly called, 'T*ts & Ar$e (T & A)'. Moving swiftly on, things got pleasanter strolling along the narrow stretch of Whitecroft amongst period cottages, hair-dressers, mobility scooters, and for sale boards. Opposite the Methodist Church, I paused for another routine check of the noticeboard...apart from the usual ads for coffee mornings, dance classes, tabletop sales and drop-in sessions, the big up and coming event advertised a "Shindig with the Wardrobe Monsters including a bar, pie & pea supper with a Grand Raffle!" In the arms of sleep, Gosforth must be full of nocturnal animals.

To follow the boundary proper would mean driving up the A595 for a few miles to Calder Bridge, where it splits off and runs parallel with the River Calder. Under the blushing hedge sides of Cold Fell through fields of enclosure on another unnamed track. Terrain streaked in cadmium orange and burnt umber, cut up, sliced open and wounded with shades of rose madder. Bathing its claws in atomic dust, planet Sellafield chases you home. Its stories ring out across the ol' muck ball littered with flocks of Swaledale sheep chewing and moping about, happily oblivious like the eighteen million holiday campers with their feet in the air and heads on the ground. Some- how it felt right to be there, standing alone on the cusp of the wild and re- mote valleys of Ennerdale, Eskdale and Wasdale. Unnoticed in the dream of music floating towards the sea...just me, the camera and Dugdale in the blue mist of late morning...

Facing off against Sellafield about five miles inland, a sermon in stone forms part of the main evidence for the Viking period in Cumbria. Standing over fourteen and a half feet high at St Mary's church, a wonderful monolith of red sandstone dominates the churchyard. It is a representation of the age of migrations in a thinly populated out of the way district. A Scando-Gothic story of antiquarian interests and mythological insights. The Vikings had arrived in the ninth century, sharpened up with their own unique brand of ultraviolence. With lashings of angel trumpets and devil trombones, they sprang the ultimate surprise visits. First written about in the late eighteenth century, there were thought to be three runic crosses at Gosforth in the old historic county of Cumberland. Pointing devotedly to heaven with the ancient hills melting away like wax on one side, the Irish Sea on the other.

While serving as a curate and vicar in Maryport, an amateur antiquarian, Reverend William Slater Calverley, became the first to claim the markings on the cross represented scenes from pagan Norse mythology. With the Igdrasil holly tree, hammer of Thor, Vala's prophecy of the Voluspa – the last battle of Ragnarok and the Twilight of the Gods. Here in a soundless churchyard was an apocalyptic vision of Good and Evil, Gods and Monsters where Danes worshipping Norse deities interacted with the indigenous Christian faith. Erected by Vikings who settled at Gosforth and converted to Christianity, the cross writ large the echoes of primaeval truth which everyone could understand. In 1887, Calverley initiated a full scale replica of the cross and had it installed in the churchyard in Aspatria, Sheila Fell's home town in the north west of Cumbria, between Maryport and Wigton.

Rebuilding work at St Mary's a few years later in 1896/7 led to the discovery of two hogbacked tombmarkers. The 'Warrior's tomb and Saint's tomb' feature a battle scene on one of the long sides with two rows of warriors armed with shields and spears. Their discovery opened up a new line of thinking about the origin of the cross though. These interpretations claimed it must have been a memorial stone for a great leader, and not a form of preaching sculpture. The main instigator of this theory was W. G. Collingwood, Ruskin's secretary and a philosopher of stone. Mainly in the art forms of Scandinavian and pre-Norman crosses of Cumbria and the North of England. He argued that the Norse settlement must have contained a powerful chief utilising the sands of Seascale to launch overseas raids, whilst hunting deer in the fertile forests of the Wasdale Valley. Collingwood also drew a map of Cumbria to highlight the distribution of monuments showing the communities and interaction of people. Intriguingly, this revealed a central core completely bereft of pre-Norman sculptured monuments. To find the region's ancient stone sculptures you have to seek out the peripheries of the present-day national park.

Another friend of Ruskin's, Canon Rawnsley (public face of the Lake District Defence Society now the Friends of the Lake District - FLD), provided numerous observations about the region's Scandinavian heritage. Especially the core of place names, interpreting Seascale as 'the huts by the sea the Viking fishers knew'. He memorably referred to the three great crosses at Bewcastle, Irton and Gosforth as 'poems in stone'.

Ultimately, the Viking settlements in Cumberland got a big one in the yarbles from English King Æthelred the Unready during the summer of 1000, when he travelled north for some payback after hearing they had snuck off to plunder Kent before sailing to Normandy to sell the booty...

Departing from the church, through a stile, I headed into a boggy field with a soft incline towards the farms at Middle and Low Boon Wood. By midday it had clouded over and the sky had turned grey and overcast. I walked past a lone gorse bush (mentioned by Dugdale) amidst familiar boundary weather into wet fields alive with the rumble of engines and bustle of machinery. Passing through Middle Boon Wood, the high-pitched whining noise of a car's slipping timing belt brought back childhood memories of the four-minute warning siren. Changing the world forever, one is all that you can score, score no more, score no more. As kids we all used to daydream about what we might do in such a short space of time.

But in the nuclear age of extremes, a different little boy led to mankind's greatest intellectual achievement. The destroyer of worlds in the new 'atomic age' ushered in by the US bombings of Hiroshima and Nagasaki. Even though a hideous moral dilemma brought an end to the Second World War, the subsequent Cold War and nuclear arms race developed some key motifs in popular culture. A steady stream of works in various media began to emanate from: Warhol's blood red mushroom clouds fading to black, Kubrick's masterpiece of political satire, *Dr Strangelove* (or: *How I Learned to Stop Worrying and Love the Bomb)* and Orwell's seminal ever-present *1984* – the blueprint for any dystopian science fiction since its publication back in 1949. Nowadays there is a Four Minute Warning app, revising both US and UK security threats in real time, giving important terrorist security updates.

Barking incessantly, an over enthusiastic collie ran towards me before I exited the farm gates and left a sea of slush and crap in my wake. Again cursing a lack of wellingtons whilst attempting to cut across pools of water in a mélange of fields gouged by tractor tyres. Crossing over a track, I entered another large expanse populated by a flock of nervous sheep. Behind them, the iniquitous pair of piles at Sellafield loomed large like a Bond villain's lair. 'Close to catastrophe' was the title of Eric Robson's *Choice* feature marking the 60th anniversary of the Windscale fire in his regular column for Cumbria Life. I'd been reading the tale of the heroes who prevented such a horrifying tragedy before starting the stage. It seems the legacy of Britain's nuclear programme is one of bunglers and breakthroughs. It's easy to create a mess, but very difficult (and expensive) to clean it up.

The fallout of Britain's worst nuclear accident in October 1957 has been the cause of considerable mistrust and secrecy ever since. For two days a national emergency threatened to set off a nuclear bomb in the huge cooling tower, known as Windscale Pile One. One of two air-cooled piles where natural uranium fuel, held in a matrix of graphite, was bombarded with neutrons, transmuting it into plutonium 239. Both operated at low temperatures, which meant that energy could build up slowly in a graphite core. A highly dangerous situation if stored energy was left in the heart of the pile. Any unplanned releases of it could escape spontaneously in a powerful rush of intense heat. The Atomic Energy Authority merely crossed their fingers and walked a sizzling tightrope as the recorded temperatures in the piles got hotter and hotter. On 10th October 1957, the setting sun threatened to light the way, when the inevitable happened and Pile One overheated in a feast of blaze. Famously, the filtration system installed on the pile had been a late addition, placed peculiarly near the top. Despite being sarcastically referred to as 'Cockroft's Folly' (after its designer Sir John Cockroft), this last-minute piece of insurance turned out to be a masterstroke. It is estimated that the high-level filters captured around 95 per cent of the radioactive dust created by the fire.

Just six years after becoming a national park, the Lake District and most of the North West could have been turned into scorched earth. Even the incredibly bold decision to try cooling the reactor by pouring in two million tons of water had little effect. It was seen as a desperate measure by the general manager, Tom Tuohy, who valiantly climbed to the top of the reactor and gazed down into a blazing inferno. If the water had produced a hydrogen/oxygen explosion, then Cumberland would have been blown off the map. In the end, switching off all the cooling and ventilation systems paid dividends and a national disaster was somehow averted. Built in West Cumbria just after the Second World War, the only bright spark from the whole episode consigned Pile One to a slow death and the eventual scrap-heap.

The price of bringing Britain into the atomic age had almost proved fatal. A vanity project hurried into existence by politicians eager to cut costs, the unique science fiction stage set assembled at Windscale was mainly designed to keep up with the world's great powers. Just as in one of Blofeld's volcanic bases, workers dressed all in white scrambled up and down ladders inside an enormous hush-hush operation. Even before the fire in the mid-1950s, rumours were rife about the levels of radioactivity contaminating Seascale during the building of neighbouring reactors at Calder Hall. Spraying radioactivity in the air for you and me...the official line said it was better to tell lies rather than alarm people with facts!

Not much has changed in the intervening years. Although, back then, the authorities also wanted to prevent folk walking round in PVC suits and plastic macs with air hoods and hoses. Now in the modern Internet age you are free to order unisex total enclosure suits at the click of a button, with a clear glass hood and inflation valve for club-wear fantasy and fetish.

As the fire in the reactor waned, a BBC voice full of received pronunciation announced that a north east wind was blowing across the site and taking away any radioactive dust to the Irish Sea – now often declared one of the most radioactive bodies of water in the world. Incredibly, even though the workers at Windscale were told to stay inside and wear face masks, no public warnings were given at neighbouring Seascale! Here, locals went about their everyday business completely oblivious to all the smoke coming out of the chimney. An unthinkable situation in the new digital world governed by social media and communications like Facebook's Safety Check (which allows users in disaster zones to show themselves as safe) or the CrisisMappers Network.

Predictably, the Government censored the report into the fire and its causes. Despite bans on milk sales for up to 150 farms in the vicinity, coupled with a steady rise in people dying of leukaemia, the radiation leaks were considered to be of no significance to public health. Up we ghost, chemical's itching. If (as many have suspected), the whole of West Cumbria was contaminated with specks of radioactive dust, then the future proof will be gathered in the sediments of lakes in the national park. "Monuments to our initial ignorance" was the poignant phrase used by Lord Christopher Hinton (head of Britain's nuclear infrastructure at the time) to describe the catastrophic piles at Windscale...

*Safer Sooner...*Built to manufacture plutonium for the atomic bomb, British Nuclear Fuels Ltd (BNFL) decided to extinguish any remaining embers from the fire catastrophe by rebadging the plant's name from Windscale to Sellafield in 1981. But since then it has merely developed into a £2 billion a year beast of burden. A decommissioning nightmare on the edge of Britain's largest national park, which housed the world's first commercial nuclear power station, and became a centre for storing highly radioactive waste from the old piles. Used fuel was also reprocessed by separating uranium and plutonium from waste materials. Incredibly, most of the highly radioactive waste amassed was unassumingly dumped into building B30 (nick-named 'Dirty 30'), which housed storage ponds several times the size of an Olympic pool. In an increasingly complex environment, a wasteland of water-cooled sludge formed out of the corroded magnox alloy surrounding the fuel rods.

*Safer Sooner...*There were two buildings at Sellafield dedicated to reprocessing different types of nuclear fuel; the Magnox and Thermal Oxide Reprocessing Plants. Almost inconceivably, the huge Magnox Swarf Storage Silo was built in the 1960s without any plans for how waste could be taken out of the building. Since then, waste built up from the dawn of the nuclear age has turned into 'an intolerable risk'. Cleaning up the mess is understandably a costly, challenging and time-consuming process. Even the LDNPA started to get a little jittery when its own branding began to be called into question as a result of plans to bury some of the waste within the borders of the national park!

Imagine...a World Heritage Site sitting on top of an atomic dustbin.

*Safer Sooner...*In 2008, the Labour Government published a white paper about creating a framework for the geological disposal of nuclear waste. It also invited councils up and down the UK to volunteer for the scheme; but the complete list of contenders included the name of just one area – West Cumbria! Undeterred by the virtual no-show, the government pressed on with its contentious plans. They courted a charmingly named geologist, Dr Jeremy Dearlove, who matched three rock volumes as potentially suitable dumping grounds. These were the Mercia mudstone of the Solway Plain along with the red/pink granites of Eskdale and Ennerdale. Without conforming to any national or international criteria, the proposals would have meant burying nuclear waste by tunnelling under mountains of hard rock. A journey beginning on the sandstone underlying Sellafield continuing across the Lake District boundary fault line and finishing at the Ennerdale granite area. Based on a French scheme, the projections showed how construction and surface maintenance buildings could end up gnawing into the very soul of the majestic and well-loved twin peaks Great Gable and Pillar. But then the futuristic bow-wow headline *'Safer Sooner'* on the final magazine cover of Sellafield's glossy annual review 2017/18 handed a new bone to the ol' atomic dog...*Bow-wow-wow-yippie-yo-yippie-yeah...Bow-wow-yippie-yo-yippie-yeah...*

Stacking up tens of thousands of three-metre cubed steel boxes in a vast shielded building. Caves on rails, time to put chemistry in a bucket. In a massively complex programme of retrievals, here was a new process likened to emptying a dustbin with a tea spoon. Against a legacy of cost overruns and time delays, the mopping-up bill was now rumoured to be somewhere in the region of £54 billion! According to the government's specially dedicated website, Sellafield is still the most challenging environmental clean-up exercise anywhere in Europe. Despite a dodgy safety record with a horrifying history of mistakes, protestors locking themselves together and consumers shelling out for new infrastructure, Britain's longest running public relations disaster has survived for two very contrasting reasons.

First, people need work. Literally thousands on the West Coast rely on the site to make a living and Sellafield plays a crucial role in keeping the local economy busy with high employment levels.

Second, the increasingly complex task of trying to decommission such a waste-ridden facility.

And in the sleep of death what dreams may come – that's the real atomic rub, even if living and working close to a nuclear organisation is a daunting prospect. Especially if you don't understand what it does and how it does it. Although there's absolutely nothing to worry about if you believe all the soundbites on the government website, which label Sellafield 'a centre for nuclear excellence' in West Cumbria, providing community needs with industry resources. In reality, the site is dying a very long-winded and very expensive death. After dominating the skyline for over seventy years, Windscale Pile One chimney is now part of the ongoing decommissioning project and set to be demolished.

Sellafield's distinctive dark towers were supposed to be making way for the potential of a new beast lurking in the shadows: NuGen's planned £10 billion Moorside nuclear power station to be built on land nearby. A site armed with a common sense of purpose, identity and commitment. With the vision, mission and values of creating safe, reliable, affordable, Low Carbon energy using so-called 'proven' nuclear technology. But the project was dogged by setbacks and delays. Initially a joint French-Japanese venture, the Japanese developer Toshiba's nuclear division Westinghouse went bankrupt in March 2017. Next up, French company Engie pulled out citing 'significant challenges'. Toshiba have since been desperately trying to flog NuGen to the Korean Electric Power Corp., but with the inevitable extra time needed to reach a satisfactory conclusion, NuGen's subsequent review threatened to cloud the deal in deathly tones...

Under agitated skies at the edge of Sellafield, I stood peering in at its grey bulk thinking about the book, *Sellafield Stories – Life with Britain's First Nuclear Plant.* A collection of stories voiced through the lives of thirty people who lived and worked in the 'heart of the nation', containing almost seventy years of momentary fragments...

"I'd rather it hadn't come..."

"I didn't have a helmet or anything..."

"The management were dreadful..."

"Nuclear waste issues are measured in centuries..."

Et in Arcadia ego...

England's green and pleasant land, turning into a melody of haunting power spread out over some 700 acres. Jarman's colourless atom, the corner-stones of lies on which successive governments have built their defence. Emotional ties, worries and opinions, atomic and political half-truths not based on any facts. In the dark underworld of fanatics the country threatens to fall asleep without the renewables of coal, gas and oil. Step forward uranium, the saviour believed to be the only way forward to keep the lights on. And what dreams may come in a no-deal Brexit land, when another new generation governed in a hostile political environment attempt to build up from nothing as in the aftermath of nuclear war...

I trudged on...over the velvet floor of a conifer wood before a strong bucolic smell alerted me to the presence of an irregular tyre wall, banked up with heaps of manure beside a large pool of brown slurry. In the middle of the sprawling agricultural works sat a large round tank. Intrigued, I looked up Ponsonby Old Hall farm later on Google. It turned out to be a Stanley Renewable Energy anaerobic digestion plant, a joint venture between Iona Capital Energy and a family-run farm. According to their website, the plant is now operated by Advantage Biogas Limited and suppplies feedstock from existing farm wastes, such as manure and slurry, complemented by energy crops. In the absence of air on the fringes of Sellafield, energy from agricultural waste offered a glimpse into a different cleaner future.

Further on at a wooden stile buried in spiteful gorse, I waited briefly for a lorry loaded up with garden furniture to negotiate a five-point turn on the narrow track to Gibb Hill Farm. From there, a right fork led directly onto a desire path (Dugdale's 'tunnel of trees'), a feral holloway, possibly an old pilgrimage route to Calder Abbey. Passages of time carved deep into the land enveloping hearts and minds beneath a dome of trees. The path rose gently uphill until it branched off to the left into a lurid-green-coloured field. From this open viewpoint the whole rhythm of the coastal walk was revealed; from the Duddon Sands in the far-left hand corner to the bulk-head of Black Combe, across the River Esk and out to the Irish Sea. Further off into the distance a clone army of big and greyish Martians waved back eagerly, whilst directly behind, the central fells curled up in an attractive bundle of World Heritage. In the air only a gentle murmur from the A595 filtered up from below the horizon, with the occasional echoes of a dog barking or the chatter of birdsong. A thick row of sticky and prickly gorse bushes surrounded In Fell before I crossed over the River Calder at Stakes Bridge.

In her *Complete Guide to the English Lakes* published in 1855, the Victorian sociologist, journalist and abolitionist, Harriet Martineau, painted a vivid picture of the same view. Engulfed by banks of ivy and ferns, the foaming russet-brown waves of the Calder swirled under the red sandstone bridge almost exactly as she had first described. Although now the mile or so to the Abbey was protected by a mixture of barbed wire and thorn bushes. All along the banks of the Calder, ancient footmarks communed in a thoroughly monastic scene. While the dreamy sound of gushing water filled the canopy lining the old hermetic route, the ruins of the privately owned Calder Abbey were hushed and hidden behind a screen of fir and yew trees. A descendant of the brutes who vanquished England in the Norman Conquest, Ranulph de Meschines, Lord Copeland originally founded it as a Benedictine monastery in 1134 for a group of monks from Furness Abbey.

Incredibly, this period is still an open wound for some supporters of Brexit, who believe the Conquest is comparable to the country's "domination" by nameless EU institutions. Way back then for a little over four hundred years the Abbey survived in relative peace. Until the last abbot, Richard Ponsonby had to surrender the abbey in 1536 when the Dissolution sent a sixteenth-century shockwave across the landscape. With my own time now rapidly running out, there was precious little scope to investigate the forgotten picturesque ruins. After stumbling into a courtyard of holiday lets, I decided to cut my losses and head back to Stakes Bridge towards the slopes of Cold Fell. Avoiding Sellafield by following the A595, the boundary then veers to the right at Calder Bridge, where it hugs Sparholme Wood before running parallel with my own chosen route all the way into Ennerdale.

Mindful of the fading light there was still about an hour to play with. But then, rushing onto the icy edges of a wooden footbridge, my right foot slipped completely and I fell hard onto my left hip bone. Ironically, I'd just taken a couple of Nurofen for a dull ache in my right ankle, but this new setback threatened to slow my progress even further. With spirits faltering considerably, I encountered a churned-up mud bath encircling Strudda Bank Farm. Stumbling around like a wreckhead, the fluffed-up treacle shaved off more valuable minutes from my increasingly tight schedule. At least I didn't fall over.

Continuing on with the River Calder twisting away on my right, another footbridge over Worm Gill allowed a brief moment to assess a sopping pair of wet boots. The last push towards Friar's Gill and Monk's Bridge promised to breathe through the souls of former routes taken by the abbots of the monastery. At the point of Dugdale's so-called 'delightful but remote glade', the rounded slopes of Capel Crag displayed the distinctive red-orange glow of autumn's tapestry. With the time now creeping towards 4.30 pm a choice loomed large like the gathering darkness – follow the boundary on the dull cut-through to Sellafield on the other side of Swarth Fell or take Dugdale's advice and proceed on the valley route to Monk's Bridge. The latter meant a couple of miles amidst the loneliest stretch of moorland in the entire walk, and soon I discovered there really was no light at the end of the tunnel…

Siding with Dugdale, the journey into darkness began on a path sinking towards the end of the world at Ennerdale Water. Twenty-eight days in a heartbeat, Boyle's zombie apocalypse at Benson's Knott. As the rage virus ran parallel with the national park boundary, ghosts of the undead burned flames throughout the night. With every tentative step, the Calder tried to warn me, but all around the night closed in. On and on, free-fall flow until the end, yes, the river knew…

Just a few hundred metres south of Farthwaite, the slightly pointed arch of Monk's Bridge was once thought to be a post-mediaeval single-span packhorse bridge over the Calder. Finding a spot in the wet bracken above a rocky gorge, I sat on a rounded boulder taking photos of the water foaming safe as milk for twenty minutes, maybe longer. Admiring the Grade II Listed monument at the end of a long day, it felt as if time had almost stopped. In the magical half-light waiting for night to fall, the still tranquility reflected whispers associated with Calder Abbey just a few kilometres downstream. Except now the red sandstone blocks were thought to have been either constructed or rebuilt in the seventeenth or eighteenth century.

With only a bike headlight to use as a guide over the saturated valley floor between Swarth Moor and Caw Fell, I soon realised I had made a huge mistake taking Dugdale's advice. For one thing, there was no path of any description to even attempt to follow. As the darkness engulfed me, a genuine sense of panic threatened to take over. After using the OS app as a guide throughout the last few hours, my phone was now out of battery and signal. The feeling of desperation got even worse after ransacking inside my bag pulled up only a badly bruised banana and a token mac-in-a-sac for emergencies. Although that was practically useless, being only ever so slightly water-resistant, and certainly not even remotely waterproof. At least the Calder offered a hint of salvation with its readymade water supply. Then it suddenly dawned on me that Dugdale's quirky hand drawings would be my only guide through the anonymous retreat.

Abruptly, beneath my feet, the spongy bog of straw-like bracken gave way and formed a sink hole. Plunging underwater from a future I'll never know.

Deeper, deeper, deeper trembling with arms outstretched into the frigid dark. The burbling of bubbles rising up towards a lantern of light illuminated amongst the greenish depths. Imprisoned in a tomb of reeds with head bowed and eyes closed, shirt sleeves rippled like a sail on the wind. With an explosion of heat, I could feel flailing arms targeting the tread on the bottom of my boots. Wriggling my legs furiously as I puffed my chest out, in the dead calm, music called from the souls of the deep. Heading towards a pallid star, muted cries charged through the endless space and grasped my flickering spirit. And then, all at once, a hand gloved in lace pulled me clear of the water's surface. Left to struggle to my feet, breaths came quickly with repeated coughs at the pale glow on the edge of the void. Looking out into the blackened landscape the echo of a familiar voice floated on the breeze...

"The earth is full of the goodness of the Lord..."

It was Lady Anne again. She had come to my rescue wearing a gown of seawater-green satin bathed in the ethereal glow of a moonbeam.

"It is much more reliable in this wild countryside to have safety in numbers, especially after dark." With a smirk on her dimpled face, she stood in front of me as beautiful as before, dark hair flowing in ribbons through the diabolical night so fast. An elevator to heaven, one woman with a dream, at pleasure, she turned her back to summon a white saddle horse wading carefully at the side of the Calder.

Mesmerised in the new song's measure, I nodded my gratitude but said nothing, savouring every moment we spent together instead. She beckoned in the same manner as before at Warriners Wood, only this time leading me toward a powerful looking creature that looked like one of Stubbs' equine masterpieces. Pressing my hand in hers again we prepared to ride the boundaries together in fear that any second could be our last. Soon enough we bade farewell to sunken fields with deathless chimes and rode for a brief spell on the open fell road. Stopping at Kinniside, our lovely creature trotted in and out of the perfect circle, eleven stones with a diameter of eighteen metres. Lady Anne hopped off athletically to stand in the middle of the circle with arms outstretched. Her voice echoed as in a sweet dream...

"In the eighteenth century when the sun was dark and silent as the moon, a farmer filled his pockets with stones, using them as gate posts..."

Picking a stick off the ground, I sat down on one of the rocks with her dark and roving eyes seeking mine...Closing them fleetingly, I suddenly saw all horrors retracing footsteps in the dark chambers of a grey land.

A swirling sea at the foot of a bed carried me down to a cell. Laying on my back a borderless sky awaited sunlight that would not come...Bringing me back, Lady Anne's low voice soothed like a huge sunlit cloud...

"Through the rain and through the mud, a Doctor Quine of Frizington reconstructed a circle under dark and empty skies which came to symbolise the burning flesh of men..."

But before I had the chance to settle, we rode off and found ourselves on the level way at Brougham toward the old Roman road sloping downwards. There the creature increased its gallop puffing through huge nostrils and snorting wild approval.

With effortless grace the great Lady held up her right hand and made the shape of a cross before speaking into a vacuum...

"The poor were our pioneers, we set them to work, curing idleness and supplying their needs." As my grip tightened round her waist, we passed castle after castle at rapid speed from Brough, little Pendragon and on to the churches and chapels at Barden, Mallerstang and Skipton.

Not even turning into the face of a steep climb slowed the rabid animal who dragged both of us uphill in another show of formidable power. On through Whinfield to Appleby Castle it raged, until finally the horse slowed on the brow of another hill.

At that moment, I knew it was the end as I parted from the Great Lady for that night and forever underneath the round arched entrance to Caesar's Tower. From the ground around me, still flowing with her blood, I waved goodbye to Lady Anne as she continued off into a halo of lunar luminescence, condemned to ride the bounds alone. I watched her slowly plunge into the shade without another word, only the sounds of swaying trees and rustling leaves. Off to bestow more presents and encouragement to her beloved Westmorland tenants. Eyes wide open between a U-shaped valley, the desolate journey back to Ennerdale beckoned. Where dream homes guarded by giant columns of volcanic rock were also shrouded in plantations descending to an isolated lake.

Up above, a memento mori reflected the red skies of atomic storms…

ENNERDALE BRIDGE
TO COCKERMOUTH

A BOGGY, UNEVEN NIGHTMARE
NO ESCAPE FROM GOD'S BROKEN MAN
SENDING OUT DREAMS CARRIED ON THE WIND
THE DAYS ARE NUMBERED
BLUR THE BOUNDARIES BETWEEN OPEN FELL
AND WOODLAND
A COCKTAIL OF AUSTERITY AND THE
HOUSING MARKET'S CRISIS OF INEQUALITY
NEW MONEY TRANSITIONING INTO OLD MONEY
UNDER THE SPELL OF A DARK AND GRIM FORCE
THE TRUTH DIED WITH A CONQUERED SOUL
ENNERDALE BRIDGE TO COCKERMOUTH

The death of hope and despair…

9 November 2017. The B-word on the radio…pulling fast ones, red lines, major issues, NHS cash pledges and the chief mover and shaker from Wetherspoon's sparking a trade war against Sainsbury's, Whitbread and… er, Nick Clegg. Allegedly for 'factually incorrect and highly misleading' statements about the impact of the Notorious B…I could already hear pot calling as I switched it off. Turning my attention to the next stage of the walk instead, all I had to fall back on were some rather dog-eared notes detailing the outline of the route taken by Dugdale. Unknowingly at the time, I'd lost the Boundary Walk during the darkened turmoil after the sink hole opened up in the Calder Valley. Buried waste high in the squelchy mass, the book must have been sucked into the hidden depths where souls drink. Fittingly, I supposed, there it would remain glowing torch-like, lighting up the secret rays of the fringes. With a last burst of energy I'd managed to haul myself out of the glacial dark towards the flowing Calder. Frozen, disorientated and thoroughly fed up, only pure adrenalin steered me across the river up and over Swarth Fell.

To borrow an old football analogy, this would be almost like a stage of two halves. Ennerdale Bridge to Cockermouth followed by the much shorter, Cockermouth to Bassenthwaite. As on the previous stage, I drove out through the heartbeat of the national park on the A591 past Ambleside, Grasmere and over the Raise before getting stuck behind a holiday coach on the slow ascent round Thirlmere. It was a beautifully crisp autumnal morning, the kind which saw ghostly vapours hug the valley floors, until they gently rose toward cloud inversions masking the lofty peaks of the Fairfield and Helvellyn ranges. Small teams of amateur photographers lined the lakeshores armed with tripods and flasks. Bringing World Heritage to the comfort of homes through a bombardment of landscape selfies on social media, with the hashtags: #Worklifebalance #landscapephotography #capturingbritain #theplacetobe…

Overtaking the coach through St John's in the Vale, I pressed on past basecamp at Keswick and the narrow stretch of dual carriageway hugging the western shores of Bassenthwaite. From out of nowhere a blend of charisma, craftsmanship and performance flashed by in the shape of an old icon. It was a red Morgan sportscar, the same colour as a Routemaste London bus, but clearly a lot quicker. On the horizon fast approaching, the bright lights and decorated sheds of the big 'city' of Cockermouth glowed like neon glitter. The birthplace of Wordsworth, custodian of the cultural landscape and father of the national park place myth. Before the simple water drinking bard's time, a leading mutineer, Fletcher Christian, was also born nearby.

Situated upon two rivers – the Derwent and the Cocker, like Kendal in the south, it lies just outside the Lake District National Park boundary, about fifteen or so miles northwest of Keswick. During my on-and-off spells in Cumbria, it was one of those places I always enjoyed exploring. But driving round and round the congested town centre looking for somewhere to park could be time-consuming. After my third futile attempt, I abandoned the idea and headed out of town, eventually finding a space down a narrow cul-de-sac next to the busy Lamplugh roundabout on the A66. Wheeling out Knightrider, I had to battle against a strong headwind and the usual wave of lorries and delivery vans, as I was cycling along the rolling curves of the A5086. Although it was refreshing to be out on such a dry and bright day, a strong strobe effect created by sunlight shining through clumps of trees played havoc with my vision.

Just after passing Lamplugh Village Hall I made a left turn onto a narrow uphill track heading for Kirkland. On the descent into Ennerdale Bridge, a freshly tarmacked section of road provided a very welcome relief from the usual rough and ready surfaces ridden with potholes. Freewheeling into the village, I was greeted by the now familiar hush of a small hamlet on the edge of the boundary. Standing at the mouth of one of the least frequented valleys, the isolated geographical position and challenging journey times have kept it relatively secluded. But those who make the effort are rewarded with a world-class setting divided by the river Ehen which meets Crossdale Beck on a journey from lake and fell. Close by, the majestic Borrowdale Volcanic peaks of Great Gable, Kirk Fell, Pillar and Steeple tower over the head of Ennerdale Water – the most westerly of all the Cumbrian lakes. Following in the same footsteps of the early Romantics, I locked up Knightrider at the Fox and Hounds pub directly opposite St Mary's Church. Once the parish chapel and setting of a Wordsworth poem, *The Brothers,* penned in 1800, the year after he moved back to his native Cumbria, to Dove Cottage in Grasmere. But the 'bare ring of mossy wall' from that time has long gone, seeing as the present-day church was rebuilt in the 1870s.

Moving away from the church, the stage started properly on an unkempt football pitch, the classic pub-team cabbage patch. A boggy, uneven nightmare, no doubt patrolled by twenty-two men who line up to kick ten lumps out of each other every Sunday morning in honour of the so-called beautiful game. Wearing my third pair of boots since the start of the walk, the river Ehen purred beside the waterlogged pitch, whilst overhead the rich blue tones reminded me of the Matisse cut-out painting, where Icarus is shown flailing to inevitable death. I feared being confronted with a similar feeling of horror and mystery advancing from Ennerdale to Cockermouth by way of Lamplugh.

On a sturdy footbridge made of metal, I stood drinking in the peace and quiet of a very different day, serenaded by the constant song of mainly blue tits, chaffinches and blackbirds, with trickles of sunlight filtering through a soft cushion of silver birch on the riverbank. After crossing over the Ehen, an uphill path through Salter Wood led out onto a road opposite Salter Hall where a cyclist sped by the gates. In my garbled notes, Dugdale described it as one of the oldest residential houses in Cumbria, built in 1586. It was situated on the border of a former extensive estate of limestone-quarrying, lime-burning and iron-ore mining that gained prominence from the mid-19th to the later 20th century. Eskett Pit, along with other mines and quarries, was first recorded in 1865, although Salter Hall Quarry closed in 1926, whilst the limestone quarry at Eskett remains open. Out on the open pasture heading toward Kirkland, the majestic view of Valley Head revealed itself. From here, the mountain peaks provided an almost 360-degree backdrop to the River Liza with a glacial valley floor littered by moraines. Pillar Rock, statuesque, magnificent and proud sending out dreams carried on the wind.

Yet in a post-9/11 world, the invisible threats of infectious diseases are the new paranoia striking western society, transmitted in the air, waiting to strike. Ennerdale, one of the remotest valleys in the Lake District, where the not-infected holed up waiting for salvation in Boyle's strange and atmospheric post-apocalyptic zombie horror. In a difficult to explain social malaise, the film had a desperately over-familiar theme…people killing people. The timing of it could not have been more poignant after the outbreak of foot-and-mouth in the same year, which echoed in real life, the issue of pandemic destruction. The rapid spread of infection quickly became a huge crisis for agriculture and the economy, putting the country into a state of panic. When perpetual dreams met reality in a blue filtered haze, a genuine situation leading to military intervention was also repeated to bloody effect in the film. The end of the world is upon us, pretty soon we'll all turn to dust. Goodbye my friends, goodbye cruel world…Exposure, infection, epidemic, evacuation, devastation, the days are numbered…

In a world gone crazy, everything seemed hazy, about to break loose… Peering in at a wild place, Ennerdale was clearly different from the rest of the territory I'd covered up to that point. In an old issue (no. 41) of the journal for all Lakeland Ramblers published in the early eighties (I'd discovered it folded up inside a book at a Kendal charity shop), M. A. Toole described a wonderfully archaic view of the solitude Ennerdale thrust upon any lesser-spotted visitors...

> Many who venture this far find the atmosphere of brooding, almost sullen loneliness somewhat oppressive, and after briefly admiring the view from the proximity of their cars, drive away to seek the less disturbing company of others of their kind, leaving the silence to descend once more...

A few years back I'd ventured out to see what oppressive silence looked like, along with the company of a fellow traveller, the landscape photographer, David Unsworth. Setting out from the damp, old cottage he rented in the Greenburn valley, which had once been painted by Kurt Schwitters, 'the Caspar David Friedrich of the Dadaist revolution'. Loading the boot with bikes, we edged past Thirlmere on the long and winding route that took in Keswick, the western side of Bassenthwaite and the outskirts of Cockermouth. Pulling in at Bowness Knott car park on the forestry track running round part of Ennerdale Water, the penny dropped that neither of us had brought any bike locks; so we had to camouflage them with branches and twigs near a small bridge. Our main objective lay straight ahead, the most direct route up to the summit of Pillar. At that time, I often used to think of David as 'the eyes of Cumbria' due to his incredibly deep-rooted knowledge of virtually any mountain, valley or crag you'd care to mention. He'd spent so much time on the fells, getting remarkable results with his im-pressive 10" x 8" large format piece of kit, that he appeared to possess an almost X-ray like memory of the landscape.

Ascending slowly and without care, green bunches of conifers contrasted with the streaky mauve and violet shadows charging across High Stile and High Crag behind us. Scrambling up through a succession of ghylls, the impressive triangular-shaped bulkhead of Pillar Rock soon loomed large in front. The Shamrock Traverse, at 500 ft, looked like a cathedral spirit in stone, and somehow its craggy mass reminded me a little of the Sagrada Familia, part of another World Heritage Site. Except Pillar marks the birthplace of rock-climbing in the Lake District, first climbed by John Atkinson from Croftfoot, only a few miles away.

When I first met David and his partner Angie, they'd just published a lavishly produced book which aimed to communicate their personal ideas and philosophy on landscape photography as a serious art form. For both of them, any days spent poking around abandoned slate quarries or just 'out on the hill', with what looked like an old movie camera, tripod, tent, plentiful supply of biscuits and a flask full of tea, was time well-spent. Prior to taking up photography, David had actually plied his trade as a painter for some fifteen years. Heavily influenced by Ruskin's 'truth to nature' and

Friedrich's 'photographic stillness', he was always full of slightly whimsical, but well-intentioned ideas for anyone visiting the area…

"I just wish everyone could slow down, spend some time in the landscape, instead of instantly reaching for a camera or phone and pointing it at the first viewpoint they come to."

"If only folk wanted to get off the beaten path and explore a bit more. It's like some of them don't trust their own creative instincts. After all, Lakeland shines in mid-distance scenes and details."

Descending from the flat expanse of Pillar's wind-torn summit, the enduring memory of that day arrived later when we wandered aimlessly into a fairy-tale piece of woodland. Incredibly, to our complete surprise, the mourning chamber of a dark conifer plantation captivated and beckoned us in. It housed an eerie mosaic of cushioned leaf; scraps of dead wood and minimal lighting that could easily have been part of a stage set for a Hollywood blockbuster. Although I guessed David viewed the pockets of columned vaults as more wrapped up with the enchanted forest of Hansel and Gretel charm or Arthurian legend. Typically, we slowed right down and spent the next hour or so exploring and taking photos in the secluded hush of our own magnetically imbued hollow.

Established in 2002, Wild Ennerdale was set up as a partnership of people and organisations led by the Forestry Commission, NT and United Utilities with the support of Natural England; all of whom are the principal landowners in the valley. Together, they had a vision to sell…"To allow the evolution of Ennerdale as a wild valley for the benefit of people, relying more on natural processes to shape its landscape and ecology…"

The 'Spirit of Place' that Wild Ennerdale describes is one full of tranquillity, ruggedness, self-will, wildness, with a feeling more of Scotland or Scandinavia. Yet it is still visibly influenced by forestry plantation and sheep-farming. Dating back to the boom and bust of the 1920s, the Forestry Commission clothed the lower slopes and surrounding fells of the glaciated valley with a breathing plantation of conifers. These non-indigenous species were framed with beech, birch and a few other embellishments. Creating a universe of leaden heaviness taking up some 3,000 acres of forest, that still overshadows the head of the valley today. Since its inception, Wild Ennerdale has been trying to soften the dominating conifers with native trees, whilst attempting to blur the boundaries between open fell and woodland. Although one part needs no form of rewilding, Side Wood along the South Side of Ennerdale Water. This unique piece of forest is a remnant of the ancient birch and oak woodland which once roofed Lakeland to some 2,000ft. It boasts a fertile habitat supporting a variety of species that was awarded Site of Special Scientific status. A more traditional form of woodland management practised for hundreds (if not thousands) of years is also evident with traces of coppicing and charcoal burning. Around the time his powerful vision of the future 'Feral' was published, George Monbiot described the British landscape as 'a burnt, blasted and largely empty land with the delightful ambience of a nuclear winter'. He also argued that Ennerdale was not particularly wild in comparison with projects in other countries, famously drawing attention to the lack of predators controlling the numbers of herbivores such as deer.

In his forceful manifesto, rewilding implied the existence of carnivores to enhance the diversity of feeding habits. A few years later, he did single out the River Liza in his so-called 'Wild-ish Ennerdale', following Desmond's storm of ignorance. Claiming that if all the rivers in Cumbria had been re-wilded in the same way (by allowing them to meander, accumulate logs and stones), then there might not have been any floods. Mainly for the simple reason that any obstructions would have held the water back, sifted it and discharged it more slowly. According to Monbiot, everyone just records spectacles and ignores the implications. Whereas those who disagree prefer to focus on the cultural landscape instead.

My own head was full of the fresh smell of sheep poop after spending a good twenty minutes or so embalmed in the landscape. Absorbing a mountain territory robed in the porticoes of forestry get-ups, where farms were surrounded by masses of sheep, and thickets of hawthorn or gorse lined the way immediately in front. Passing over a narrow stream, on my left an uphill grassy slope formed the gateway to a wood fenced off around the perimeter to shield the bleeding heart of a giant crater. It formed some old limestone quarry workings. Scampering through fields of rocky outcrops full of Swaledales, I detected the first appearance of a dry-stone wall, which naturally felt quite new compared to the standard lines of bushy hedgerows I'd been used to seeing.

Joining up with the right of way at High Stowbank, it was only a short distance to the old mining village of Kirkland. A small neighbourhood which local estate agents laud as a village on the edge of the national park with spectacular, uninterrupted views of Ennerdale Lake and the surrounding mountains. Looking at the plain rows of terraced housing, it felt more like I'd stumbled into Percy Kelly's *Crosby Villas* along an empty road in the midst of bare fells. With their blue hands touching me, all these things in all positions, all these things will one day take control. Detached dormer bungalows completed the circle on the opposite side, many of them featuring enclosed lawns, mature perennial borders, paved walkways, patio seating areas and summerhouses. In-between the terraces I caught a glimpse of straining washing lines next to a kids' play area dwarfed by basketball hoops and a muddy goalmouth. The way of modern life – family, second or holiday homes rubbing up against one another. According to the Commission for Rural Communities Report (December 2005) the LDNPA's 'Review of Second Home Data and Assessment of the Effects Second Homes are Having on Rural Communities' (available to download on their website, but already well out of date)…' It was noted that a sense of community was extremely important to people. Many felt that this was becoming progressively eroded in rural areas and there was a genuine fear of rural areas becoming retirement villages for the affluent elderly, or dormitory villages for commuters and second homeowners…'

At least in the dormitory village of Kirkland, on the fringes, there was still a sense of community in amongst a cocktail of austerity and the housing market's crisis of inequality. All these things coming to fruition, fudges will not communicate the chocolate box against poverty and isolation…

I passed underneath a disused railway line, the three-mile long Rowrah and Kelton Fell Mineral Railway, a tiny obscure track that once serviced the iron-ore mines of West Cumberland from the late 19th century until the early 1920s. Even though it ran within a couple of miles of Ennerdale, it was better known for carrying rich materials rather than any wealthy passengers. The boundary crept into play again on the Loweswater road above Smaithwaite Farm. Until we bumped into each other at Felldyke, a small hamlet in the shadows of Blake Fell made up entirely of holiday cottages. There was a small roadside car park there too, for the track up to Cogra Moss, created as a reservoir in about 1880 with artificial water retained by a substantial dam across Rakegill Beck. Surrounded on three sides by Forestry Commission planting on Lamplugh Fell and Knock Murton, it was discontinued as a public water supply in 1975. These days the little tarn is a popular spot with anglers who visit to catch brown and rainbow trout against the peaceful backdrop.

Immediately, as I stepped inside the national park, the public rights of way network shifted up a gear. Ease of use and accessibility are obviously national park buzz words, but I could clearly see the difference as the signs and waymarking along with the surfaces of the tracks were a cut above anything witnessed outside it. After passing through the farm buildings at Dockray Nook, I kept to the right of more conifer plantations mentioned as a new feature back in Dugdale's day. The track eventually led out onto gently trundling grassy fields, where I decided to eat my cheese sandwiches before entering the ancient village of Lamplugh. A bucolic paradise that consisted of a rambling collection of farms and idyllic country homes on the very edge of the national park, handy for Sellafield commuters, second-home owners, holiday lets, the big city lights of Cockermouth, or the high-siders and jam-eaters of Workington and Whitehaven. A village without a true centre, but one where I imagined everybody knew everybody. It was scattered from the northerly A5086 (running between the market towns of Cockermouth and Egremont) to the narrow lanes beside St Michael's church. Old guide books speak of 'sweet meat pies' and 'Lamplugh pudding' (buns soaked until soft in hot ale and served with seasoning and spirits to taste) eaten by hill farmers after long, wet days out on the fells. It was also thought to have been part of an area entirely covered with trees, stretching across the coastal plain to the Irish Sea, as in the long-standing couplet:

From Lamplugh Fell to Morisbee,
A squirrel could hop from tree to tree...

Intriguingly, the lane running from the church towards Loweswater also forms the national park boundary, with any properties on the east side of the road part of the vibrant communities of the World Heritage Site. Although most of the other houses in Lamplugh do not come with the same world-class price tag (costing on average about 105% more), seeing as they are outside the national park. Even so, compared with the relatively modest terraces and bungalows of Kirkland, there were a few extra layers of affluence on display. Tucked neatly behind picturesque screens of beech trees, verges of cow parsley and red sandstone walls topped with blobs of moss and white lichen, were a series of large Grade II listed barns, luxury detached houses and custom-built lodges. Living for today and tomorrow. With a number of the exteriors displaying newly rendered stone walls refreshed in off-white masonry paint. Typically, some retained traces of the old village ways, with names like Byre House or Moss Side Cottage, from a period now vanished, new money transitioning into old money.

About halfway down, the trees were set further back from the road, behind wooden fences shielding around half a dozen attractive contemporary builds. Unfolding directly opposite, the picture postcard scene included fields of cows surrounded by a painterly backdrop of softly rounded hills enveloping Cogra Moss. A little more modest by comparison, several bungalows appeared further away from the church, next to new executive conversions. Looking up one of the properties online, I noticed it was up for sale at just under a cool half a million, with a long blurb of accoutrements branding it a rural paradise: sun room, zonal under-floor heating and showpiece galleried landing with vaulted ceiling, oak and chromed balustrades...

Lamplugh, renamed 'Crossbridge', featured in *Without a City Wall* and *The Hired Man*, a couple of novels published in the late 1960s by veteran Cumbrian broadcaster and curator of the nation's cultural treasures – Melvyn Bragg. Both were set in the old remote Cumberland village and provided vivid glimpses into the pulses of change framed by independence, passion, determination, desperation and self-respect. In the books, Crossbridge is described as a fairly typical fell village, located at the bottom of a range of interlocking fells, which shut out access to the nearby Solway Plain and frame the surrounding lakes and peaks in a wholly distinctive presence and beauty. A place where every sort of man passes from the sea to the hills, almost as transient as the landscape which changes and swirls with the light on the fell sides.

The Hired Man also portrays a time when annual hiring fairs were held in nearby market towns like Cockermouth. Held around Michaelmas, these events were opportunities for agricultural servants to gather, in order to bargain with potential employers, in the hope of securing a position for the subsequent year. During the same period, West Cumberland 'sat on coal', with 9,000 men employed by 43 collieries producing over two million tons of the black stuff. Of course these days everything connected with the pits has long been closed down, whilst the only buildings to survive from the same era are the church, a school, a pub and village hall – the carpenter, tailor, blacksmith and shoemakers all lost to the modern world.

But the terror of knowing what the new world was about foamed with blood in Lamplugh in June 2010.

Pressure...a recent grandfather nicknamed 'Birdy' running wild with a 12-bore sawn-off shotgun, a semi-automatic .22 rifle (fitted with a telescopic sight and silencer) plus loads of ammo. In the mid-summer dawn, no one could have had any idea what life had in store for them, on a day when everything would change for several communities at the mercy of one man.

People killing people...Derrick Bird, a quiet, nice and pleasant guy from the neighbouring village of Rowrah. According to those who knew him, he was a relatively sociable taxi driver who spent all of his 52 years living in West Cumbria, where he also got married and had two sons. After leaving school, a job as a joiner arose at Sellafield, but in the early 1990s the break-up of his marriage was soon followed by accusations of wood theft at the nuclear plant, which ultimately cost him his job. He then became a self-employed cabbie living alone in a modest pebble-dashed two-up, two-down mid-terraced home, before something snapped on that fateful sunny morning. The complex backstory of the so-called 'Cumbrian Shootings' is one of money problems, Inland Revenue investigations, Sellafield grudges, the unrequited love of a Thai girl, family feuds and disputes with other taxi drivers. A country and local community in shock sought answers to the same question splashed all over the national front pages – *Why?*

Some of Bird's friends pointed to a 2007 incident involving an unpaid fare as a possible catalyst. It happened after he challenged a teenager with a group of three friends who knocked him unconscious. This violent event was said to have changed his behaviour and led to increased bouts of heavy drinking. Other motives singled out three of his twelve victims as former employees at Sellafield, alluding to some form of revenge for a 12-month suspended sentence after the wood-theft allegations. Yet in reality, by the time he sped by his former workplace in the midst of the madness, the plant had been put in lockdown mode for the first time in its history.

Then there was the Thai girl he'd sent money to, who dumped him by text message after they'd met on holiday in the resort of Pattaya. But a dis-pute over his father's will and an ongoing investigation over unpaid tax were understood to be the real reasons for the build-up of pressure. It was rumoured he had developed an irrational fear that his twin brother, David, and the family's solicitor were conspiring to send him to prison for tax evasion. This paranoia came on top of the constant jibes and wind-ups about the state of his cab and personal hygiene from fellow colleagues on the taxi rank, some of whom he'd also rowed with about touting for fares on the eve of the shootings. Fuming as he left them, a final chilling rebuke was issued, "There's going to be a rampage tomorrow..."

During what the police referred to as phase one, under the spell of a dark and grim force, Bird drove three miles east from his home at Rowrah to his twin brother's High Trees farmhouse at Lamplugh. Arriving there under cover of darkness, just after 5am, he entered by the unlocked doors at the back, quiet as a mouse. Finding David semi-clothed in an upstairs bedroom, he shot him repeatedly eleven times, a silencer on his rifle to curb the noise. Blood was set to pour across West Cumbria, and at 10am events moved up a gear, as he set off for Frizington to kill the family solicitor, Kevin Commons, on the driveway of his farmhouse. Only this time, he neglected to use the silencer. At the sound of gunshots, police were summoned, but Bird was already speeding towards the centre of Whitehaven that had been draped in flags of St George in readiness for the up-and-coming World Cup.

Phase two marked the hour or so afterwards, between 10.30am and 11.35am, when a 45-mile rampage began at his place of work, the taxi rank on Duke Street. Soon enough a manhunt along the West Cumbria boundary of the national park was underway, after Bird struck horror into the heart of the coastal town. Calling innocent victims over to his car, embarking on a killing spree mercilessly shooting victims, seemingly at will. He shot fellow taxi driver Darren Rewcastle in the face, a crawling Donald Reid in the back, before speeding off to draw level with another taxi driver, Terence Kennedy. Smiling as he pointed the shotgun in his face, pellets were also sprayed over his terrified passenger.

From Whitehaven the chase was on, but without the use of a helicopter, Cumbria Police had to draft in others from the neighbouring Lancashire and Yorkshire forces. By now Bird was already several minutes ahead of the 42 armed police officers deployed in what became the biggest massacre in the UK since Dunblane in 1996. But they appeared powerless to stop the carnage unfolding on the West Cumbrian streets and fields, with shots pouring out of Bird's Citroen Picasso as it moved at speed from place to place. For the next couple of hours the flames of terror roared on a deadly spree taking in St Bees – Egremont – Wilton – Gosforth. After claiming the last of his innocent victims, with the brutal shooting of Jane Robinson in Seascale, he crossed over into the national park and entered the Eskdale valley teaming with people during half-term week. Marked by darkness and blood, Bird was now severely hampered due to the front offside tyre flying off the wheel of his car after repeated collisions with other cars and dry-stone walls. With armed response vehicles closing in, he abandoned his vehicle in the bright sunshine at Low Birker Farm, nearly three hours after the mayhem had started; walked into the woods, unscrewed the silencer, knelt down, jammed the .22 rifle under his chin and fired.

People killing people.. The death of hope and despair. Somewhere in the afterglow of a larch wood near the village of Boot, the truth died with a conquered soul...

At Moss Side Cottage on the edge of Lamplugh, a Mercedes 4x4 flashed past. It was the first sign of life I'd seen on the sedate walk along the boundary splitting part of the hamlet in two. From there, I set off over a crumbling wall stile for the next village of Mockerkin, across brooding fields of bog with decaying field barns creating a melancholic fantasy, like those awash in the ruins of a Salvator Rosa painting. Only the high-pitched tones of a sparrowhawk patrolling the hedgerows filled the temporarily dark and empty skies. After safely negotiating the sticky mud of the valley bottom, I entered another quiet village full of farm buildings that had diversified into holiday lets with a nominal triangular strip of grass for a green. As in most of the other places I'd already encountered, the ads on the noticeboard instantly demanded attention:

The Derwent Fells Local History Society – talk by Grevel Lindop, Architectural salvage, Private language tuition, Quality boarding kennels, Coffee morning and the Marie Antoinette Diet – "Eat cake & still lose weight!"

Exiting right on the narrow road toward the next hamlet of Sosgill, I was grateful for the sure footing the dry surface provided. Having cleaned my boots on the grass verge, I decided to ignore Dugdale's route across the marshy flats and stayed on the track walking past more farms, holiday cottages and new-builds in-between vast swathes of forestry plantations.

At a bend in the road, I pulled up sharply to observe a kestrel hovering near a hedge in the corner of a field. Its black silhouette contrasted perfectly against the sudden flash of late afternoon sun, but it was the majestic, wonderful and silent manoeuvring on the currents that enraptured me. Suddenly, as it fanned its long tail, it began to flap its wings, whilst its head remained perfectly still. Edging a little closer, I could just about make out a greyish-blue-coloured head with a light brown body. But then from nowhere, the awe-inspiring scene was gatecrashed by a pair of carrion crows. Spoilsports, whose late arrival, with gaping mouths open, filled the murky air with rasping cries which resonated all the way into Cockermouth...

COCKERMOUTH
TO BASSENTHWAITE

THE MILLENNIAL ART OF SMOKING
A MAN WITHOUT A COUNTRY
FAST DYES, THIN FLAX AND SHORT DRESS LINENS
ON THE BORDER BETWEEN URBAN AND RURAL
A SMALL POCKET OF THE INDUSTRIAL
DREAMSCAPE
MORE OF A RIGHT AND NOT A PRIVILEGE
THE FAMILIAR CROWING AND DRUMMING
PARACHUTE CLOUDS AND SKELETAL TREES
POURING OUT A TOXIC COCKTAIL
STRIPPED BARE AND BROKEN
COCKERMOUTH TO BASSENTHWAITE

The past is prologue...

The second half began with a drive north through Keswick, out under the shadow of Skiddaw on the A591 before turning off onto North Row for the descent into Bassenthwaite village. Parking opposite the Methodist church on the Avenue, I lifted out Knightrider's muddy bulk and gathered the necessaries once more. Loitering in the cold morning air by the car for a few minutes, watching the early autumn sun set the frosty fields alight, the colours of the ash and beech trees had turned a showy copper, with only a solid ring of oaks retaining their usual verdant hue. Heading back, opposite Armathwaite Hall the fields were flayed by a ghostly horror and mystery that dug deep into the silence of the road. Raking through my backpack I pulled out the camera whilst still perched on Knightrider. Leaning gently on the prickly hedge to my left, I desperately played with the settings trying to capture the alluring torches of morning light. Skiddaw's fleshy shoulders burned brightest in the distance, Russell's 'God Made Manifest' keeping watch over Keswick and beyond. From the Ouse Bridge Guest House, I turned off the B5291 to ride parallel with the booming A66 on the Peil Wyke Castle Inn back road. Undulating for a few small stretches, but much quieter, I soon whizzed past Embleton and eventually arrived in Cockermouth via the old castle ruins on Castlegate. Taking a left, straight onto Market Place, I stopped to lock Knightrider up outside 4Play Cycles – a large bike shop with a playful tagline, 'Put some fun between your legs.'

Eighteenth-century, like some town of Portugal;
Doorways faced with stone, proportionate windows,
And painted black and white or gayer colours;
A scale perfectly kept, appropriately small.
'Cockermouth' – David Wright (b.1920)

To take stock, I found a lime-green-coloured bench shaped like a cup and saucer on the pavement opposite. This stage marked the beginning of the end – homeward bound with over half of the route now covered. New things, famous streets, favourite sons – Saturday morning in the last outpost of the boundary looked almost as bright as the early morning sun. The past is prologue. Cockermouth – a department store of independent shops, a hub of creativity and aspiration along with some of the most famous figures from literature and history. For the well-heeled it stands as a shining light of resilience, heartbeat of the countryside and symbol of the national park's urban snobbery.

A place of historic significance in Cumbria, but not the Lake District.

Staring at a selection of A-boards and potted plants adorning boutiques, homeware stores and hotels, a colonnade of light blue and pink pastel coloured Georgian scenery disappeared round the bend. Sitting in the shade of a fine day, I had been beamed into a Jane Austen novel full of petticoats, cravats and hessian boots. But the Regency dandies have been replaced by hipsters pushing prams or carrying kids in padded back packs on winding streets. Discover your Cockermouth – the centre of its own world, like a big brother to the toy township of Broughton-in-Furness. Twinned with Marvejolsin the Lozerre region of southern France since 1983, in 1995 representatives of the Council of Europe awarded a plaque of honour to the town in recognition of its efforts for European Unity. In 2000, it gained the higher honour of the Europe Prize, awarded to the town most active in promoting the European ideal. How times have changed…

Gone – along with the sight of sheep in pens at the Mitchells Auction site (now a Sainsbury's), three petrol stations and no obvious flood defences, Cockermouth residents (like most of Cumbria) voted in favour of Brexit. Although (according to the tourist information website) the vote was 50-50 between Remain and Leave in all wards except Highfield, which voted 75% for the last throes of Empire.

Old traditions continue to play a part in the annual Woolfest and Cockermouth Agricultural Show, too. There's also a Local Produce and Crafts weekly market, with cosy town shops including a sprinkle of antique dealers, art galleries, an ironmonger's trading for over 180 years, several bakers and fishmongers. Newer events include the Taste Cumbria food festival and the Malcolm Wilson Rally. But there is still a strange mix of the old and the new all down the line on Main Street, and in the streets off to the side. With umpteen scissor-happy hairdressers mixed in amongst estate agents, kebab houses and charity shops. However, the big guns like Boots and Greggs seem relatively unobtrusive in contrast to bits of Kendal, (its fellow outsider in the south), and many other soulless clones on the high streets of Britain living on borrowed time and borrowed money.

Moving on, most of the voices on the street were from teams of soldiers rattling collection boxes for Remembrance Day. Further down, I paused at some large windows next to a toy shop. Behind them were apothecary bottles on shelves with coloured water, encased in aluminium and pharmaceutical packaging and painted MDF. It reminded me of Damien Hirst's site-specific installation 'Pharmacy', but it turned out to be part of a chain of shops (with others in Maryport and Whitehaven) dedicated to the soaring popularity of 'vaping'. The millennial art of smoking dictates operating a flashing Silicon Valley USB stick.

Every market town must have a 'big imposing house', and further down the west end of Main Street with two storeys limewashed in eye-catching apricot built for a Sheriff, was the NT's Wordsworth House. The main pull for Lake District tourists prepared to venture north of Keswick, if costume maids are your thing. If not, then they sell the poet's birthplace as a rare example of a fine Georgian townhouse that was home to the Wordsworth family until 1783. After losing their mother five years before, the death of their father caused the departure of the five children to seek accommodation elsewhere. In 1776, William and Dorothy attended a Dame school in Penrith, where the poet met his future wife, Mary Hutchinson. A couple of years later, William was sent to Hawkshead Grammar School with his brother Richard, whilst his dear sister Dorothy went to stay with relatives in Halifax. One of the key ingredients for World Heritage Status, it was in his own *Guide to the Lakes* that Wordsworth famously prophesied the creation of national parks.

As in the pageantry of a dream -
The gleam - The shadow - and the peace supreme...

Saved from becoming a bus station in 1937 by the Wordsworth Memorial Fund, the house was donated to the NT a year later, and opened to the public on 3 June 1939. Some eighty years on, I discovered it had fallen foul of the fake review market on TripAdvisor...

"Hidden national trust property
We came across this national trust property by chance.
It is in the centre of cockington."

Discover your Cockington? No wonder it was hidden...Anyway, as you'd expect from the NT, there was an ongoing programme of poetry readings, talks or tours, a revolving exhibition space, working kitchen and a Georgian garden filled with plants contemporary with Wordsworth's time. Back in 2003-4, the house and garden underwent a major restoration and is now firmly ensconced on the West Cumbrian bucket list as a hands-on, interactive Georgian experience. Facing a flank of Wordsworth House is a cottage in Low Sand Lane that was once home to the astronomer, Fearon Fallows. Sent to St. John's College, Cambridge in 1808 he was a contemporary of Palmerston, Herschel and Playfair. In 1821 he became the director of an observatory being built on the rocky headland at the Cape of Good Hope at the southern end of Cape Peninsula, Western Cape province, South Africa. Despite dying early at just 43 years of age, he was thought to have made a considerable contribution to astronomy by cataloguing the principal fixed stars from the Cape, whilst listing 142 new ones.

Another individual with a connection to Wordsworth and the town is John Dalton, born at Eaglesfield near Cockermouth in 1766. At 16 he formed a close relationship with a blind Quaker scholar named John Gough, who Wordsworth immortalised in *The Excursion* – a portion of his longer poem, *The Recluse*. Labelled a dissenter, Dalton went on to teach mathematics and philosophy at Manchester New College in 1792, later undertaking research in chemistry and securing the role of president of the Manchester Literary and Philosophical Society. During this period he prepared his principal communiqués on atomic theory, which was the first complete attempt to describe all matter in terms of atoms and their properties. It was through conducting this significant research that modern theories of chemistry and physics were formed. Ironically, nearly two hundred years later, his pioneering work would take on huge significance just down the road from where he was born, with the development of Sellafield. In a further twist, it is alleged that John Dalton's cottage in Eaglesfield was the first property to receive power when Calder Hall power station was officially opened by the Queen in 1956.

Two years before Dalton's birth, Fletcher Christian was born on a farm down the road in the same village of Eaglesfield. Appointed chief mate under Captain William Bligh on the *Bounty* in 1787, the ship's infamous voyage set sail for Tahiti to collect bread-fruit trees and deliver them to the West Indian colonies. Angered by Bligh's ill treatment of both himself and the crew, Christian famously became the chief mutineer responsible for overthrowing the *Bounty*, and setting Bligh adrift. Marlon Brando played the part of Christian as a haughtily foppish Dandy and aristocratic second-in-command, for the 1962 film, *Mutiny on the Bounty.*

True... Turbulent... Tremendous! Not all the critics agreed with the tagline though, with most of them judging veteran director Lewis Milestone's film 'over long and unattractive'. Yet it was supposed to be more of an examination of the status gap between the socially lower Captain Bligh (played by Trevor Howard of *Brief Encounter* fame) and Brando's often problematic Christian. In one of the key moments after the mutiny, Bligh baits Christian as 'a man without a country,' now a present-day sentiment shared by many since the morning of 24 June 2016.

Nobody really knew what happened to Christian in the end though. There are theories that he was killed on Pitcairn Island after leaving Tahiti four years earlier or even that he returned home and visited his family in Cumberland. These days, modern-day visitors and locals can take the wind out of their sails by toasting the world famous mutineer at the newly refurbished Fletcher Christian pub. However, it's not all pure ghetto gold on Main Street, with a number of For Sale boards feeling the graze against their skins. One of the most prominent is the closed 'Wordsworth Hotel'.

Like many other businesses the last tenants were also victims of the floods which blighted central Cockermouth in November 2009, when the river Cocker (from Crummock) and Derwent (from Bassenthwaite) rose to a level that left vast amounts of damage and most of the shops, restaurants and pubs completely devastated – some of them never recovered. Finally pushed into action, the Environment Agency built walls, embankments and flood gates along the rivers to help protect vulnerable homes and businesses prone to taking in water. But when the wicked beat of Storm Desmond arrived to wreak further havoc in December 2015, it was the fourth time Cockermouth had been severely hit since 2005.

At Bridge Lane, I followed the signpost 'To the Memorial Gardens' crossing over Miller's Bridge into the old industrial quarter. Derwent Mill, looming large on the right-hand side on the bank of the river of the same name, a legacy of the town's nineteenth century textile industry. A Victorian boom, exporting and prospering; fast dyes, thin flax and short dress linens. Derwent Mill was constructed on open ground to the south east of Low Gote Mills to accommodate the expanding business of the Harris family of Quakers. In its heyday they had showrooms in London, Manchester, Birmingham and Paris until the depression of the early 1930s put an end to linen production.

Next up, another family – the Millers from Great Yarmouth moved in, employing 1,100 people to manufacture sandals, boots, or ladies and children's shoes. But amid various accusations they ceased trading in 1990, when the receivers were called in. Like many relics of recession, this former Victorian sweatshop has been turned into swanky flats commanding average prices of up to half a million. Beside a large car park on the left I met Wakefield Road which curved toward Derwent Mills Commercial Park. One of the modern day replicas from a US export dating back to the peak of Thatcherism in the 1980s. When Britain first welcomed commercial parks, it began a new trend that saw the corporate world initiate its own private revolution by moving out of town to the fringes. In oceans of floor space they even started to enjoy such perks as free parking! Yet, similar to the industrial mills before them, many of these parks became increasingly obsolete.

Rounding the bend, I walked through the middle of seven single-storey workshop units. But the original landscaped courtyards were already becoming a classic form of self-seeding edgeland, typically on the border between urban and rural. Just over the river, away from the untainted Romanticism of Georgian Main Street, a small pocket of the industrial dreamscape. Modern life holding on for tomorrow with strands of barbed wire stacks, empty wooden pallets, wild shrubbery and pockets of rubbish. There's a dead end waiting at the rotting oasis...

For most of this stage I followed a section of the Allerdale Ramble. From the A595 road above Cockermouth to Scarness halfway along Bassenthwaite Lake, via Redmain, Blindcrake, Isel Hall and Simpson Wood, roughly eight miles in length. Before getting into the rhythm of the walk, I stood in a field directly above the factory units breathing in the urban sprawl of Cockermouth, spread out under clear blue skies full of contrails. It was a warm, pleasant day, one of the best I'd had so far with the low sun making the last remnants of morning dew glistening on the grass, almost to a white-out. A little further up the slope, on the left, was Hames Hall, built in the early nineteenth century in Gothic style by the leading architect Sir Robert Smirke, who had updated the design of Lowther Castle as his first project aged just 25. However, he was best known for working on the monumental British Museum (1823–47) and Covent Garden Theatre, a couple of Neo-Classical public buildings in London.

These days the former Victorian mansion has been turned into a care home. The information on the Lakeland Care website reads more like that of a hotel – set in three acres of its own grounds, en-suite showers or baths, a spacious wet room, easy-access Jacuzzi bath, original period decorative features including ornate covings and panelled ceilings, whilst at the back there is a palatial conservatory and garden room. Not to mention a full menu with a range of choices served every day, with home-cooked dishes using locally sourced ingredients. No one can blame anyone for wanting the very best care available to a loved one if they can afford it. But I couldn't help feeling that care should be more of a right and not a privilege, especially when I looked over at the house with its extensive grounds.

Climbing out of the Derwent Valley through Wood Hall Park, it was time to meet the boundary again on the asphalt of the A595. With several accident black spots it is understood to be the most dangerous road in Cumbria (along with the A66). Back in Roman Britain, Carlisle was linked to the forts of Old Carlisle and Papcastle in West Cumbria by a very direct south-westerly road that is mainly obscured by the present day A595. Entering the national park again, the route headed for Redmain and involved a small section marching beside the perilous highway full of trucks loaded up with agricultural machinery, whilst various other vehicles zipped by.

With no pavement either, I had to follow a random shred of grass verge predictably cluttered with empty crisp packets, various beer cans and bottles, hi-energy drinks, Coke cans, discarded lighters, Starbucks cups and torn up McDonald's packs.

Conserve, Enhance, Opportunities, Enjoyment...

Former traces of British settlements and place names can be found in a couple of areas on the fringes of the Lake District. On this stage I found evidence of them in the small village of Redmain, located near the River Derwent that loops away on the right hand side toward the tiny historic hamlet of Blindcrake. Its name derives from the Celtic, *Blaen Craig*, which means at the summit of a rocky outcrop and probably referred to the nearby ridge of limestone, Clints Crags. Owing to a mediaeval field strip pattern understood to be the last remaining example within the national park, the LDNPA designated the historic village a Conservation Area in 2001 *(a conservation area is defined as 'an area of special architectural or historic interest the character or appearance of which it is desirable to preserve or enhance).*

I'd entered Blindcrake on a quiet Back Lane or 'lonning', which once gave access to the strip fields. A summary of the main features of the village includes two distinct clusters of historic farmhouses, farm buildings and cottages north and south of the village green; with a prevalence of stone roadside boundary walls; modern farm buildings behind historic farmsteads, with some former agricultural barns inevitably converted into holiday lets, enclosed 'green' approaches from all directions and open fields sweeping directly up to the limit of the houses.

In the late morning hush, I ambled along the main road through the village. Grey stone predominated, surrounded by softly rolling pastoral farmland divided by a network of low hedgerows and limestone walls which followed the rising and falling countryside. Moving away from the centre, the road eventually forked downhill through Ellers Wood toward the river and nearby hamlet of Isel. In the dense foliage, I heard the first sound of gunshots reverberating through the woodland. Followed by the familiar crowing and drumming of wings from two distressed male pheasants, like Bonnie and Clyde, John Lewis-Stempel's ornate jungle fowl were on the run again.

Isel Hall, once the centre of the manor and parish, was a Grade I listed building with a fourteenth century pele tower residing on the northern banks of the River Derwent. A long history of ownership dates back to the reign of Edward II, and the Leigh family who passed it to the Lawsons in the late sixteenth century. A line that finally came to an end with Margaret Austen Leigh's death in 1986, when the house was left to her friend and champion of the arts, Mary Burkett. A formidable lady who was once said to have been introduced to the Prince of Wales as 'the maddest woman in England' for taking on a house fallen into such a state of disrepair. But Mary had a mantra, 'Everyone's mind needs art whether they know it or not', and she spent much of her lifetime vigorously promoting the arts in Cumbria and North West England.

In 1966 she was appointed director of the Abbot Hall Art Gallery in Kendal, a position she held for twenty years, bringing a significant number of new donations and purchases to the collection, including George Romney's *The Gower Family* and the towering triptych *The Great Picture*. She was also a passionate supporter of many unsung artists, advocating the work of Dadaist Kurt Schwitters, a German refugee during the Second World War who came to live in Ambleside. She also promoted Cumbrian artists, such as Sheila Fell and Percy Kelly. In 1981, barely a couple of years after Fell's tragic death in London aged 48, Burkett mounted a fitting retrospective at Abbot Hall, *A Tribute to Sheila Fell*, which included 36 of her paintings alongside works by her great friend L. S. Lowry.

Five years before, after chasing him for a long period of time, she had finally managed to persuade Kelly to stage an exhibition there in 1976. Throughout all of his life he apparently hated exhibiting his work and could be very difficult and frustrating to deal with. That didn't perturb Burkett whose persistence finally paid off; although Kelly's desperate financial plight at the time was thought to be the real reason for a change of heart. The show featured 70 paintings, with Abbot Hall adding several to their permanent collection. Kelly also wrote exquisite letters to his friends, which Chris Wadsworth (the owner of Castlegate Gallery in Cockermouth) memorably called 'paintings with words'. When Burkett died aged 90 in November 2014, 140 of these letters (dating from 1971 onwards) featured in a sale of her personal collection by the auctioneers Mitchells of Cockermouth. Many of them had been used in the 2011 book *Dear Mary, Love Percy – A Creative Thread*, edited by David A. Cross.

The end was in sight now, as I plodded further into the national park through a series of conifer plantations, with the sound of gunfire waging a warlike song that spelt doom for any feathers of coppery magnificence. After the track entered Isel Old Park Wood it soon closed alongside the Derwent, where I stood for a moment admiring the still reflections of parachute clouds and skeletal trees on the water's surface. From here the only way out was to follow the river on a section known as the Buckholme Lonning track under coppiced trees, with wire mesh on the left and an old stone wall on the right. Between the rattle and hum of shotguns I spied a solitary roe deer before the crackle of a twig alerted it to my presence. Standing wonderfully still for a moment, the slender red-grey creature sized me up and then kicked off unimpressed into the wood.

Feeling the burn, I scoffed some ham sandwiches and drank a Spar chocolate milkshake between lengthening strides. After seeing nobody for hours, suddenly the walk took on a wilder side with civilisation about to close in. A hustle here and a hustle there...Through the wire mesh something with black and white stripes moved menacingly close as shouts mixed with laughter drifted across the wood. It turned out I'd found what Dugdale called – 'Trotters and Friends Animal Farm'. Now it has been rebadged as the Lake District Wildlife Park, housing beasts of every land and clime in 24 acres of parkland. Things change. And just as I was checking out their website I came face to face with a pair of brown cattle equipped with massive horns. A quick Google revealed they were Ankole-Watusi cattle, a heritage breed from Central Africa. Chewing nonchalantly on pinches of tobacco, Del Boy and Rodders didn't ask questions. Yet they made me realise I hadn't been to a zoo for over twenty years. The last time would have been to Regent's Park in soaking conditions similar to those during the final unforgettable scene of *Withnail and I*. Now it seems that as well as the admission fee you can also buy experiences: Meet the Meerkats, Hawk Walk. Lemur Encounter. Pre-Booking is essential. The 'modern' zoo's noble aspirations: species conservation and education, also attempts to lull families into buying add-on curios. With the wire fence between myself and all the premeditated fun, even on a fairly dull section of the walk I was relieved to be passing by.

Emerging from the woodland near to the B5291, I proceeded to walk headlong into a pageant of old cars (some classic) parading round parts of the zoo before heading off into the grounds of Armathwaite Hall, next door. Once home to landed gentry who turned it into a country gentleman's residence, the hall narrowly escaped demolition some thirty years ago. Since then a massive overhaul has seen it mutate into an hotel, spa wedding venue and hangout for the corporate world. The Armathwaite Experience includes a glut of themed events aiming to create dazzling memories mirrored in flutes of the finest bubbly. In spurts of movement, the cars lined up with brake pads screeching and smoking exhausts poured out a toxic cocktail inspiring the odd wave of nostalgia. From Talbot Sunbeams, Ford Cortinas, Porsche 911s, MGBTs, some old Volvo numbers and even a string of old Alfa GTVs from the 1960s.

My own circuit was almost complete by the time I passed the exact spot where I'd stopped to take photos on Knightrider earlier that same day. Turning left through the tree line masking the eastern side of Bassenthwaite Lake, the national park waymarkers signposted a footpath to Scarness. This was the only stage on the entire boundary walk where part of it went round a lake! As I moved through a sequence of squelchy fields dominated by the brooding Skiddaw massif directly in front, the tops were covered in billowing clouds performing an ever-circling dance. For the first time in a while, my right ankle started to throb again, so I stopped for a break and took some photos of a unique symbol evoking Friedrich's Abbey among Oak Trees. A blasted tree stripped bare and broken, haunting the foreground, a symbol of the inevitability of death…

BASSENTHWAITE
TO HUTTON ROOF

A MORNING OF SILENCE AND BELLS
MIRED IN THE NONCHALANCE OF OBLIVION
FULL OF AMBIENT OCCLUSION
LIVING ON THE EDGES OF TWILIGHT ZONES
ERASING MEMORIES IN AN UNWINDING FIRE
THE SOCIAL CONTRACT OF KNITTED JUMPERS
THE DRIFT INTO MATERIALISM AND THE
COMPLEX INTERCHANGES OF INDUSTRY
A BLOODY EYE THAT PULSED AS IT STARED
OLD WORLDS SEEN THROUGH NEW EYES
A DARK AND GRIM FORCE LAUNCHED
AN UNNAMED SORROW
BASSENTHWAITE TO HUTTON ROOF

In the gentle throes of daybreak…

This was where it could have all gone a bit wrong. Still without Dugdale's book to refer back to, I had to devise my own routes for a while. Although a quick glance at the OS map revealed Bassenthwaite to Caldbeck took care of itself by following the Cumbria Way footpath for pretty much the whole stage. But then later on, after completing the first part to Caldbeck, I made the awful discovery that my voice notes for that part had been deleted! How and why, I'll never know. The only consolation was that I found out straight away. So, grabbing an old trusted notebook and pen, I quickly cobbled together the main points whilst cursing my feckless methods and technology.

Sunday morning in tidy attire. Cold, but clear first thing, I had to scrape ice off the car windscreen before setting off. Driving north again under the wallowing hippo forming Helvellyn's bulky silhouette through a landscape blending earth and sky together. Preparing all things to rest, a sprinkling of snow had issued its first broadcast of the season on the spiky tops. Down below, a stone-cold wind moved leaves on the vine of time. In the gentle throes of daybreak only a few hardy joggers and dog walkers lined the empty pavements. It was Remembrance Sunday, a morning of silence and bells.

Weaving through St John's in the Vale, Blencathra's perilous height engulfed the Penrith to Keswick A66 autobahn, the Eden Valley accident dread zone. Outside in the cold distance where wildcats used to growl, a blue tomorrow shone into Mosedale, a station on the cross of Quakerism. Moaning winds staggered with a sense of arrival entering the marshy trough of the Mungrisdale valley. Soon enough I pulled up opposite the Kirkland village shop in Caldbeck in view of the Oddfellows Arms, 'a proper' Lakeland inn offering a subtle palette of rustic romance and natural minerals in the centre; new ideas for well-behaved dogs, cyclists and walkers. Before opening the car boot, I wondered where all the inhabitants of the historic village were, but then we were still in the B&B breakfast zone. The two-hour window for families and weary walkers gathered round a cosy arrangement of tables for the full English, the colour guide books, a good fill and stagger back up to their porous cocoons.

Situated on the flanks of Skiddaw, in the graveyard of St Kentigern's church dating from the early twelfth century, a must-see beauty rested alongside a famous huntsman.

I'd passed it as I drove through a huddle of cottages and bungalows mired in the nonchalance of oblivion. Tucked underneath a lamp post, there was a 1990s BT KX100 phone box at the end of the line opposite a lone petrol pump. Two landmarks destined to become heritage assets or converted into tourist information points or even a defibrillator store.

With one last tweak of Knightrider's oily set of brake cables, I pushed off with the prospect of a nine-mile lumpy ride along the B5299 to Bassenthwaite. In the clarity of bright morning sunshine, swelling hedgerows screened the enclosure of Cumberland's commons surrounding the hamlets of Whelpo and Uldale. The latter being the occasional home of Judith Paris, the heroine from Sir Hugh Walpole's *Herries Chronicles* (the saga of a Cumbrian family penned in the 1930s). Thumbing two fingers at any literary critics awaiting in the undergrowth, Walpole described it as 'a fine, queer book in the big manner'. In 1924 he settled in the Lake District, moving into a house under the round bottom of Cat Bells near Keswick. In *Apple Trees*, a rare volume of reminiscences (published at Christmas in 1932), he spoke in Wordsworthian tones of the debt he owed to the landscape of Cumberland...

> I sat with my mother in a field above Ullswater. It was a perfect summer evening. They were bringing in the hay, with singing and laughter, and light spinning as with the murmurous flash of a million golden insects sparkled upon Ullswater...This was in fact recovered country, for as children we had been brought – my sister, my brother and I – year after year to Sower Myre Farm near Gosforth – a village between Wastwater and Seascale. The years of our childhood are of course the foundation of all our life. We never altogether emerge from them...

With views of Skiddaw's northern forest, I passed through little wooded valleys streaked with silver birch and dashes of yellow gorse. A long grumbling strain uphill provided the odd snippet of mountain grandeur, whilst further in the distance I spied the edges of Bassenthwaite Lake. Turning off at the Rake, I settled into a slow and dreamy rhythm. Arriving in the white-washed village of Bassenthwaite my legs were wound in elastic bands as I crawled over the old stone bridge by the Sun Inn. A village marked by the loss of wool production, mining and farmers blooming into jack of all trades. A multitude of trades replaced and being sunk by the slow death of hotels, B&Bs, holiday homes and caravan sites.

After a few minutes spent idly pedalling up and down an avenue of colourless cottages and farm buildings, I decided to head out and lock up Knightrider at the recently refurbished Bassenthwaite Parish Rooms. A swanky new build funded by Lottery money replacing the original hall built in 1908 for a group known as the Skiddaw Humane and Friendly Society.

In February 2014, the parish council published a 'Community Plan' providing a snapshot of village life on the margins of the national park. Dog-fouling, road safety, a lack of footpaths, sympathetic views on affordable housing, the needs of young families and concerns over the number of holiday homes were top of the list. At the back, a summary table of action points cited housing problems as the highest priority and sought to remedy them by working closely with Chief Executive Leafe and the Lake District National Park's 'High quality of life for all' strategy. Under a long-term timescale (how long no one knows), the parish council's action key words were suitably vague:

Explore control measures. Encourage provision…

Yet in a complex economic world full of ambient occlusion, the highest priority is rarely discussed in public, and often ignored to protect the free market. What chance can anyone have of establishing a foothold living on the edge of a twilight zons, where scrutiny is potentially harmful. Despite acknowledgment of the problems, there is still a conspiracy of silence in relation to any ideas or solutions, while those that can continue to look the other way, believing holiday homes are the best way to invest their money. #Dogfriendly #Luxury #Cottage #NoOneKnowsCumbriaBetter…

I locked Knightrider to the only bike rack in the village, and turned to grab my backpack just as a family of three pulled up in a red Nissan. We nodded at each other and exchanged the usual banal business of seasoned fell walkers:

"Lovely weekend."

"Where you headed to?"

"Have a good 'un'…"

Making up almost a third of the mountain core, the Skiddaw Group is formed of mud rock believed to be amongst the oldest in Europe. At more than 3,000m thick they were laid down in relatively deep water, over a long period of time. Folded and cleaved they have a very complex structure, whilst distinct zones and trending faults outcrop in a wide belt across the northern and western fells. They also pop up to form the sphinxlike Black Combe in the south west and as inliers across the lower limits of Ullswater and Haweswater. Bassenthwaite, with two lakes beating as one (in times of flood), lies firmly in the northern part of the national park lying on Skiddaw slates. In one of the emptiest landscapes in the area, a shallow valley made up of the less assertive rocks found in the Back o'Skiddaw country – bare and open. Norman Nicholson's 'great stretch of moorland curved and moulded like a dollop of clay in the hands of a sculptor'.

This stage would also be a journey blowing a bugle through the land of John Peel with scarcely another soul or frond of bracken in sight. With combed mountain tops of conifer acres planted in regulation straight lines, monocultures and acid rivers; rebuild and maintain. Ennerdale, Whinlatter, Upper Eskdale, Rusland Valley, Dunnerdale and on ridges of Skiddaw above Bassenthwaite.

The Forestry Act, ushered in by the post-war upland despoilers and new guardians of the periphery. In modern times talk has switched to environmental resources, restructuring and development of the Forest Design Plans. Restoring native woodland, broadleaf planting and help for threatened species. Dissenting voices spoke up about plans to asset-strip the country's national heritage. A chorus that grew louder in light of the coalition Government's botched sell-off plan for the Forestry Commission in 2010, but the so-called 'Environmental Vandalism' was put on hold. Just a year later, the National Forest Inventory announced post-war decline was officially halted, with a reported 13% tree cover across the UK. Since then, Britain's woodlands have been quietly regenerated into a wide range of recreation and tourist facilities, from deer-stalking to rallying, and historic sites including barrows, forts and mediaeval villages. To the traditional sounds of the English summer, estates are filling up with landscaped lookouts, hot tubs and little fluffy towels.

Under the finest blue skies, clouds caught the last vestiges of autumnal sunshine. Transfixed by their unique painterly appearance, I watched their undergarments glow with a transparent flash through a gap in the foliage lining School Road. For one moment, the sky washed everything away, erasing memories in an unwinding fire scraping away at my mind. Then, from nowhere, a grey squirrel darted out of the large grassy field on the right and paused, looking back from the middle of the road. As quickly as he appeared, Timmy Tiptoes soon lost his nerve and vanished in a fitful gust. The sleeping mists were starting to clear from the valley floors at the same time as the sunshine poured into the boundary, burnished as on the previous day. Under perfect conditions for walking I headed back into the village, taking a right at the green before entering some empty fields lying to the northwest. I was headed in the direction of Great Cockup – not the best of omens...

Kestrel Lodge campsite has operated under many different guises since Dugdale's time when it was plain old High Close Farm, a working eighteenth-century farm with a black sheep-herder by the name of Bracken. Now it has warped into an old-fashioned campsite with a few mod cons, all in safe staggering distance of the nearest gastro pub. Out here tents plug in and change the world while the fire pit of the campfire headphase provides moments of clarity. At a T-junction past the camping grounds, I took a left and joined the Cumbria Way footpath. A seventy-four mile pilgrimage scything through the heart of World Heritage, starting in Stan Laurel's Ulverston down in the Deep South before heading to the northern ballast of Carlisle; the historic border city hewn out of old red, where love and hate fought with burning hearts.

Park Wood was crossed by two footpaths and designated as both open access land and a 'Plantation on Ancient Woodland Site' (Put your PAWS up!) In the new climate of restructure and development, plans to phase out the dense coniferous cover and encourage recolonisation by native broadleaf species were already in motion. Under the mature larch canopy in the eastern end of the wood was a healthy natural regeneration of native broadleaved species including hazel, birch, rowan, holly and oak. Previously owned by the Forestry Commission, it is now in private ownership. Robin Hood Wood similarly privately owned and crossed by a footpath connects with Park Wood to the west.

On the fringes of the plantation is the High Close holiday home enclave. Since the mid-1970s the park has offered those with metal cards and laser-etched signatures a chance to build their own Grand Design in accessible seclusion. Chic-looking spacious high-tech framed prefabs made out of timber, like an elegant Tardis to defy all the usual caravan clichés in the fantasy world of highways and byways. The social contract of knitted jumpers and the horror of Britishness infused with noisy teenagers, litterbugs, dewy grass in the gloom and wafts of sewage. 'If the caravans a rockin' don't come knocking.' Ben Wheatley's *Sightseers* partly filmed in the Lake District, a pitch-black caravan caper that turned an even harsher shade of dark. Folk Horror: an atmosphere, a mist, the evil under the soil, the terror in the backwoods of a forgotten lane, and the ghosts that haunt stones and bands of dark, lonely water. A growing subgenre with roots in the late 1960s and early '70s through films like: *The Witchfinder General, Blood on Satan's Claw* and *The Wicker Man*. Wheatley's 2012 film actually included scenes shot not that far away at the Pencil Museum in Keswick and Long Meg's stone circle near Penrith. In one particularly gruesome moment, a NT member and stereotypical Daily Mail reader (played by Richard Lumsden) meets a violent end after daring to speak out about dog poo!

In one of his more poetic moments, Dugdale described the steep climb through the closely-knit conifers of Whitefield Wood as 'dark and sepulchral', a clinging silence broken only by the chattering stream tumbling down through the trees. Moving through the sporadic shafts of light, I found that like most of the journey so far, no one else was around. There were certainly no dog walkers or horse riders, supposedly the main users of road and paths. But the waterfall's song still echoed through the melancholy treescape, filtering amidst the same pondering shadows the forest seer meets in the transcendental rapture of Emerson's *Woodnotes II:*

As sunbeams stream through liberal space
And nothing jostle or displace,
So waved the pine tree through my thought
And fanned the dreams it never brought.

At Orthwaite, after scooting round the northern edge of Little Tarn across a rough slope flecked with gorse, I took a photo of a group of cottages. Lying in the painted shadows of the road, they would have made a perfect writer's retreat in the middle of so many competing factions. Nature, cultural heritage, the drift into materialism and the complex interchanges of industry. A language older than history. The migratory sound poem of the boundless shade.

Heading north on the Cumbria Way, passing by Over Water, a nutrient-rich small tarn owned by the NT surrounded by wet grassland and closed canopy woodland; once a natural water body, it was dammed in 1904 to increase its size. Now it acts as a reservoir supplying water to Wigton further north. It is also an SSSI supporting a wide variety of flora including yellow and white water lilies and water lobelia. Over Water also has a long association with breeding birds, including great-crested grebes, grey herons and reed warblers. The tarn is also noted as a feeding place for the fish eating ospreys which breed beside Bassenthwaite Lake. With characteristic slow wingbeats the peerless bird of prey with dazzling white underparts and long narrow wings had initially nested beside Bassenthwaite in 2001, the first to breed in the Lake District for 150 years. The flight zone over Bassenthwaite Lake can be surveyed from the outdoor viewpoints at Dodd Wood (about three miles north of Keswick off the A591). From here, high-powered telescopes and binoculars are provided by the Forestry Commission, who furnish the viewpoints with the obligatory money-spinners: car-parking, toilets and a tearoom. Yet the ospreys' busy gladiatorial theatre of conflict also spans the flowing tides and shifting sands of the South Lakes estuaries. By playing at *Big Brother* you can catch up on them at 'osprey watch' in the Whinlatter Forest Visitor Centre. Here you can watch live pictures in high definition from a camera focused purely on their nest.

Another reservoir flashed by, Chapelhouse, just before Longlands, where I joined up with the old road and headed out on a wing under Longlands Fell. The magical cries of sparrowhawks circling overhead lit up the blue skies and cast a stain of red throughout the air. A token cyclist rounded a corner and dulled the growing lethargy of my steps for a few minutes.

Emerging out onto the open fells felt very strange after all the enclosed territory of the fringe destinations. Up to this point I'd been mainly used to scattered villages on narrow winding roads, a few farms surrounded by miles of boggy fields, burial grounds, unnatural treescapes, firing ranges and poisonous industries in pools of oily water. This designated path absorbed in smooth and soft grassy slopes bathed in a glossy sheen quickly became a slow-motion reminder (in Lake District tourism terms) of being on the wrong side.

Still, I had no choice but to keep going on the low-level stretch of the Cumbria Way path. Whilst a background triptych of the Uldale Fells – Great Sca Fell, Great Cockup and Meal Fell – joined together to form one vast sheep pasture. I remembered looking at the OS app at this point, barely a mile away from the boundary, in one of the quietest parts of the national park. The mystery at the edge, rubbing its eyes in the steps of yesterday…

At the slightly larger hamlet of Fellside (predominantly made up of stone-built seventeenth century farmhouses), two strands of the Cumbria Way converged. Positioned south west of Caldbeck, Fellside is a small community supporting a primary school, pub, church, doctor's surgery and a post of- fice/store. Rush-hour souls need to hit the neighbouring metropolises of Carlisle, Wigton, Penrith, Keswick or Cockermouth.

There was a residential centre though, formerly a private residence, now owned by Cumbria County Council. According to the council website, the old secluded farmhouse can accommodate up to 38 people with direct access onto the Northern Fells close to Caldbeck for rambling and hiking, given the importance of strenuous open-air holidays. This isolated place also marked my departure from the Cumbria Way, as I branched off to the right, away from the life-changing path many young people will embark on. Personal and unique journeys framed by living history and outdoor learning in the shades of autumn, from one of three bases in the Northern Lake District offering Duke of Edinburgh expeditions and training.

The northbound track to Caldbeck was calling and so was one of the Lake District's famous sons (even though most of his hunts were held outside the modern-day national park). *D'ye Ken John Peel?* Born of farming stock at Caldbeck in 1777, the first of thirteen children to William 'Cock and Bacon' Peel and Lettice Scott. John's father was a chicken and pig farmer who farmed at Ireby. Soon enough his son followed in his footsteps. They lived in an age when predators were hunted down brutally as farmers up and down the land invited huntsmen with packs of dogs to hunt the foxes on their land. Said to be an exceptional horse rider, John had something of the night about him. Even though mining for lead and copper was also prevalent during this period, the young rogue (like his father and grandfather before him) stuck with farming instead.

In his twenties he took off in the dead of night with Mary White, a local girl from Uldale, to get married over a blacksmith's anvil at Gretna Green in Scotland. Once settled, he continued to make his living from general farming and horse dealing, which brought him into contact with other huntsmen. John Peel like a bloody eye that pulsed as it stared. With a '*Tally Ho!*', pine martens, hares and the odd fox would be in his sights, sometimes on hunts lasting for up to three or four days. On low-lying land over the bleak and wild country, hounds ran with music sounding an unnerving whine like distant cries of human grief. Above Uldale across to the heights of massive Skiddaw, where the thirsting Peel would be forced to abandon, often running the pack for the whole day.

Even though hunting was his main focus, he also gained a reputation for heavy drinking, sometimes going on two-or-three day benders after a hunt. He famously wore a heavy overcoat, the Iveson Grey (not gay as some might say) made from wool known as hodden, handwoven locally at a Caldbeck mill. After hunting hounds for over fifty years, Peel died aged 78 in 1854 and was buried in the churchyard at Caldbeck. But it took a friend of his, John Woodcock Graves, to immortalise him in the local ballad *D'ye Ken John Peel?* Ironically, Graves ended up disliking Cumberland so much that he emigrated to Tasmania in 1833.

Animal welfare and animal rights are still amongst the most controversial issues sure to create a 'them and us' scenario today, especially between vegans and livestock farmers. As in the story of John Peel, the history of fell farming is interlaced with tales of hunting. Many saw the fox as vermin, to be 'pursued to destruction', other farmers viewed the hunt as more of a social opportunity to meet up with other farmers, especially over the solitary winter months, while some farmers never approved of the hunt.

In the intervening years after the untold havoc and trauma created by foot-and-mouth disease, interest in the way food is produced along with the treatment of animals in that process has grown considerably. Since the Hunting Act of 2004, hunting foxes, deer and hares with packs of dogs has been banned in England, Scotland and Wales. However, the quintessential British institution of 'traditional hunting' and the thrill of the chase have not gone away. Instead, it has been reinvented as 'trail hunting' following an animal-based scent trail (using fox urine, according to the hunters) which is laid in areas where foxes or hares are likely to be. But if the hounds pick up the scent of a live animal by mistake then there is obviously a high possibility that they will stray from the original trail laid down and chase the real one instead. With a knowing nudge and a wink, the hunt can then claim immunity by not telling those controlling the hounds where the scent has been laid.

However, you've always got to tread very carefully if you want to be accepted in the country. With the term 'drag hunting' conjuring up alternative images of Dom Joly's Weird World of Sport, 'dragging the countryside for the strong scent of a transvestite – running as fast you can in nine inch heels up river and down dale'. But 'drag hunting' is a legitimate sport which also uses packs of hounds, although it existed before the hunting ban and is not intended to mimic animal hunting. In this version the hounds hunt an artificial non-animal scent (typically aniseed) pulled by a drag that has been laid down over a prearranged route. After the vision of chasing Paco Rabanne-scented divas on the Caldbeck fells had worn off, I turned right then left and left again alongside a fence.

In the evening of the day, strands of fading sunlight fondled the hedges and burnt leaves on cross-shaped oaks forming an avenue pointing to the B5299 between Whelpo and Caldbeck. Out in the fields, a sweeping troop of jackdaws tore through the air as if they were about to form part of some strange nightly feast. Not to be outdone, a murder of crows abandoned their sombre perches and joined them to make a thunderous din. As I stood watching the unfolding drama, right on cue, a fox trotted out slowly near the hedgerow in a dim corner of the same field. Carefully marking its territory whilst waiting for the silence of darkness, the look it gave pulled the curtain away, *'You will be the death of me…'*

The next part of the stage began in damp drizzle with a creeping mist pouring through the bottom of the valley floors. Heading out on the A66, all dipped headlights, poor visibility, nothing but a ghostly blanket closing like heavy eyes. The moment I arrived at Hutton Roof, a long downpour felt more like abandonment. A tiny elevated hamlet, grey like the weather, dominated to the west by outcroppings of limestone, now forgotten and badly in need of some form of renewal or exorcism. Three hundred metres above sea level, but only ten miles away from Junction 41 of the M6. Pure noir. It was the kind of place where folk walk beside themselves just to pass the time. Pulling to the left through broken windows stuffed with loo roll, I saw rows of wooden sheds behind chicken wire. They were next to a stack of pallets opposite the building site of the Old School House.

In the eerie silence after a mini-flash flood had battered my car, I wheeled out Knightrider and cycled to a dilapidated stile in front of a field of long grass housing a soggy wet picnic bench supplied by the perennial pressurisers, FLD; a token gesture left to rot opposite a defunct small pond ringed by tussocks. Behind the sludge-coloured sheet of water, a cattle grid gave access onto a long driveway leading into the courtyard of Brow Top Farm, the most prominent series of buildings in the village. Cut off from the rest, here they announce themselves from a lofty perch to the River Caldew and below into Mosedale and Mungrisdale. Locked off from the world, a place off limits with a warning marked up like Otto Kruger's Judge in *High Noon* "This is just a dirty little village in the middle of nowhere. Nothing that happens here is really important."

I needed to make a move before the light drizzle settled in to a much heavier rhythm, so I turned round and pedalled back south through the village. Under a token street light toward Wham Head Farm House (Wham being derived from the Old Norse word, *hvammr* meaning a marshy hollow), which was formerly the home of Richard Richardson, who also built the first school house in 1830, it burnt down in 1905. Open skies, dark and vast and full of rain nipping at my wheels on the long, narrow straight roads over the five-mile dash to Caldbeck. Whispering trees echoed their sighs in conditions perfect for waterfalls. Somewhere just before the long village green of Hesket Newmarket, I took a right turn and was immediately engulfed by a flock of Swaledales spilling out of an open field gate onto the road. At the sight of Knightrider's bulk they duly fell into line following my hand signals as I motioned to the side where the safety of the stone wall was.

"You're doing well there, d'ya want a job?"

A whistling farmer in a flat cap with long bushy sideburns gave me a toothy grin as he sped by on a black quad bike – miraculously, a pair of collies somehow clung on to the back. Swaledales, tough as old boots, all horns and ears, first introduced to the Lake District not that far away at the Mungrisdale Ram Show back in 1929. Now they are also the iconic emblem of the neighbouring Yorkshire Dales National Park.

When I entered Caldbeck it was as quiet as it had been the week before on the Sunday morning. At least I managed to find a proper place to lock up the bike next to the Old Smithy Tea Rooms, something of a rarity in most of the other places I'd been to. Beside Fell View Primary School the up and coming big event on the noticeboard announced the Caldbeck Players lavish production of the *Wizard of Oz* at the village hall.

But I was off to see the Howk or the Fairykirk, a wonderful grotto with a Fairies' Kettle! A cataclysmic experience and must-see! – according to Dugdale. Yes, the maestro had returned after I'd managed to hunt down a copy of his *magnum opus* in a local charity shop – now I owned the Boundary Walk! The Howk was a limestone gorge with hanging trees, a series of foaming pools and odd recesses eroded out of rock. Its name being aptly derived from the Cumbrian dialect to 'scoop out'. Coleridge, no stranger to measureless caverns, had first discovered the, 'Fairies' parlors and fine

Cathedral seats overhung by the rock' in October 1800. It is a place the national park had initially set up as a site of special interest with a wooden footbridge suspended above a section gauged into the rock. They also put in a sturdy steel and stone fence on the bank opposite festooned with ferns.

Old worlds seen through new eyes. The battle is over but the war's not yet won. I shut my eyes and listened to the powerful sound of regeneration frothing in deep grooves of rage. *Cald beck* derived from the Old Norse for 'cold stream'. Crossing over its pulsing sobs the ruin of the former Bobbin Mill at the bottom of the deep gorge presented a hollowed out skeleton entombed with nineteenth-century ghosts. Still breathing beneath the scars, the heavily weathered and decaying English Heritage and national park interpretation board was hardly an advert for World Class Heritage. The green lungs of the Murley Moss treatment factory had missed a trick. Why not ask for a three-figure donation and install a simple QR code instead. Sponsor the park close to your heart, all items are available…

Horse and cart and ancient coppiced woodland provided the raw materials for the site, which began production in 1857. A huge water wheel (thought to be the second largest in the country at the time) measuring 42 feet 5 inches (13.1m) in diameter was powered by water from the beck. The initial owners and managers of the mill were John Jennings, who leased the site to a Mr W. Helme, owner of Low Mill in Caldbeck. I hung around on my own in the damp conditions for a good half hour, taking photos of the parallel lines formed by dark shadows in the two-storey coppice shed. Opened doorways that housed rippling rooms of colour ornamented with smooth textures like those in Rothko's large Colour Field Paintings. Mythic art, a yearning for transcendence and the infinite. A uniformity of blood-red tones blurred with an even, flat consistency, evoking a feathery, ephemeral dreaminess. Nature's artistry had remained a souvenir for the inns and alehouses, cloth and clog-making, brewing and mining industries along with the mills powered by the *Cald beck* faithful to the end, like a devoted corpse.

On the footpath to the old Matthew Rudding Farm the bells of the primary school rang out across the tranquil village in delicate whirls, to replace the earlier thumping beats of dripping engines. Barely a mile out, in the dreamland where murder ballads stroke on drums, with undulating shame a farm locked up in darkness hid a dead mother lying on the kitchen floor. With the father nowhere to be found, a dark and grim force launched an unnamed sorrow. Two days later he turned up and was immediately arrested and charged with the murder of his wife. She'd been strangled, robbed of her life by 'wilful murder'. The husband, Billy Stalker was branded 'dangerous' after his recent release from a mental asylum. Drifting from land to land amongst the mines of the surrounding fells and isolated communities in the late nineteenth century. There were five deaths and several more falling ill at the Dale Beck Smelter. Nineteen taken from all age groups, among them many children, foul deeds will rise and really get a small town going.

After I'd passed a row of whitewashed cottages, boundary weather invaded the valley floors with a thick grey mist throwing its arms around the fields. Sorting out the sheep from the goats, some of them were being repainted with milk; a helping hand that's the rural charm in the country. Skirting round the market town of Hesket Newmarket, the geological setting proved far more interesting than the boredom of trudging through an endless succession of enclosed mud-spattered fields over and over again. A landscape made by man for man out of the confines of the original forests, but with gates surrounded by a repugnant ring of muck, my interest had started to fade whilst everything smelt of faeces.

Just north of Caldbeck and Uldale, the underlying rock consisted of limestones, sandstones and shales from the Lower Carboniferous age. The fault blocks which practically encircle the Lake District with marine environments dipping radially outwards. In the Caldbeck area rocks vary greatly in their character as limestone thins to the north east between the enclosing walls of the Skiddaw massif in the west and the Pennine range in the east. Looking out from the brow of Hutton Roof earlier, I'd noticed how the western area was dominated by a ridge that includes the three battalions of Blencathra, Bowscale Fell and Carrock Fell. With the rocks predominantly belonging to the Skiddaw slates, in the south east Blencathra and its gentler cousin, Souther Fell, are the boys from the black stuff. In dreams, a scattered troop of ghosts from the eighteenth century gathered a phantom army that was once spied on Souther Fell.

On Midsummer Eve 1735, several gentlemen following horses at a distance, first believed to be huntsman, were then surrounded by an army vast…crowding on and marching off bathed in the light of dread dissolving over the mountain…on the same eve ten years later preceding the 1745 Rebellion, the same vision returned. But this time villagers believed it was an apparition of Bonnie Prince Charlie's attempted uprising. Some even-climbed the mountain top the next morning looking for signs of hoof-prints.

Years later the mirage would be dismissed as an optical illusion, a spectral army caused by the Prince's rebels performing manoeuvres on the West Coast of Scotland. Yet the spirit of '45 marked the passing of a way of life. Which led to Sir Walter Scott lighting a cultural beacon encompassing novels such as *Waverley, The Heart of Midlothian* and *Ivanhoe* to help romanticise elements of Scotland's rich past. Tartan, stags and Highland scenery, a new sense of cultural heritage and identity printed onto a tin of shortbread. Now it forms an assemblage of tart-tat kitsch piped into Edinburgh's Royal Mile presenting a sterile conundrum similar to the vibrant world-class tourist traps on offer at bubbly Bowness. #ScotlandIsNow #theplacetobe...

From Street Head Farmhouse the featureless terrain took me over a number of dilapidated stiles as I made my way gently across sopping wet fields. Against a backdrop of crows that filtered off high and to the right, reminding me a little of Van Gogh's masterpiece, *Wheatfield with Crows*. Like small black flowers that grow in the sky under vast troubled and swirling clouds. Their rasping voices competed with the splish-splosh of my boots squelching in the muck. The painting had been completed just a few months before Vincent walked into a field and shot himself in the chest with a revolver. Although he managed to stagger back to the inn at Auvers, he didn't realise that he had fatally wounded himself. His last reported words, 'La tristesse durera toujours' (the sadness will last forever), were quoted in a letter from his younger brother, Theo, to the second of their three sisters, Elisabeth, who had the rather Machiavellian nickname of 'Lies'. Like a leaf in the autumn, forever delayed the scream to a sigh…

The view from nowhere. There was still no sign of the weather lifting, despite a forecast which said it should have brightened up by now. After I'd been spoilt by the clear blue skies of the last few stages, the pale and dismal milieu mixed with the broad swampy fields had put a large dent in my wavering enthusiasm. The repetition of moving from one isolated farm to the next was starting to take its toll. Even turning to Dugdale in my hour of need didn't prove to be inspiring either…"It becomes readily apparent on this section of our walk that the north east corner of the national park between the Caldew and the northern fells is rarely crossed by walkers." Although I had to strongly disagree with his comments praising the 'well-maintained' stiles. Wandering and condemned in a landscape across the boundary wastes, yanking boots out of the abyss, following the OS app like a bloodhound on the trail of Dame Edna.

Eventually my southerly progression led to the deep trench of the Caldew Valley, and ran into the mountains westward from Mosedale, cut in grey grits and the igneous rocks of gabbro and granophyre. From Hat Cliff View, I gazed fondly at the naked purple breasts of Carrock Fell. At two thousand feet, spectacularly remote amongst the rocky boulders and crags, an Iron Age hillfort is exposed on the top. Built on the margins of the present day national park with a commanding view over what became Inglewood Forest and the passage into the Eden Valley. Film director Tom

Browne's intimate family portrait, *Radiator,* featured scenes shot in nearby Mosedale at his late parents' cottage. About halfway through, one of the main characters escapes to the summit of Carrock Fell after a particularly troubled episode with Leonard (Browne's father in the film). Following a homecoming screening at the 2015 Keswick Film Festival, Browne spoke of the barren terrain whilst filming in the area:

"I am very fond of the Northern Fells, they are wilder and far less popular than the more celebrated fells of the central Lake District and their desolation compliments the film..."

HUTTON ROOF
TO POOLEY BRIDGE

THE GATEWAY FOR BUSINESS OR PLEASURE
REPLACED BY FARMING AND
THE GREEN-TARTAN EFFECT
THE RUSTIC ANTENNA OF COW SNOUT WOOD
ENCHANTED VIGNETTES INTO A NETHER WORLD
EXCITEMENT MIXED WITH DREAD
STRAIGHT INTO THE DOG SHIT OBSESSIVE ZONE
THE JOY OF THICK VERSUS THIN CUT
SWEETEN THE BITTER AFTERTASTE OF BREXIT
HUTTON ROOF TO POOLEY BRIDGE

Thou shalt not poop!

After the muck and desolation of the excursion round Hutton Roof's environs, waking up to yet another wet and dreary morning didn't exactly stoke the boundary fires. Turning on the morning brainwash, a Tory MP was urging Theresa May not to "play Santa Claus" by handing over billions of pounds to the EU. But Downing Street had a new hollow soundbyte up their sleeve: "nothing's agreed until everything's agreed..." The B-word divorce bill.

Suddenly, I'd found all the motivation I needed to get out and hit the next stage, heading south toward Pooley Bridge at the northern end of Ullswater. A little honey-pot of national park tourism, made up predominantly of pubs, gift shops B&Bs and hotels that once split the old counties of Westmorland and Cumberland in two. More recently, Storm Desmond's cursing terror washed away the sixteenth-century bridge over the River Eamont, which flows out of the lake until it reaches the River Eden past Eamont Bridge. Setting off early, in poor visibility on a new route over the A592 Kirkstone Pass, tackling a mountain corridor at nearly 1,500ft above sea level, allegedly riddled with ghosts. A suitably atmospheric mist brushed the fell sides and hid the tops in a thick white vapour. Enflaming the sky, the conditions certainly added to the myths as I wound my way up a number of twisting corners from Troutbeck before reaching the Kirkstone Inn.

The Lake District's *Slaughtered Lamb* and haunting ground of Ruth Ray, a soul turned upside down, said to warn any travellers of the dangers lurking there. Enchanted hearts immobilised in the heavy snowfall of a winter's day on the way back from Patterdale. A phantom frozen and full of light, yet somehow a baby wrapped in warm cloth survived beside her mother's sleeping corpse. Dropping down beside Brothers Water, I ended up stuck behind a Biffa lorry after breezing through Glenridding on the lakeside road round Ullswater. Pulling up in Pooley Bridge some twenty minutes later, I soon encountered the financialisation of society, welcome to rip-off Britain.

Driving up and down the village trying to find somewhere charging half-reasonable rates. To survive the hungry predators of the British holiday trade, tourists must either be wedged up or clued up in this part of town. The weather got worse on the rolling ride from Pooley Bridge to the Hutton Roof dead zone.

Showers came and hovered just above my bike as the rainwater kicked up from the road, sending splats of mud onto my backpack at the same time. On a slight incline passing through the village of Dacre, a group of three or four builders cutting down strips of wood outside the Horse and Farrier pub looked inquisitively at my big boots and bulging backpack before breaking out into titters. Putting their barefaced show of smugness out of my mind for a moment, I soon discovered the cause of their amusement. On a narrow track surrounded by farmland lined with telegraph poles, shaved hedgerows and the odd stretch of stone wall, a red triangular road sign suddenly warned of a one in six (18%) gradient! Ouch...

After blowing hard zig-zagging my way up the steep empty road, the dubious reward was a first encounter with the A66. Get your kicks on the gateway for business or pleasure. Part of the Roman invasion of stone, from Scotch Corner to Penrith and on to the western outpost at Cockermouth. Crossing over a hazy surface full of spray, I pushed on through the long, straight roads of the Greystoke area. With rain and hailstones slanting into my face, from nowhere a stocky lady in a mac and wellies appeared on the left-hand side shackling two panting black labs...

"Not very nice weather is it!" she offered with considerable understatement. Arriving at the junction leading up to the scarp of limestone at Hutton Roof, I decided to lock Knightrider to a sign on the verge. Every minute saved in the unrelenting mizzle felt like a two-fingered riposte to the weather gods.

Behind me the boundaries of the medieval Inglewood Forest marked a drop eastwards from a height of about 1,000ft in the Hutton Roof area across a drift-covered limestone plateau to around 500ft at Carlisle. One of England's largest hunting preserves, the ancient royal forest included Anglian farmers who had crossed the Pennines into the Eden Valley, whilst the ancient British formed a muscular core in the sandstone hills at Penrith. However, the 'Wood of the English or Angles' once famed for its timber had been slowly replaced by farming and the green-tartan effect of coniferous plantations.

Wet through at the start of a ten and a half mile stage, I ignored Dugdale's route over a brown sea dotted with grass-topped islands. Trying to keep the screen of my phone dry was nigh on impossible, so leaving voice notes proved tricky. For the first time in a while, I started on the boundary, striding down the middle of the road under large skies with a cordon of grey cloud encroaching upon everything. Following the distinctive landscape of the Georgian enclosure, there were no landmarks, just a grid of nameless roads lined with copper-coloured hedges topped with wiry birch branches that screened traces of old stone walls, which at one time encircled the 5,000-acre Greystoke Park.

Flat empty fields of enclosure protected by modern wire fences and metal gates had been scoured with tractor marks and buckles of mud. At Scales Farm, I turned left off the road, taking a field track signposted to Scales Plantation, cutting through a rectangular patchwork towards the rustic antenna of Cow Snout Wood. In Dugdale's time he claimed it to be a remnant of what it once was, with half of the wood cut down in a First World War no man's land. But I was just grateful to shelter from the driving rain under the upright Sitka spruce trees, standing to attention like rows of soldiers. Suitably refreshed, I followed the soft solitary path covered with needles and cones through the wood. In some anonymous retreat, small pockets of light framed by dark silhouettes emerged like enchanted vignettes into a nether world. Stirred by the spark of possibilities, I took out my camera and attempted to capture the ghostlike monoculture. The blurred images reflected tear drops seeking the first breaths of the boundary's confession.

The exit from the wood led out onto open moorland and straight back into the wet and wild conditions. A cold blue-grey fog had descended as the wind and rain slanted across the expanse, with Greystoke Forest away on my left, and a long, straight track over to my right passing through a succession of farms towards the A66. Before I reached the road I encountered every walker's nightmare – a large herd of cows with calves. Before I had the opportunity to change course and give them a wide berth their collective radar had locked onto me. There was only a small gap to aim for to get round them and exit through the stile positioned in the bottom right-hand corner of the field.

It reminded me of a similar moment when I'd confronted some black cows in the darkness coming back from a late walk over Cunswick Scar, near Kendal. Foolishly, I attempted to play chicken with the herd and usher them away from a narrow stile in the corner of the field. The cattle had gathered there on a patch of higher ground and it soon became clear that they were not for budging. Holding the line, I pressed on, believing they would magically part, like a miracle of the ages, but to my horror they began to charge downhill instead! In the ensuing panic, I ended up becoming the chicken instead, jumping over the nearest dry-stone wall to avoid the moody cows. Often, I can still remember a large black eye caught by the moonlight glaring at me over the top of an old stone wall. Crouched down in the muck, I could only pray that the herd wouldn't attempt to jump across.

I turned my attention to the south and the A66, as a new determined mood absorbed me on the road through Berrier, after leaving behind the shifting clouds and lashing rain on the open grassy plateau. The views Dugdale mentioned of the Mungrisdale Trench and the striking upthrust of Carrock Fell had been lost to the worst type of boundary weather. Instead, I upped my pace on the C2C cycle route with the distant sound of dogs barking at a kennels hidden in-between a sequence of farms. Broad ridges, old stone walls, rowan and hawthorn trees unfolding parallel to an old Roman road, out on the fringes of Greystoke Forest.

Loitering behind, a dense rectangular block of coniferous plantations, swaying to and fro in a rain of tears. Stay in the 'heart of the Lake District', so the tagline for the picture postcard Whitbarrow Village and Leisure Park goes. Excitement mixed with dread. A dream of dark and troubling things, full of country charm including all mod cons, hot tubs, frisbee golf, a duck pond, entertainment and a bottle of Taittinger on arrival. But there was another greeting next to the CCTV and litter warning signs at the entrance. Formed out of an assemblage of material forms, but mainly spirit bottles with crumpled beer cans and fag packets, Tony Cragg's key to a past time which is our present. You never know what you might find lying around doing it for Van Gogh. Thankfully, I didn't stumble upon a lopped-off left ear like Jeffrey Beaumont did in the strange world of *Blue Velvet*, but I half suspected one might be there.

Type 'Motherby' into an Internet search engine and the results will yield just a couple of pages full of B&Bs, self-catering accommodation and property for sale. Once a street village of grey farms, some from the late seventeenth century, it is now the new pollution ornamented with bird feeders for over-fed birds, spray-painted flowers and kitsch prints of Lakeland cottages in plumes of smoke framed in walnut veneer. Up and coming on the village noticeboard there was a new production to look forward to: The Pirates of Watermillock & the Chasm of Hades! Entering Penruddock, (like Pen-rith) a name formed from the Welsh prefix pen, meaning a head or summit, I walked straight into the dog-shit obsessive zone. With £1,000 penalty warning signs and 'Scoop that Poop!' flyers stuck to the backs of lamp posts everywhere. Maybe they could try seeking some more divine inspiration as an alternative similar to the Cathedral of St John the Divine at the northern end of Manhattan, in the US, whose campaign printed in bold neo-gothic, read 'Thou Shalt Not Poop.' It proved so popular they even started making signs as laptop covers!

Out here in the Penrith suburbs, the back gardens consisted of a curious mix of football nets and topiary hedges. I'd like to think it was a nod to the pleasure gardens of Renaissance Europe that featured mazes and labyrinths evolved from parterre and knot gardens, where the goal in each case was to reach the centre of the garden. The noise of traffic was a reminder that everything passes by the small village on the way eastwards to Penrith about 5.5 miles away, or westbound to the former heavy industries on the coast at Workington. Route 66. A constant flow of trucks, HGVs, 4x4s and SUVs. A land of confusion, collisions and crashes. I typed 'traffic on the A66' into a search engine and the following list appeared:

> accident on A66 cumbria today, is the A66 open today? accident on A66 near keswick today, penrith A66 crash, A66 accident yesterday, A66 accident update, A66 crash death...

The story goes back to the upgrades of the road network in 1971, when the Department of the Environment's proposal to replace the A594 with the A66/M6 Penrith bypass came at the same time as the downgrading of the rail network. One of the main east-west links in the UK, the hundred-mile trans-Pennine odyssey has since been dubbed 'Britain's Worst Road'. Before the M6 opened the floodgates to the north (and put over 20 million people within a few hours' drive of the national park), most Anglo-Scottish traffic used Scotch Corner to avoid the unrelenting grind of the A6 Shap summit. As a result, it became the key location where traffic heading for the west of Scotland left the Great North Road by cutting across the Pennines to get to the A6 at Penrith.

Although this section of the A66 (like many Roman roads) looked fast and furious on the map, it was in fact relatively narrow in places. Many of these 'pinch points' have become modern-day accident black spots. Big wagons, bad weather, higher ground, lower temperatures, heavy traffic, more delays, strong winds, exposed stretches, long diversions and big queues on Bank Holiday weekends. A fatal list for a tourist hot spot in dire need of an upgrade. I had to wait patiently at the road's edge for a few minutes before a momentary lapse of scorching rubber provided an opportunity to cross safely. At least the rain had started to ease a little. On the footpath to Dacrebank, mottled clouds drifted across the sky whilst a grass slope led down to a secluded back lane. From there I aimed left at an abandoned field barn, with slits for air to keep the hay dry, close to St Mary's Well, as the sudden cries of a pheasant running off into a wood surprised the hell out of me.

Time was now the enemy, but at least the escaping tones of Dacre Beck helped to shut out the ongoing assault of the fury road barely 100 yards away. Dacre – 'a trickling stream', a village set in a hollow just inside the national park. Limestone affected by iron staining resulted in a delicate grey-coloured rock that used to be quarried there. This was used to great effect in the Georgian frontage of nearby Dalemain House on the banks of the River Eamont. A grand stately home more renowned for jars of the sticky stuff these days, with its annual Marmalade Festival. The joy of thick versus thin cut, cold toast or mixed with a Martini, something so quintessentially British, it inevitably ended up featuring in the dreaded B-word negotiations reported in a piquant *Financial Times* headline: "Marmalade Brexit row spreads as German MEP preserves humour..."

The irony of allowing marmalade to be called marmalade again in a proposal to help sweeten the bitter aftertaste of the notorious B for many EU citizens...

In the year of Our Lord 698, the Venerable Bede, a spiritual writer from a murdered town, mentioned Dacre as the site of an Anglo monastery. The present Norman church of St Andrew was thought to have been erected on the same spot and features a tower rebuilt in 1810. Soaked through, I wandered inside the old red sandstone construction, with my hood up, carrying a heavily laden backpack. In an idle corner, I sat on one of the long wooden benches sniffling and collecting myself, staring at the stained glass. Everyone needs a Willie – as in Whitelaw, Thatcher's right-hand man. The most recent window had been dedicated to the old Viscount, MP for Penrith and the Border for almost 30 years, and the last commoner to be created a hereditary peer.

There are fragments of two pre-Norman Viking cross shafts, which include the figures of Adam and Eve carved alongside animals and two scenes featuring the tree and the serpent. The restored tower houses three bells: a tenor bell dedicated to St Bartholomew, a middle bell, known as the Blessed Mary Bell, and a treble bell. In the sanctuary, an effigy of a crusader knight from the mediaeval period. There were even traces of proud northern Lady Anne, with links to the time of Edward Hasell of Dalemain, her erstwhile steward. An Elizabethan silver-gilt communion cup that she gave to him was later presented to Dacre Church. It is now in the Treasury at Carlisle Cathedral. Lady Anne also gave a special lock dated 1671, which is still fixed on the south aisle door.

Moving outside, I came face to face with the Dacre Bears, four stone statues believed to be marking the boundary of a sacred pagan site. A puzzle located in the churchyard that has dogged the village for centuries. With the rain punching holes in the sky once more, I cast my eye briefly over a noticeboard brimming with holiday home/parish council services: Lakeland Decorators, Sally's Cottages, Penrith Joinery & Contractors, Cottage House Cleaning and a public meeting about street lights (for Stainton, Newbiggin, Blencowe and Dacre) – "You will have read in the newspaper that if parish residents wish to keep the street lights it could mean an increase in the parish rates. So the parish council wants to know your views!" Someday soon the only light will come from the moon...

I took another short detour to take a couple of photos of Dacre Castle, a relic from the middle of the fourteenth century built as a fortified pele tower and defence against marauding Scottish Borderers. This place marked the point in Dugdale's odyssey where he included a 1967 William

Rollinson drawing of the 39 pele towers around fourteenth-century Lakeland. A hark back to the Age of Destruction, when the whole of the north of England was a treacherous frontier zone in a permanent state of turmoil. Now we have the legacy of George Osborne's Northern Powerhouse, a lacklustre idea full of empty rhetoric that includes renewable generators named after Bond villains. Size mattered like never before, until Osbo received an Asbo once the country voted in a new Age of Self Destruction in 2016.

Still, the castle at Dacre became unique for its 'Room of the Three Kings', where the Kings Athelstan of Scotland, Constantine of Scotland and Eugenius of Cumberland were believed to have met to sign a treaty. Tucked behind a wooden fence with a few sheep merrily grazing near the stream, I left the castellated ramparts and continued left down the road to Dacre Beck, before entering the Eamont Valley filtered by deadly mists within sight of Pooley Bridge at the bottom end of Ullswater.

POOLEY BRIDGE TO KELD

A WINGED VICTORY FOR THE SULLEN
FORMING A SLEEPLESS MILITIA
STARING INTO A METALLIC ABYSS
A NEW LIVING ABSTRACTION
GET TANKED UP ON BEAUTY AND GRANDEUR
THE EVILS OF LATE MODERNITY BREED
A HOTBED OF CRIME
FOR BEAUTIFUL UNIONS UNDER
MIDNIGHT SKIES OF BLUE
EVERYTHING IS LANDSCAPE
DRIPPING WITH THE BLOOD OF NATURE'S DESIRE
POOLEY BRIDGE TO KELD

"There must be some kinda way outta here…"

Pooley Bridge – the hill or mound by the pool. Formerly a fishing village shaken out of its quiet seclusion by the arrival of the Lancaster to Carlisle railway line in the mid-nineteenth century, which brought tourists within a few miles to the head of Ullswater; the Z-shaped polished mirror, about nine miles long, England's second largest lake. The penultimate stage with roughly around 130 miles already covered. All around, familiar weather with grey chinking loops of damp drizzle fashioning a winged victory for the sullen. Out through Kendal on the A6, taking a new route on the right shoulder of the national park.Into the misty void where pylons slowly emerged, forming a sleepless militia, the new watchman of the fringes.

After a fruitless parking debrief in Keld, I turned round and edged into a space just off Main Street at the northern end of Shap. Time was now against me on the long cycle over narrow tracks and B-roads to Pooley Bridge. I soon realised I'd be covering most of the same route on the walk back as I set off on Keld Lane out through a maze of fields ringed by ancient dry-stone walls. The route crossed over the River Lowther onto Wide-worth Farm Road, then past an old red phone box marking some of Cumbria's finest film heritage, eventually hooking up with the B5320 onto Pooley Bridge High Street.

It was a long ride in horrible wet weather, with hilly sections against a strong headwind, everything Knightrider was not designed for! Pulling into an empty national park car park opposite Granny Dowbekin's tea rooms, next to a temporary bridge construction, I locked the bike with dampened spirits in body and mind, contemplating a ten and a half mile stage. Not ideal, so I downed a Muller rebranded Choco-Hazelnut Frijj shake, feeling disappointed by the thinner, less sweet and more watery flavour – not a patch on the old school sugary Spar numbers. Moving round a bend in the road to the left, the sixteenth century bridge marking the county boundary between Cumberland and Westmorland had been washed away in the foaming waters as a result of Storm Desmond's visit. But we know his ilk will come calling again, waters will rise through the earth, bringing landslides and sweeping torrents that flood homes and shops. Once more the streets will be piled high with furniture and white goods forming modern day Towers of Babel. Never Forget. Never Forgive.

In recent years it didn't help that the Sweeney Todd-led Coalition slashed flood defence budgets by 27% in 2010. Not one to mince his words, Richard Ashley, Professor of Flood Resilience at Sheffield University, went on record to expose the fallacy of the Cameron/Osborne freak show, "Extreme weather, political dishonesty, institutional chaos, slack planning, dodgy developments and a continuing refusal to accept that climate change is driving this – we are all working together to create a disaster…" Ultimately, Desmond's legacy was a £123.6 million infrastructure recovery programme, including 1,600 early surveys, 1,234 repair schemes, 174 highway jobs, 754 bridge repairs and 306 civil projects. Even though the wound at Pooley Bridge had been cauterized with a provisional structure, a new bridge would take another five years to be lowered into place.

In the early morning melancholy, pushing to the heart of the present, I stood for a moment to take pictures of a visual homage to Vorticism. Industrial urbanism in a sturdy womblike environment that was unexpectedly providing lines of communication. I had hardly expected to find a 'New Living Abstraction' full of Cubist fragmentation reflecting modern technology. But that's exactly what I saw when staring into a metallic abyss plunging into the heart of the replacement bridge structure.

Founded by the artist, writer and polemicist, Wyndham Lewis in 1914, Vorticism was propelled by a magazine called Blast. Although only two issues were ever published, it was the uncompromising manifestos written by Lewis 'blasting' the so-called effeteness of British art and culture that grabbed the attention. Whilst proclaiming the Vorticist aesthetic, 'The New Vortex plunges to the heart of the Present – we produce a New Living Abstraction'. His artworks combined cubist fragmentation with angular imagery derived from the machine and the urban environment, in a British equivalent to Italian futurism. Other artists involved with the group included the sculptors Sir Jacob Epstein and Henri Gaudier-Brzeska. However, the divine hammer of the First World War quickly brought Vorticism to an end, although Lewis tried another attempt to revive it afterwards, in 1920, with the short-lived Group X.

Tourists arrive on Main Street from one of the Ullswater steamers connecting Howtown and Glenridding. The heritage passenger fleet working towards a sustainable future for the national park. Set sail in Wordsworth Country and get tanked up on beauty and grandeur. Experience the wonderful world of purchasing power in the small gift shops – ice creams, souvenirs, rubber dinghies, guide books, cigarettes and alcohol, all within the shadows of the national park's fantasy world. There was even an air of the seaside about the place as I made my way under scudding clouds between a mixture of signage for B&Bs, pubs and cafés. Some had sprawling patios full of wooden tables and umbrellas, offering home-cooked food and real ales, where you can let the kids run wild and watch the next batch arrive from the jetty.

Old Red made another appearance at St Paul's Church and the Parkin Memorial Hall built in 1911. Regular users read like a roll call of middle

England, with the WI and their famed jam and Jerusalem, craft fairs, a flea market and Lake District National Park slide shows. On the noticeboard outside I discovered a curious mix of adverts featuring Christmas coffee mornings, afternoon tea with carols, "Scoop the Poop" and a £5,000 reward for suspicious person theft leading to the successful prosecution of the perpetrators and safe recovery of such stolen items as: a Honda quad bike, a Scott mountain bike, a strimmer and a chop saw. Even beneath the supposed genteel façade of World Heritage, the evils of late modernity breed a hotbed of crime.

In the late November rain there was hardly another soul about. Only the odd dog-walker and a postman carrying two weighty bags chock-a-block with parcels, the spoils of late-night clickers on phones or tablets, for whom every day is Prime Day. Apart from events like the winter droving two-day festival, the living light of the village is in lockdown mode after the Easter-October season, when the clocks go back and the long winter silence puts everything into slow motion. It's easy to see why the chills and horror of Storm Desmond still slide and writhe around communities that can only repair, regroup and search the sky with sorrow-laden eyes.

Zooming out the view from above on Google maps, Dunmallet's Hill (a name which means 'hill of slaughter' – Wainwright's 'simple after-dinner stroll') was on the other side of the Eamont from Pooley Bridge. What looked like a large head of broccoli was a steeply-wooded conical-shaped fell covered with various types of trees, from conifers to broadleaf, surmounted with Druidical remains. Directly opposite the cloaked woodland, above Howtown, the heavy-backed Swarth Fell rose gruffly from the edge of Ullswater. Vacating the benign fantasy world, I moved out of town from the Memorial Hall onto Roe Head Lane, passing the hidden residential realm of bungalows mixed with a familiar gathering of B&Bs, holiday lets, campers and caravans.

The view started to open up as I gained more height, with dark clouds circling menacingly over Ullswater, whilst immediately behind the autumnal hues lit Dunmallet Hill with a fiery orange and red glow. Striking out onto Moor Divock, a wooden way marker signed to Heughscar Hill signalled my entrance onto the Ullswater Way. After the carnage wrought by the December 2015 storm, a new walking route around Ullswater was devised. Signalled on wooden signs ornamented with a daffodil logo reminiscent of *The Good Life* opening-title sequence, the route brought together existing footpaths with a handful of new rights of way, taking walkers away from the road, particularly on the western edge of the lake.

The 21-mile loop of Ullswater formed part of a national park pilot project set up to identify opportunities and ambitions for a local community within a Lake District Valley.

In 2014, after a six-month consultation period including workshops with local people, the Ullswater Valley Plan was hatched. Since then, the 'Vibrant Communities' slogan has been rolled out, with the Ullswater Way providing 2.5km of new public footpaths while creating a sustainable visitor attraction in the local area. It felt strange to be walking on a designated path surrounded by lakes and mountains, with bare rock underfoot, breathing in the clean, prosperous air of the national park. The complexities of organic life, changeable weather, and the way man continue to shape the landscape.

What all this immediately signified was the introduction of other people! My boundary solitude came crashing down when I began to be confronted with a steady procession of walkers, dogs and fell-runners. Where they all came from and how they all got there I would never know. But in the strange sequence of sunshine and showers, I felt my spirit dissolve into the mountain, shining behind sparkles of bright-coloured rainbows. Compromised through the desolate dreamscape, a violet-grey mist glided off a mosaic carpet of red, yellow ochre, burnt umber and ultramarine. On the soft grassy path, the huge open skies full of cumulus clouds punctured by glowing shafts of light brought a sense of the awe-inspiring nature of the sublime.

Turner developed a taste for the same kind of scenery during his tours of Britain and mainland Europe in the late eighteenth and early nineteenth centuries. Part of the Tate's Turner Bequest features a *Tweed and Lakes* sketchbook that is the principal record of a wide-ranging tour he made up to the Scottish Borders, in the autumn of 1797. Significantly, it marked his first attempts to tackle 'Sublime' landscapes on anything like the kind of grand scale he would become known for. Even though it was thought he still depicted the scenery from a more picturesque point of view, there were several partially coloured drawings that suggested imposing weather conditions or extravagant light effects. He also produced numerous horizontal drawings of Ullswater, mainly along the western shore of the lake showing the cascading Aira Force waterfall. There was a scene looking south from the shore near Stybarrow Crag, towards Patterdale and beyond. Intriguingly, Turner's inscription mistook Hartsop Dodd for Helvellyn, which would not have been seen from his viewpoint.

According to Dugdale, Moor Divock is overrun with ghostly disappearances and visible remnants of Bronze Age antiquities. The principal one of three circles is the Cockpit Stone Circle, a large bank which includes 75 stones brought by the first settlers, who were stone carriers.

Following signs for Askham Fell, I crossed over 'High Street', the Roman highway linking their forts at Brocavum (Brougham Castle) and Galava (Ambleside). It's believed to have followed the line of a much older, prehistoric track, while the highest fell it traverses is named after it. At Sandwick (originally the Old Norse settlement of *Sandewic* derived from 'creek in the sand'), near Howtown on the eastern shore of Ullswater, a group of Roman soldiers were said to have vanished completely after dropping by to fetch drinking water. They were thought to be part of a group who were in the area to build High Street nearly 3,000 feet above the lake. But legend dictates they never returned and not a helmet, sword or shield reflecting the flashing of the light has ever been uncovered.

Passing to the right of Heughscar Hill, the weather turned colder and more unwelcoming, as the bare beauty of the open moorland turned into a mash-up of *An American Werewolf in London* and *Withnail and I*. Plodding on, there were no birds and scarcely any sheep, and according to the OS app I was now walking through a landscape peppered with 'shakeholes', which I would later discover signified a telltale sign of limestone country. I found an old definition of them on a very archaic BBC website page, "A shakehole is a depression in the limestone landscape. In some limestone areas there is a covering of boulder clay about two or three metres thick. Shakeholes are formed where surface water washes the boulder clay down into cracks or fissures in the limestone under the boulder clay. They are usually found in groups..."

With the wind gathering for a final assault, it had become impossible to record voice notes on the exposed approach to the slightly phallic-shaped Cop Stone. A grey glacial erratic about five feet high, leaning slightly northwards, it was smooth and flaked with shades of yellow ochre. Looking out over the top of the stone I could see off into the near future where the reflective chimneys of the Shap granite works belched out new power chords high up into the turbulent skies. After a brief pause to take some pictures, everything darkened black as pitch. Puffing with venom, the most luxurious avalanche of the day was then duly unleashed. But I could find no hiding place dropping down off the moorland towards the southern edge of Helton – 'a place on the side of a hill'.

Now I was heading into the heart of *Withnail* country, after crossing the River Lowther and skirting the small hamlet of Whale. Entering the Lowther Valley had also marked a geological shift from carboniferous limestone to the more craggy Borrowdale Volcanics, mostly found in the central areas. I walked swiftly on a track lined with either hedgerows or moss-covered stone walls surrounded by large patterns of enclosures dating back to the late eighteenth century. For the first time in ages, the reassuring song of sparrows, robins and blue tits made their presence felt, darting in amongst the handful of withered trees and bushes lining the route. I kept on, striding through the flat, relatively barren environment of ol' Wicked Jimmy's back yard. Once again under shifting skies, moving from farm to farm walking parallel with the river.

Heading for Knipe, with the well-known speech of crows debating noisily amongst themselves, as if they owned the place. As I scooted past a conifer plantation a gruesome sight reared up on the road; ceased to exist, giving its goodbye. It was the carcass of a rabbit, with tufts of fur and bits of skin scattered on the road. Its neck looked to have been mangled while the chest had a few puncture marks. With the tall conifers just up the road to perch on as a lookout, it bore all the hallmarks of a buzzard kill. But I hadn't heard or seen any for a while. I felt sure they wouldn't be far away though, especially with such rich pickings left out in the open.

Further on, at the bottom of a downslope, the mowed lawns and manicured driveway of Knipe Hall emerged. An early seventeenth-century, Grade II Listed period farmhouse, set in three acres of private land, for beautiful unions under midnight skies of blue. It was a wedding venue with self-catering accommodation attached, where guests can turn a whiter shade of pale in the old hayloft now a 'party barn'. Next to a stone wall, one of Gilbert Scott's cherished emblems of Britishness had been turned into a community information hub...

"Welcome to the phone box at Knipe. Have a nice day and please come back again."

There were notes about walks in the area and also an advert for the Bampton Remote Cinema, but with no film listings or any other details. Descending carefully through a field submerged in water, I headed over the River Lowther on a bouncy footbridge pursued by a mysterious dog-walker who had unexpectedly surfaced out of some trees. Thankfully, he was no madman on the prowl with eels. I soon lost sight of him on the elevated muddy embankment close to the edge of the river, moving ever closer to another red phone box, a modern-day site of film pilgrimage. But, I have to admit, Bruce Robinson's semi-autobiographical masterpiece used to drive me up the wall when working alongside former colleagues who would try to quote it word for word. Usually very badly and always after a few ales of course!

It seems strange to think why *Withnail and I*, a low-budget film about two failed actors trudging around the outskirts of the Lake District, would endure for so long. But it has...Now I could truly empathise with the main characters, having been submerged on a similar walk, (minus cake and fine wine). One of the best British cult movies ever made, it's still hard to believe Richard E. Grant (a lifelong non-smoker and teetotaller) played a flamboyant alcoholic in a trench coat throughout his first ever major film role!

The film also featured one of the most famous trophy boltholes in Cumbria, albeit without a regulation welcome pack. These days, most places provide either fresh fruit or herbal teas, hot chocolate or even a glass of prosecco, all of which might have helped soothe Withnail's "bastard behind the eyes". Oddly enough, a few days before embarking on the stage, I caught a snippet of a Desert Island Discs episode with Christopher Nolan, who had picked the track 'Marwood Walks' from the original soundtrack as one of his choices, whilst reflecting on the underlying melancholy in the film that he had noticed more and more as the years went by.

Standing in a steamed-up Bampton phone box on Wideworth Farm Road, I began leafing through all the film quotes left behind by fans in the 'signing in book'. Dating back to 2016, the list was endless, a quirky tradition burning bright for a country still coming down from the modern B-word trip...

"Scrubbers, scrubbers, scrubbers..."
"What do you think of Desmond Wolfe?"
"Came a long way to see this phone box – are you the farmer?"
(all Dave & Steph)
"I found this by accident...I came on holiday by mistake" (Womble)
"Flowers are simply tarts; prostitutes for the bees..." (Constantine)

Bampton – the place of the beam...A small village just over four miles west of Shap, near the point where the river Lowther is joined by a stream from Haweswater. The former reservoir with a hollowed-out lake had previously been a U-shaped valley completely transformed by the building of a dam and the raising of the water level. Everything is landscape in the immersed village of Mardale, mercilessly eroded by water deeper than tombs. Removing the boundary between the natural and the artificial, trying to suit the almost unquenchable demands of the urban sprawl. 'Architecture as constructed ground', Alvar Aalto's approach, the Finnish designer who viewed painting and sculpture as "branches of the tree whose trunk is architecture".

On the outside of the stone shelter, next to the phone box, the noticeboard was already gearing up for Christmas with adverts for coffee mornings and a concert by the Penrith Singers. In the window of the tea shop in the heart of the village, a display had been cobbled together with Polaroids of Bampton and notelets, jars of Blossom Honey, a short break to the Lake District guidebook (with routes), some bottles of Lakeland Lager, Hawkshead beer, Kendal Mintcake and, with characteristic detachment, a perfunctory Withnail/Bampton greetings card. Half a mile away, Bampton Grange contained cottages dating from the early eighteenth century undergoing several refurbishments, along with a rare Anglican Church dedicated to St Patrick, said to have walked there in 540AD after being shipwrecked on the Duddon Sands.

In steady rain, I stood to watch and listen to a farmer on a quad bike barking out orders to his two collie dogs. He was attempting to herd a flock of Swaledales through a narrow field gate. Fat wheels, a mud splattered vehicle and a mob compressed into a tight spot. I noticed while one of the dogs barked and chased, the other stayed perfectly still, giving the sheep such an evil look they duly ran in the opposing direction.

The end of all our dreams...In the rapidly fading light, the ruins of Shap Abbey cried out from the misty gloom of early evening. Religion's message clear: denial, guilt and fear, prayers of the naive and the lies people believe. Walking parallel with Rosgill Hall Wood, the wet conditions of the Lowther Valley worsened, hindering visibility to a filmy veil. In the bleak expanse leading up to the Abbey, I started to wonder whether I would actually see anything through the scattered troop descending all around. But slowly the compact outline of the western tower started to reveal itself, gently poking over the screen of limestone crags overshadowed with trees, like a ghost rider in the sky.

The grey ruin of the Premonstratensian order, once an important hospice for any weary travellers on the way to Carlisle or the south. For a moment, I started to entertain thoughts of slithering down the muddy slopes to try and find a way in. But then quickly dismissed such ideas as foolish fantasy when I remembered the retreat was owned by the English Heritage warm bath of expensive nostalgia. Above a line of trees, I took a handful of photos as the site's haunting scent swung roughly in the swelling breeze. Fragments of the thirteenth-century church remained, although Lord Wharton plundered the lead and roofs in the dissolution of 1540. Stuart House situated close by sheltered a retreating Bonnie Prince Charlie in December 1745, after the ill-fated Jacobite Rebellion. In the seventeenth century, the Abbey was raided again when stone was brought to the village to build a market hall.

Awakened from the drift, a strange grinding sound distracted me from the monastery's lost souls. It turned out to be coming from a solitary crow perched in a dark, scrawny tree, about twenty yards further down the valley to my right. Next to it, crammed side by side onto the main cross branch of a sturdy oak, a committee of unkindness sat in deathly silence. I turned back to the broken and breathless bird suspended on its own gallows pole, my staring eyes dripping with the blood of nature's desire...

KEEP
OUT

SHAP
TO PLUMGARTHS

THE SMOKING GUNS OF A
BORN-TO-RULE MINORITY
DISINTEGRATION LOOPS
BIGGER AND BETTER
THROUGH THE ARSE-END OF NOWHERE
A BARREN GRAVEYARD FOR DAMNED SOULS
ANOTHER EMPTY SLOGAN FOR THE
ULTRA-LOCALS
INDUSTRY AS THEME PARK
SCATTERING JOYS AND SORROWS ON IMPULSE
LIKE NATURE IN ITS BLACK ORBIT
GNAWED BY THE SORES OF HALF-TRUTHS
SHAP TO PLUMGARTHS

Here's where the story ends...

> "To Shap! What on earth can take you to Shap?
> There are no shops at Shap."
> (Alice Vavasor's Grandpapa, in A. Trollope's *'Can You Forgive Her?'*)

Anthony Trollope's 1864 novel featured a society in which the main routes into power were for the one per cent born into money and influence (rather than talent or truthfulness). Something that is still a depressingly familiar theme in today's heavily divided country. Especially given that more than half of the donations made in the 2016 EU referendum campaign came from just ten wealthy donors, according to the open government organisation, Transparency International. "Take Back Control" said the small millionaires club of the ultra-wealthy elite. Where six of the top ten donors who supported the Leave campaign gave almost £9.5 million, whilst the overall donations stacked up to £17.5 million – almost exactly one vote for every pound given towards the B-word delusion. Even the Remain donations totalled £14.2 million. All of which meant that just over half of the country voted for 'a series of possibilities' funded by the smoking guns of a born-to-rule minority; who chose to focus ruthlessly, blatantly and often disgracefully on immigration.

In another fantasy land...The Pet Shop Boys borrowed Trollope's book title for a single that featured a video of the duo wandering around a CGI landscape dressed as Coneheads, while feeding bread to a fat gaggle of geese in Battersea Park. The disintegration loops of yesterday, today and tomorrow...

On the way through Kendal, it was one of the few mornings I'd had to scrape a heavy frost off the car. Fern was talking tripe on Radio Cumbria. On this occasion, it was the chambers of the stomach variety – Would you? Could you? For once, I agreed with the son of a Butcher, 'Hell no!' Dashing along the last stretch of the A6, waving goodbye to the sweeps of Skelsmergh, Longsleddale and Low Jock Scar, I held hands with the boundary for the last hurrah. Just before a series of snaking bends, I pulled into a layby to park up. Hoisting Knightrider out of the back, staring up with considerable trepidation at the steep route directly ahead. The A6 over Shap summit. *A true snorter...*

Pedalling circles passing rock after rock, granite-grey as morning. Although freezing, the weather had played fair, with bright, clear blue skies and only a minor headwind. In truth, once I'd found the lowest gear possible, it became just another case of head down; build up the rhythm without looking up. On the long drag uphill, the main hindrance came from the odd van or truck, often accelerating past a little too close for comfort. On the summit a memorial stone paid tribute...

> To the drivers and crews of vehicles that made possible the social and commercial links between north and south on this old and difficult route over Shap Fell before the opening of the M6 Motorway. Remembered too are those who built and maintained the road and the generations of local people who gave freely of food and shelter to stranded travellers in bad weather...

Directly opposite the entrance to the Cemex Blue Quarry, I locked the bike to a parking sign, downed another chocolate milkshake and crossed over the A6. Wickers Gill flowed behind the grassy bank where I'd left Knightrider, zigzagging toward the River Lowther swelling with excess water from the triangular shaped Wet Sleddale reservoir. On land once owned by Shap Abbey, the manmade construction supplied fresh water to Manchester, while extracted water was carried through tunnels to the neighbouring Haweswater. It was also overlooked by Uncle Monty's infamous holiday home – Crow Crag. Another site of pilgrimage for *Withnail* fans, who gather in the courtyard to pay homage to their sozzled heroes at sold out screenings of the film every July.

Suitably, the final stage meant linking with the other two extensions made to the national park boundary on 1 August 2016. The national park labelled them the 'East extension areas', which included Birkbeck Fells Common, Whinfell Common, Bretherdale and Borrowdale within the parishes of Orton and Tebay. Bigger and better – no longer inferior, now the unduly forgotten fringes were part of the vibrant centre, armed with the designated badge of World Heritage to boot. Passing through the soft tones of Wasdale to Borrowdale Beck, my own song was nearly ended. Shap Fell itself, wild and uncultivated, a wasteland connecting nothing with nothing. Early in the morning of 28 November 2017, standing in the middle of the A6, identifying with Alice's Grandpapa, wondering what on earth was I doing there?

Avoiding all contact on another walk into a long stretch of time, the shadowy depths where no shelter grows to shield. Don't get me wrong, I have always been captivated by the desolation of open moorland, especially on an expanse swathed in ghostly manifestations. "Gaan ower Shap" was a time-honoured memory, along with the haunting appearance of a shape-shifting phantom, long associated with a death omen. In *Shappe in Bygone Days* (1904), Reverend Joseph Whiteside reported the existence of a 'dobby' or bogey that took on the form of a large black dog. More recently, in 1988, J.A. Brooks set about reinforcing the old legend where local people believed fatal accidents were foretold by the sighting of a black dog, due to the hazardous conditions in winter. It would always appear in the same place, running in front of cars for a few yards before leaping over a stone buttress to a drop some 300 feet below. Shap Fell, once described as, "the southern boundary of our civilisation...passing south of it is only for the brave, the mercenary or the foolish."

At that moment, I too felt a little foolish. After cycling through the arse-end of nowhere, into the echoes of silence cast adrift from the national park place myth. Under the shadow of pink and igneous rocks, a barren graveyard for damned souls and broken-down vehicles, a rarely visited rat-run for home delivery vans and trucks loaded up with aggregates. A little over twenty years ago, Andy Goldsworthy retraced a route from the Scottish borders across isolated areas of Cumbrian hillside. It was for a project designed to mark some of the drove roads in which sheep and cattle were once driven over the border to markets in England.

Using maps to identify the ancient sites of sheepfolds, Goldsworthy paid particular attention to those vital layers of rural history in order to select locations for a symbolic arch he would construct at various points on the journey south. At first, he made a red sandstone arch at Spango Farm, Dumfriesshire, out of blocks from Locharbriggs in Scotland. After leaving it overnight, it was photographed before being dismantled, with the rocks placed on a trailer and driven down to Longtown, the first site in Cumbria. So began a ritualistic trail of goodwill that stopped at places in Carlisle and Penrith, eventually arriving by a stream at Shap Beck Quarry, where a wash-fold once stood. On the curve of carboniferous limestone north and west from Ravenstonedale to Cockermouth, Goldsworthy stood his arch with one foot in the beck, the other on the bank. It was placed within earshot of the A6, moving south to Shap, next to where a steel bridge carried the West Coast railway line over the beck.

The next arch took shape in the layby of a ten-metre high quarried limestone face near Shap beside a large cattle-float and trailer – pens-on-wheels. The modern day drovers bringing slaughter for fuel, only a few years before the temporary halt of movement for all animals. An event that occurred after the shit hit the fan during the foot-and-mouth outbreak. Day in, day out, from dawn to dusk. The mental anguish of watching thousands upon thousands of animal carcasses destroyed as life fell to dust. One, maybe two, sometimes three farms a day were visited by slaughter teams who brought silence to livelihoods in the space of just a few minutes.

At the time, part of Nick Utting's role as the General Secretary of the National Farmers' Union in North Cumbria became relaying the brutal effects on the lives throughout the rural communities affected. Mostly to outsiders (including politicians), who naturally found it difficult to understand the devastation caused by such a terrible plague. The subsequent NT document, *A Vision for the Lake District after Foot and Mouth,* was thought to be a 'watershed' moment for the area. Just over fifteen years later one of the 'biggest' ideas from it has now been realised, with the designation of a cultural landscape World Heritage Site. But the social, economic, environmental and cultural issues, especially the problems of local housing and the restoration of a viable, sustainable, local economy, are still as prevalent as ever.

Goldsworthy placed his third arch just outside the national park on Main Street in Shap town centre. On the pavement in damp and grey conditions, in front of a trio of arches on the Market Cross, a charismatic building dating from the time of the Market Charter in 1687. He described his own arch as "another animal of the same species", even though the cross's many eyes and brows were captured by the building, while his "was still free". At one time the three arches were open, containing the stalls of towns-folk selling their produce. During the nineteenth century, the building was a dame school that eventually went on to accommodate the Shap library service until 2002. Now the coursed rubble, slate roofs and stone ridges house regular monthly meetings of the parish council, the remnants of Cameron's 'Big Society', yet another empty slogan.

Another location Goldsworthy used included the M6 between Shap and Tebay. Here, the sandstone arch lodged on two glacial erratic boulders that flowed down the Vale of Eden some 400 million years ago, swinging to the west around the northern Lake District. With one side higher than the other, steady rainfall turned the sandstone arch a deep red, contrasting perfectly with the crushed tarmac of the bleak motorway behind.

Nearby, between the bastard countryside of the Lake District and Yorkshire Dales National Parks, Tebay Services provides fugitive couples with a chance to elope. An escape to the middle of nowhere, a couple of minutes off the M6, in the poetic edgelands of Farley and Symmons Roberts, Tebay was the new Gretna Green.

At the start of the chain-linked public footpath through Blue Quarry, I was confronted by a map. Industry as theme park – roll up, roll up…please adhere at all times to the prescribed routes. It had been put up next to a small hut (presumably the site office) surrounded by an iron fence protected by a set of barriers. Highlights on the tour included the West Mainline track, a Hippo-wash that swallowed mud, and great big charcoal-grey dunes formed by the gravel and extraction-supply spaceports. Theirs was a blend of style and substance, 'Building Better Into everything – the needs of the built environment balanced with a firm set of commitments to the natural environment.'

An eerie silence engulfed the empty car park; the only other sign of life came from a handful of sheep munching away on the moorland arcing south outside the site. Alongside the perimeter fence a public bridleway was sandwiched between the tilting sickness offered by the Pendolino trains and the free-flowing sparkling movement on the M6. Over on the other side, the A6 roller coaster rattled gently into retirement. Shap granite, one of the finest and most distinctive rock types in Cumbria, is known for its coarse texture and large pink crystals, the main features are the megacrysts (a large well-formed crystal set in a fine groundmass), and its separation into darker and lighter variations.

Blue Quarry sits on the Dent Subgroup, underlain by lavas and tuffs (volcanic ash) of the Borrowdale Volcanic Group. Whilst the Shap granite outcrop is a small intrusion and broad metasomatic aureole (metamorphic changes caused by chemically active fluids penetrating and migrating through rock) beginning at the junction between the Borrowdale Volcanic Group and the Windermere Group to the south. The rock of ages became widely used across the UK as a building stone, particularly with the advent of railways in Victorian times when the Albert Memorial, St Pancras Station and Piccadilly Circus were all constructed out of it. From Eros to graveyards, polished Shap granite headstones and monuments started to appear frequently in Victorian and Edwardian graveyards as well.

Intriguingly, a quick look at the OS app informed me that the boundary ran directly through the centre of Blue Quarry, before following the southern route of the A6 over Shap Fell and beyond. My own route passed underneath the ranks of a formidable bank of pylons stretching their fingers out across the Pennines into ethereal bounds. With a new sense of renewal I strode away from a future hewn out of ancient rock, heading for the starry spheres of a somnium continuum, where memory stripped a kaleidoscopic dreamscape, and one note soothed souls banished to off-world colonies. Out here a familiar choice presented itself – north or south over the 1,350 foot summit to the other side.

Exiting the quarry, I continued on the straight track of original coaching highway past a small coppice resonating with birdsong. The open moorland habitat encompassed a complex mosaic of blanket bog and dry heath. Pink bell-shaped *Erica tetralix* flowers (cross-leaved heath), enrobed the upland, intermingled with dense mats of compact bog moss displaying an autumnal mix of yellow, orange and brown. A shimmer of pink heather, the bushy *Calluna vulgaris* dwarf shrub was also dominant, along with tussocks of purple moor grass, *Molinia caerulea*. Crossing a threshold I came to a sheep-holding pen constructed out of corrugated iron protected by metal barriers. Sprayed in gold on a set of wooden doors locked with rusted bolts, a warning, "Keep Out", accompanied by a couple of question marks to add a sense of bewilderment. In the eerie tomb-like ambience, I half expected something to start rising out of the ground, just like at the end of *Carrie* when a hand comes out of the grave.

The events section of the modern day Shap Wells Hotel website looked like a roll call from *Phoenix Nights*. Showcasing a series of Irish Country Music gigs, disco nights, various tribute acts with Showmadymady, Badness and the pseudo Scandinavian fiends – Swede Dreamz. The hotel originally opened in the early nineteenth century when it quickly gained notoriety for the remedial properties of the waters pulled out from the well in the grounds of the current building. It was closed in 1939 and opened as a prisoner-of-war camp in 1941, during the Second World War, after the Government requisitioned the premises for officers, NCOs and petty officers, mostly from German U-boats. It didn't reopen for hotel business again until 1947. Incredibly, after the war, some of the imprisoned German officers brought their families over to stay in the same bedrooms they had occupied whilst incarcerated there.

Continuing south over the access track leading down to the hotel, I kept straight ahead for half a mile or so, eventually meeting the A6 again. Another large conifer plantation had come into view on my right below Long Fell, at around the same time as I issued a final lament to voice notes. In the washed-out valley raked by an uncontrollable beast, the wind was all powerful and destructive, scattering joys and sorrows on impulse. On a well-used public bridleway, the steady gradient led toward Packhorse Hill. Entering the 'safety corridor' of a rejected and ignored landscape littered with warning signs, patrolled by zones of power sheltering forestry workings. There was even an abandoned fridge next to some frayed cables and a few hefty slabs of grey rock.

I stood next to them for a while, charting a mutant juxtaposition of roads, traffic, trains, quarries, pylons, plantations, fells, streams, becks and, slicing through it all, the national park boundary. In the science of patterns I had found a true in-between place within vaults of unredressed melancholy. Like nature in its black orbit, we were slowly being destroyed and projected into the music. Directly opposite, stood a hunk of intrusive rock now a geological conservation area.

Singing up the boundary, Shap Pink Quarry – a concept in the mind just like Uluru/Ayers Rock, but this was a song scattering a trail of columns and façades throughout the north of England and beyond.

Birkbeck Fells Common – motorcycles and 4x4 vehicles prohibited! A pattern of marked contrast with abandonment and loss, blocks of coniferous forestry, networks of masts and lines of intrusive pylons – simple, open and relatively unbroken. The fells offer a far-reaching and vividly alluring 360-degree panorama of the surrounding upland areas incorporating the Howgills, Orton Fells, central Lake District, North Pennines escarpment and south to Bowland. Hard to access, wild and remote, the decay and renewal on the exposed moorland was highlighted with isolated stone buildings or disintegrating enclosure walls in need of repair. Solitude and tranquillity in the margins emptied of people. Lakes to Dales…In Natural England's 2009 Boundary review of the Birkbeck Fells and Whinfell Evaluation Area, the main incongruous features were the presence of pylons, the noisy M6 corridor and West Coast Mainline railway…along with the lack of tree cover and its elevation (being similar to or slightly lower than the constant hum of energy and communication).

From afar in the lonely wilderness I could just make out the faint cries of a voice. It called with shadowy echoes from the middle and north of the moorland. Stretching all true realities, a dead soul was pleading for someone to take away a dream that had failed to measure up to reality. In a chill of hopelessness the ghostly sounds started to circle a ruin, gnawed by the sores of half-truths and empty promises. Harsh words, broken lives, burning bridges, a prayer for the dying…

In the middle of the empty road I watched a puff of purple haze blow over the summit of Shap Fell. A storm seemed poised to hit as I stared out onto a sombre landscape twinned with the cover of Springsteen's *Nebraska*. A place where time still flowed as sluggishly as the vans and trucks did in the 1970s. When engines whined and overheated prior to the winds of change that shepherded in the M6.

Moving on past an isolated repeater station, housing a creature lodged in ice taken over by *The Thing*. For some reason it reminded me of the Norwegian base in John Carpenter's classic. *Anytime.Anywhere.Anyone.* Especially for those unfortunate enough to be stranded overnight in the dead of winter when the A6 can be snowbound and impassable.

With the light starting to ebb it was nearly time to say farewell to the boundary, so I descended off a silhouetted Whatshaw Common, before dropping to the valley floor. Here I saw a fine example of a monkey-puzzle tree at Hause Foot Farm, next to a bridge over Crookdale Beck. Hemmed in on all sides by the imposing Shap Fells, with only one track in and out, strangely I felt more of a keen sense of isolation here than on the bare summit loitering above. But then, right on cue, a red post-office van hurtled towards me on the access road. Entering the lesser known Borrowdale Valley and crossing over a beck of the same name, the steep ramp up to Hollowgate brought me back onto the A6 again. From this vantage point a huge panorama opened up looking southwards towards Kendal into Yorkshire, and out into the white-out of the Irish Sea. By contrast, Ashstead Fell, to my left, had been given a Mohican, with both sides of its conifer plantation shaved off, the boundary remained an area of non-conformity right to the end.

When I eventually reached the car and collected Knightrider, I would be completing the final few miles by road, with Dugdale's spirit occupying the passenger seat. Passing through the quaint little hamlet at Garnett Bridge, populated with old mill cottages next to the River Kent. The last fragments mired in Desmond's legacy, with bridges and road closures almost two years after the event. For the first time in a while I would see sparrowhawks patrolling the hedgerows, their high pitched *giu giu* cries sounding strangely comforting, along with the familiar subsong from grumpy crows. The last kickback would come from a heavy rain shower, slanting into the windscreen on the narrow lanes around Bowston. With the spray kicking up on the A591 past the Whalebones, in the rear view a rainbow formed over both sides of the road. Back at the will-o'-the-wisp headlights of unseen spirits at Plumgarths, tuning into Radio Cumbria blasting out the air-punching "Alive and Kicking", stay until your love is...

Before the final illusion with the story about to end, I trudged the last few steps round the corner of the aptly named Muddy Brow. Suddenly, a hot dog packet caught my eye on the grass verge barely a few yards in front. *Nature Vibe*, it's that little souvenir...Cautiously picking up the predominantly black card packaging, I soon realised my naive mistake.

"A bestseller: 17cm long, 3.5cm in diameter with throbbing veins. Sometimes gentle, sometimes impetuous – whatever your needs at the time."

Tossed aside by the girding chorus of George Shaw's dithyrambic nymphs, hedge porn, patrolling the edges beating timbrels with high-fives.

Discover. Explore. Inspire.

One twist of the regulator is enough...

NATURAL VERSUS CULTURAL

EXPAND THE BORDERS
LAKES TO DALES
HELSINGTON BARROWS, SIZERGH FELL,
LYTH VALLEY, BIRKBECK FELLS COMMON,
WHINFELL COMMON
POETS, PAINTERS AND (EVERYDAY) PEOPLE
BREXIT - 56.4% VOTE LEAVE IN CUMBRIA
GHOSTS OF NOSTALGIA'S PAST
#THEPLACETOBE #WEARETHELAKES
SECOND-HOME SYNDROME
LOVE THE LAKES
LIFE ON THE MARGINS
TOUCHING THE BOUNDARIES
NATURAL VERSUS CULTURAL

Natural versus Cultural:

Like most things, it all started on a Monday...
When Britain's largest national park formerly opened on 13 August 1951. In the same year George VI opened the Festival of Britain, The Archers began, zebra crossings were introduced and Tottenham Hotspur were crowned champions of the old First Division Championship and the long road to World Heritage Status had just been initiated. Expand the borders; boost the pearl of rural tourism, everyone's a winner (unless you happen to reside on the outside of course). But then, for the next sixty years or so, nothing much happened, size-wise.

In the first ten years the tinkling of electricity to the valleys sparked the sound of a dreamscape. Poles and pylons – contentious blots on the landscape flowing with tensions and disputes. The answer – screen them with trees wherever possible, otherwise introduce a zoning scheme. But the landscape and visual aspect issues refused to go away.

In 2016 the National Grid's plans to build giant pylons the size of Nelson's column highlighted the divide between the inside and outside of the national park. Cumbria became a county of two halves, pastoral and sublime versus nuclear. The shock of the new. From the outside looking in, the National Grid had a bright idea – route the lines underground within the national park, and remove any existing pylons forming part of the current line. But then let them re-emerge on the outside, within tens of metres of the boundary for some eight miles or so – crossing divides. Conservation groups such as FLD (along with other campaigners like the American author Bill Bryson) claimed the beautiful national park countryside doesn't just end at a fixed boundary.

Before sparks flew across the margins, the old met the new in late autumn, October 2015, when approval for expanding the boundary in three different places was finally granted. Lakes to Dales, time to slip on the corporate jacket and talk landscape sense. Chief Executive Leafe cited the 'many people' who dubbed the historic moment sixty years of 'unfinished business', from the original drawing up of the national park boundary. But the landmark decision had not come easily; it had been the result of what he vaguely called 'many, many years of work'. Yet, what did all these years of work really add up to? For the LDNPA a tiny increase in size of 3%, or 27 square miles to be precise.

Leafe's reaction to the news was filmed up the road from their Murley Moss offices next to ASDA in Kendal (just outside the boundary). Smiles and special places go hand in hand on the new perimeter and, with it, an additional 300 cheers rang out. From Helsington Barrows down to Sizergh

Fell and onto the Lyth Valley, along with Birkbeck Fells Common to Whinfell Common. Now a new total of some 41,100 lived inside this unique corner of England. By contrast, the Yorkshire Dales National Park grew by almost a quarter at the same moment. With the M6 forming a new boundary between the two national parks.

According to Chief Executive Leafe, the decision taken by the Department for the Environment, Food and Rural Affairs was a firm vote of confidence from both government and public alike. Now there would be even more recreational opportunities and even more outdoor activities. It also provided another shot in the arm for Cumbria Tourism's Adventure Capital plans. Widen the paths and ready the zip wires.

#WeAreTheLakes...

But the conservationists disagreed, not everyone wants to live in Disneyland, Cumbria. The Sandford Principle applies – if there is any conflict, protecting the environment must always take priority. After all, butterflies only come to pretty flowers. Poignantly, conservation body Natural England had first suggested the Boundary extensions in 2009, with a public inquiry launched in 2013. As a result, more than 3,000 objections and representations were submitted, before the recommended extensions got the final thumbs up.

It proved quite a turnaround from earlier on that same year, when the cash-strapped national park attempted to sell off some of its best-known assets. In the shop window, the most eye catching amongst all the properties and woodland areas became available for a measly guide price of £20-30,000. Yours for the equivalent of four top-notch quad bikes, the much loved Stickle Tarn, situated below the iconic Langdale Pikes. Bringing to an end with a single stroke the old 'You can't put a price on that' adage. Leading the chorus of disapproval, the local South Lakes MP finally had a purpose. An admirer of Her Majesty's selfless service to Britain, he likened the situation to selling off England's crown jewels. Facing repeated calls for his head, the chief executive attempted to downplay the predictable boos and hisses. "There is nothing unusual in the transfer of public to private." But petitions were raised, signatures gathered, and the spirit of Beatrix Potter summoned – national park or nationalised park?

Nature had been thrust back into the English imagination once again. In response, the beleaguered national park authority adopted a belt and braces approach. Public access would be woven into any deals. "Trust us!" they pleaded, whilst more sell-offs were being plotted at the newly dubbed, *Surly Moss* joke factory. Somewhere in amongst the slings and arrows came the real truth, "Our model for running the national park is not based around the principle of public land ownership." Still mired with the fall out of austerity, while nursing the impact of savage Government cuts, hard heads were called for. In the end, it turned out to be a phoney war. Yet who owns the national park is still the number one, frequently asked, question on their own website. Surprisingly to some, the LDNPA owns a meagre 4%. The power in the land is still dished out amongst organisations such as the NT, United Utilities, Forestry Commission and private landowners. And then, back in December 2010, an old sideshow rolled into the heart of the aspiring Adventure Capital...

After a comprehensive spending review, the new Coalition Government formed in 2010 slashed the LDNPA's budget by 28.5% over the next four years. In-between the inevitable staff cuts and land sales that followed, they also shortlisted the Lake District for nomination to UNESCO as a World Heritage site. Back the Bid, but don't expect us to shell out for it. Ultimately, it proved to be third time lucky after two failed bids in the latter half of the 1980s. Some said it was the three Ps that won it – poets, painters and (everyday) people. The butcher, the farmer, the ranger and then - makes no difference what group I'm in. Once again, they rolled out Leafe to heap praise on a momentous decision, "It puts us right up there with some of the world's most iconic landscapes and buildings."

Almost immediately, they sought a special kind of person to oversee an ambitious Management Plan aimed at solving all the long-term hot potatoes: climate change, upland farming, affordable housing, the nuclear industry and volume of traffic. Yet quite extraordinarily, the omnipotent B-word did not merit a single mention amongst the 700 odd pages supporting the bid. A fact not lost on national park tormentor-in-chief, George Monbiot, who pointed out, "The entire vision relies on the economic viability of the farming system – which depends in turn on subsidies from the European Union."

Monbiot believed the British countryside was headed for a Grim Reaping. With the fallout from Brexit casting a long shadow over sheep farming, due to a potential £3bn black hole. Suddenly, animals and words were treading the same careworn paths. Unexpectedly, the deep pockets of rich landowners could suffer. The more land you owned, the more subsidies you stood to lose.

Media darling Monbiot was certainly no stranger to controversy. He has long questioned how what he calls the Lake District National Park Authority's 'sheep museum' would be sustained. Whilst putting a muddied boot into the award of World Heritage Status at the same time. Infamously calling the area an 'ecological disaster zone, shagged by the white plague.'

Paradoxically, Monbiot (the great agent provocateur and King of the sound bite) believes that one day, national parks could become the great rewilders.

On 23 June 2016, 56.4% of people in five out of the six areas of Cumbria voted to Leave the EU. Only South Lakeland (the area predominantly in the national park) voted to Remain. Immediately, as the pound faltered, eyebrows were raised due to the sky-high price of some necessities. Ever since the triggering of Article 50, trade across European boundaries threatened to wander aimlessly into no man's land. The ghosts of nostalgia's past had turned a blind eye to over seventy years of peace. Somewhere between the shadows and whispering voices lay a whitewashed pandemonium nobody voted for. If you wanted a vision of the future, imagine piles of empty coffee cups, stacks of dirty pots, unwashed linen and unwiped arses. Should I stay or should I go now? Hard, Soft, Deal or no Deal, In or Out. With the constant threat of fewer staff to choose from, low wages and high rents, the post-Brexit landscape gave the national park a new set of mountains to climb.

How the overall outlook has changed since 1995, when things were supposedly about to get better on all fronts. Back then, the new Environment Act aimed to set out the buzzwords for national park criteria.

Conserve, Enhance, Opportunities, Enjoyment.

Meet these goals and the holy grail of economic and social wellbeing would be within reach. Fast forward to the present-day pressures and up to eighteen million visitors arriving on an annual basis.

'It smileth upon the beholders and giveth contentment to as many as travaile it'...

With the busy bees among the tourists blowing off steam either swinging in the trees or splashing about in #theplacetobe. During the peak (Easter and summer) holidays or even at weekends, most are sucked straight into the centre. Junction 36 of the M6 becomes a homing beacon; impatient wheels burning rubber on the dual carriageways until the rocky descent into Plumgarths comes into view. Anyone would think the landscape is awash with magic-money trees. Like those shaken around the national park's so-called thriving communities of Keswick or Bowness-on-Windermere. Yet, a longstanding elephant in the room is still prevalent, with the status symbol of second-home or holiday-let ownership as high as 60–70% in some villages. The milk-snatcher's dark legacy – Thatcher's materialistic individualism and the rise of divisions. Look at my wad 'Loadsamoney' and the housing-fuelled booms of the 1980s. What's that smell? The smoking ashes of 'Second Home Syndrome' bursting into flames again. Tensions against incomers remain as high as the rents.

The buy-to-let boom may be coming to an end for tax reasons, but it's still not known how many there really are. According to the Office for National Statistics, 3.5% of the population have a second home in the UK.

Even though the Lake District National Park initially unveiled plans with a strong focus on the needs of locals, this is hardly a new phenomenon. Since 2000, a 30% increase in multiple-home ownership has put house prices way beyond the reach of mainly young people existing on much lower incomes. For many, this period has coincided with an acceptance that if you can't afford to buy a house it's because you aren't good enough. Inevitably, social life and the vitality of several villages have declined, along with demand for local shops, schools and transport.

A legacy of loss waving goodbye to grocery stores, bakers and fruit and veg shops. Replaced by the growth of lifestyle-driven cafés and gift shops run on coffee, sarcasm and lipstick. In the national park, house prices have risen by a whopping 80% since 2002. By comparison, household incomes increased only a modest 14% – simple economics and politics. Falling fertility rates and uncertainty in the labour market. The desire to nest tempered by the endless merry-go-round of renting one place after another.

Lives on pause, child or career, local needs fall on deaf ears. Planning must be controlled and the environment protected. Sandford tugs hard on the zip wires round these parts. Unable to afford what little housing is on offer, many locals of working age are inevitably forced to seek 'opportunities' in urban areas. Add to that a touristic economy ever more reliant on part-time and zero hours contracts, where a full-time job is often the modern equivalent of Shangri-la. Problems with the roll-out of superfast broadband for homes and businesses have not helped ease the situation either.

Especially with the Government admitting it is struggling to meet its own minimum targets of 10 megabits per second. Add to the mix an ageing workforce and population, expensive transport costs and little or no mobile coverage in some spots. A slow decay brought on by the baby boomers occupation. But the smart money is now on millennial travellers embracing the 'Airbnb' revolution. Digital lovers soaking up the shining sun of memorable and unique experiences rather than inheriting family holiday homes.

Elsewhere in the national park another story exists, one of hard cash and credit cards made out of metal. Inherited money, driven by huge guzzling 4x4s or SUVs tearing up the narrow roadways, garnishing the slate-ridden drives of woodland or Lakeshore mansions. Where poor public transport links mean more noise and less natural landscape. Open the bi-fold doors, rev up the intelligent heating and follow the LEDs towards a steel-and-glass stairway. Help us to protect your national park, but ignore any whispers about the B-word, second homes or holiday lets. Gaping affordability gaps don't apply to designated settlements reaping all the economic benefits of inflated house prices. Parallel lives without a need to engage with those who aren't really like you. To keep the visiting millions onside, the high-flying centre bulges with an assortment of gift shops, cafés, pubs, hotels, restaurants and outdoor shops.

Changes, trends, issues and gaps.

The 'State of the National Park' annual report monitors employment, housing provision, services available and the vibrancy of opportunities. In a period of rising concern about inequalities, house prices and social change, the pressure for reform is real enough and has been building up for a generation.

A World Heritage landscape wrapped up in so many wide-ranging issues, I felt a close affinity with Chatwin at the end of *The Songlines*, always longing for a place that can never be found...

Acknowledgements

I am deeply grateful to Julian Hyde for his unequivocal support, reference material and research - a parallel path continues...

Many thanks to Iain Sharpe for creating such a fantastic set of drawings.

Thank you to Chris Hayton at Full Point for the cover design and to Gerard Hearne for his expert proofreading - I make an exclusive claim to any remaining errors...

My thanks to Richard Skelton and Autumn Richardson, Dr Will Smith, Dr David Cooper and to Graham Dugdale for producing the initial boundary walk.

Finally, my heartfelt thanks to Tina Smith for encouraging me to keep going and to friends and to family, both here and gone.

Select Bibliography

Helen Babbs - *Adrift:A Secret Life of London's Waterways*, 2016
Maurice E. Baren - *How it all Began in the Lake District*, 2001
Roger K. Bingham - *Kendal:A Social History*, 1995
The Chronicles of Milnthorpe, 1987
Ron Black - *Hunting Songs Volume Two: Lakeland Songs*, 2012
Bernard J. Bradbury - *History of Cockermouth*, 1981
Melvyn Bragg - *Cumbria in Verse*, 1984 - *The Hired Man*, 1969
Geoff Brown - *Herdwicks: Herdwick sheep and the English Lake District*, 2009
Alan Bryant - Towns and Villages of the Lake District and Cumbria, 1994
Bruce Chatwin - *The Songlines*, 1987
Edited by DJH Clifford - *The Diaries of Lady Anne Clifford*, 2003
Edited by the Countryside Commission - *The Lake District National Park*, 1975
Ian Crofton - *Walking the Border:A Journey between Scotland and England*, 2014
The Cumberland Geological Society - *Lakeland Rocks and Landscape A Field Guide*, 1998
Hunter Davies - *Sellafield Stories: Life in Britain's First Nuclear Plant*, 2012
Graham K. Dugdale - *The Lake District Boundary Walk*, 1996
Charlie Emett - *Eden Tapestry*, 1995
Paul Evans - *Field Notes from the Edge: Journeys through Britain's Secret Wilderness*, 2015
Richard Fortey - *The Wood for the Trees:The Long VIew of Nature from a Small Wood*, 2016
Sean Frain - *Hunting in the Lake District*, 2010 - *Murder, Mystery and Mischief in the English Lake District*, 2016
Recorded by Jack Gillespie - *Our Cumbria The Stories of Cumbrian Men & Women*, 1989
Andy Goldsworthy – *Arch*, 1999
Edited by Caz Graham - *Foot and Mouth Heart and Soul*, 2001
Cate Haste - *Sheila Fell:A Passion for Paint*, 2010
Jacquetta Hawkes - *A Land*, 1951
Paul Hindle - *Lakeland Roads*, 1977 - *Roads and Trackways of the Lake District*, 1984
Martin Holmes - *Proud Northern Lady: Lady Anne Clifford, 1590-1676*, 1975
W. G. Hoskins - *The Making of the English Landscape*, 1955
Derek Jarman - *Chroma*, 1994
Grevel Lindop - *Literary Guide to the Lake District*, 1993
Karen Lloyd - *The Gathering Tide:A Journey around the Edgelands of Morecambe Bay*, 2016

Richard Mabey - *The Unofficial Countryside,* 2010
J.D. Marshall - *Furness and the Industrial Revolution: An Economic History of Furness (1711-1900),* 1958
Terry McCormick - *Lake District Fell Farming: Historical and literary perspectives, 1750-2017,* 2018
Roy Millward & Adrian Robinson - *The Lake District,* 1980
Edited by F. Moseley - *The Geology of the Lake District,* 1978
Adam Naylor - *Neat, Though Not Sumptuous: Lowick Hall - a Chronicle,* 2013
Arthur Nicholls - *Kendal in Bygone Days,* 2011
Norman Nicholson - *Rock Face: Poems by Norman Nicholson,* 1948 - *Portrait of the Lakes,* 1964
Nick Papadimitriou – *Scarp,* 2012
Stephen Read - *Luck to Levens: Glimpses of a Westmorland Parish and its Inhabitants through time,* 2014
Michael Symmons Roberts – *Edgelands,* 2011
Eric Robinson - *The Later Poems of John Clare,* 1964
Neil Rollinson – *Amphibians,* 2007
Shap Local History Society - *Mardale: Echoes and Reflections of a Lost Lakeland Community,* 2011
John Sharpe - *Colourful Characters of Cumbria's Eden Valley,* 2015
Marion Shoard - *This Land Is Our Land,* 1987
Iain Sinclair – *London Orbital,* 2002
Colin Smith - *A Guide to the Milestones, Mileposts and Toll Buildings of Cumbria, 2011* - Mungrisdale Heritage Trails, 2009
Kenneth Smith - *Cumbrian Villages,* 1973
John Lewis Stempel - Meadowland: *The Private Life of an English Field,* 2014
Kate Thurston - *Curiosities of Cumbria: A County Guide to the Unusual,* 1994
Matthew Townend - *The Vikings and Victorian Lakeland: The Norse Medievalism of W.G. Collingwood and his Contemporaries,* 2009
Dominick Tyler - *Uncommon Ground: A Word-Lover's Guide to the British Landscape,* 2015
Chris Wadsworth - *Hercules and the Farmer's Wife: And Other Stories from a Cumbrian Art Gallery,* 2009 - *Percy Kelly Line of Beauty: A Retrospective,* 2017
John K. Walton - *The Making of a Cultural Landscape: The English Lake District as Tourist Destination, 1750-2010,* 2013
Mary Welsh - *Walking the Lakeland Fringes: The South-West,* 2000
Jennifer Westwood - *Haunted England: The Penguin Book of Ghosts,* 2008
G.C. Williamson - *Lady Anne Clifford,* 1922
Margaret Erskine Wilson - *Wild Flowers of Britain: Month by Month,* 2016
Jan Wiltshire - *Cumbrian Contrasts: A Vision of Countryside,* 2016
Angus Winchester - *Cumbria: An Historical Gazetteer,* 2016 - *Lake District Field-Names: A Guide for Local Historians,* 2017

William Wordsworth - *Guide to the Lakes*, 1977
John Wyatt - *The Lake District National Park*, 1966
Flora of the Fells: Celebrating Cumbria's Mountain Landscapes – 2003
Oil Paintings in Public Ownership in Cumbria - 2013

BOUNDARY SONGS: NOTES FROM THE EDGE OF THE LAKE DISTRICT NATIONAL PARK

David Banning is a writer based in Cumbria. His previous works include a guidebook *An A-Z of Cumbria and the Lake District on Film* (Hayloft, 2016) and the prose poem *Song of the Road* (Voices in a Lane, 2018).
He has completed a BA History of Art at Goldsmiths College, University of London and studied Lake District Landscape Studies to postgraduate level at Lancaster University.

PHOTOGRAPHY by David Banning
DRAWINGS by Iain Sharpe

Lightning Source UK Ltd.
Milton Keynes UK
UKHW010633280920
370651UK00001B/11